Commerce

of

the

Prairies

American
History
Landmarks

Edited by

David Freeman Hawke

Josiah Gregg

Commerce
of
the
Prairies

A Selection

The Bobbs-Merrill Company, Inc.
Indianapolis & New York

Josiah Gregg, 1806–1850

Commerce of the Prairies was first published in 1844.

Copyright © 1970 by The Bobbs-Merrill Company, Inc.
Library of Congress Catalog Card Number 78–120184
Printed in the United States of America
First Printing
Designed by Starr Atkinson

Contents

Commerce of the Prairies

BOOK ONE

BOOK TWO

Editor's Introduction

Josiah Gregg never desired, so he said, "to be considered an odd fish," but he was just that—a "crabid" man, to use his own word; also shy, introverted, antisocial, and, being fearful perhaps of woman's eagerness to domesticate, a lifelong bachelor. He abandoned society as a young man, and though he tried once or twice to return, the pull of the West proved irresistible. He died on the edge of the continent in the forests of California, a loner to the end. But as odd fish often do, he left a mark on his times. Gregg's *Commerce of the Prairies* was the first great book—some would say the greatest—written about the American West; and though it pictures a world long gone, it remains as readable today as it was to those who read it when it was published in 1844.

Even as a youngster Gregg revealed what his brother called "some quite peculiar traits of character." He never, so far as his brother knew, succumbed to "boyish freaks" or childish frivolities. He never displayed a sense of humor nor perpetrated a practical joke and "never could be induced to tell an untruth—not even in jest." He judged people for "what he esteemed their moral worth," and his high standards gave him few friends. (But those few, his brother noted, found him generous and warmhearted; "he never forsook them, nor they him.") He never experimented with profanity or smoking. He enjoyed school and "books were his principal companions from infancy." In short, on the surface he was the sort of boy Aunt Sally would have loved and Tom Sawyer detested. Perhaps Huck Finn alone would have sensed a kinship with the solemn, lonely Gregg. Huck reckoned he had "to light out for the Territory ahead of the rest, because Aunt Sally she's going to adopt and civilize me, and I can't stand it." Gregg aired the same sentiment some forty years earlier when he confessed he had "striven in vain to reconcile myself to the even tenor of civilized life in the United States."

Gregg's eagerness "to light out for the Territory ahead" seems curious for one who never, even by Huck Finn's standards, knew much of a civilization to escape from. He was born in the wilds of Tennessee in 1806, the fourth son of a farmer for whom the grass always seemed greener somewhere else. When Gregg was three his father moved the family to a plot of land along the Mississippi opposite St. Louis. Then in 1812, when what westerners called the "Indian War" began, he moved into the Missouri Territory, settling along the Indian frontier at Cooper's Fort. (Indians raided the fort when Gregg was eight, killing an uncle and abducting a cousin.) One final move remained—from Cooper's Fort to a farm near what would become the town of Independence, the starting point for the way West along the Santa Fe and Oregon Trails.

Two of Gregg's brothers early became involved in the Santa Fe trade, but the family expected something better for Josiah, who by the standards of the frontier seemed to be a genius. He had taught himself French and Italian, read virtually everything that drifted his way, had a bent for science, and appeared to know more about mathematics than anyone else in Missouri. When eleven he made a quadrant out of wood, which he used effectively enough to astonish schoolmates. (He with great certainty would call out the height of a tree and they, eager to prove him wrong, would climb to the top and drop down a rope to check the measurement, usually an accurate one.) Later he taught himself surveying and in the process became a skilled cartographer.

Gregg first put his varied talents to use as a school teacher. That experiment lasted a year. Next, he thought of medicine, but the physician he wanted to apprentice himself to rejected his application. A frontier society offered a limited choice of careers to a young man, and Gregg now had only the legal profession left to try. The attempt to become a lawyer proved disastrous. Later he admitted that law was the only subject he ever sought to master in which he failed "to make reasonable progress." He abandoned the struggle in 1830, when his health collapsed, leaving him for several months a "reduced and debilitated" and bedridden man. There appeared to be nothing organically wrong, but his body refused to mend. The doctor thought a long trip might put him back on his feet, and in the spring of 1831, perhaps influenced by his brothers' accounts of their adventures out West, he joined a wagon train headed for Santa Fe.

The belief that travel could cure what ailed a man was not unique with Gregg's doctor. Most physicians of the day, confronted by an illness that mystified them, advised a change of scenery as a matter of course. Unwittingly the baffled physicians were contributing to American literature. Three important books published in the 1840's resulted from such medical advice given to three young men in ill health—Charles A. Dana's *Two Years Before the Mast*, Francis Parkman's *California and Oregon Trail*, and Josiah Gregg's *Commerce of the Prairies.*

2.

When Gregg set out in 1831, the Santa Fe trade had flourished for less than a decade. Captain Zebulon Pike had first aroused interest in its possibilities in 1807 when he brought back to Missouri "exciting descriptions of the new El Dorado," but those who responded to Pike's enthusiasm received a frigid welcome in Santa Fe. The jailing of several Missouri traders as interlopers spoiled any dream of quick riches. The damper on commerce remained until 1821, when an Indian trader named William Becknell learned that Santa Fe, oppressed by the high price of goods imported through Mexico, now welcomed American merchants. Becknell returned to Santa Fe the following year with $5,000 worth of goods on which he reaped a sizable profit. On the way out he pioneered a new route directly across the Cimarron Desert. By avoiding the tortuous trip through Raton Pass he opened a trail passable for wagons, which could carry more goods, and more cheaply, than the packmules that had been used up to now. The first wagon train to make the eight-hundred-mile trip from Independence to Santa Fe traveled out in 1824, carrying some $25,000 worth of merchandise. The traders, among them two of Gregg's brothers, sold their cargo for nearly $200,000. From then on the Santa Fe traffic expanded steadily. The year Gregg joined it, one hundred thirty wagons loaded with $250,000 in merchandise set out across the prairies.

Gregg left Independence so weak that friends literally had to lift him into a wagon, as if he were an invalid. The chimneys of Independence had hardly dropped behind when Gregg revived, and within a few days he was riding his pony over the plains, sharing guard duty at night, joining in a buffalo chase, and eating as never before. The headaches, dyspepsia, and other ills that had long plagued him vanished, never to reappear except during his brief returns to civilization.

Gregg came alive on the prairies, but the open spaces gave him more than a sound body. There, unexpectedly, he found the chance to use skills and interests he had accumulated since childhood. His surveying experience and knowledge of mathematics had trained him to be a superb navigator through the sea of grass; and his skill at cartography made the map he later drew for his book the best yet done of the southwest, blemished by incredibly few errors. His knack with languages allowed him to become fluent in Spanish with little difficulty. His once blighted interest in medicine now made him an honored member of every caravan with which he traveled. ("Such was his reputation in administering remedies that not only his men, while on the plains," said his brother, "but many of his friends and relations at home would not consent to have a physician called so long as he could be induced to attend the patient.")

Where back on the Missouri frontier Gregg as a physician or lawyer or shopkeeper would have been forced to channel his energy in a particular direction, the prairie gave full scope to his various interests. Paul Horgan, who has written the best biographical sketch of Gregg, has remarked that "he was neither wholly a trader, nor an artist, nor a scientist, nor a physical man, but a thoughtful combination of all these; and on the frontier, where judgments were simple and likenesses were apt to be crudely reckoned, he was a puzzling creature." He still puzzled and annoyed his traveling companions, but now he was too absorbed to care about or be disturbed by their ill-feeling. The Indians fascinated him, and he studied—and would write about—them more perceptively than anyone previously had. He studied the flora and fauna of the prairie, and between trips he corresponded with scholars to clarify what he had seen. In New Mexico he found a people whom he did not annoy and who did not find him puzzling. "The Mexicans—both high and low—always evinced the highest regard and most unbounded confidence in him," according to his brother. Their respect may help to explain why a puritanical Protestant like Gregg could not repress his fondness for these ebullient Catholics and why, though he found much in their culture to disapprove of, he could write of it with an understanding and respect that it had never before received from an American.

Gregg remained nine years on the trail, and during all but one of those years the volume of trade with Santa Fe declined steadily. More goods than the small New Mexican population could absorb accounted largely for the drop off. By the mid-1830's few traders averaged more than forty percent profit and many little more than ten percent, a dismal return for the high risks involved in the trade. By 1839-1840, Gregg's last year on the trail, traders were so disillusioned that only thirty wagons—compared to one hundred thirty the previous year—went out, and they carried only $50,000 worth of merchandise. Even that amount apparently exceeded what Santa Fe could purchase. In order to beat his competitors, Gregg pioneered a new route out that year; then, after skimming the cream from the Santa Fe market, he traveled southward to Chihuahua to tap that source. The hard scramble required to unload his cargo in 1839 may have convinced Gregg the time had come to drop out of the Santa Fe trade for a while. He did so reluctantly and clearly only for a spell, for six years later he was on his way back to Santa Fe when the Mexican War forced him into another field of action.

3.

After the last trip over the prairies, Gregg visited his brother in Van Buren, Arkansas. He was an uncomfortable guest, constantly restless and uneasy. "Nothing seemed suited to his taste," his brother remarked, "nothing adapted to his genius." The summer of 1841 found him in Texas, trading for mules; and though he bought a parcel of land, no thought he may have had of settling there ever materialized. He returned to Van Buren still at loose ends. A year passed. Near the end of 1842 he "commenced preparing notes for the compilation of a work on 'Santa Fe and the Prairies,' " which he expected to have ready for a publisher by summer.

Summer came and the book remained far from done. In July Gregg traveled to Philadelphia, planning to buy merchandise for a new trip West while he finished the book and searched out a publisher for it. The city distracted and disturbed him, and he wasted considerable time shifting from one boarding house to another in search of quiet. He became ill, first with a "chronic affection" in the nose, accompanied by severe headaches—more than likely he had sinusitis—then his hair "commenced shedding as fast as a horse in the spring." Gregg had never known such misery as he worked, buried amidst the rattling bustle of an alien city, attempting to capture his beloved West on paper. "The job is surely ten times more tedious and laborious than I had supposed," he confessed. "Had I anticipated it, I would hardly have undertaken it. But my motto is 'Go Ahead.' "

In November, the book done, he went to New York to find a publisher. "My confidence has sunk as the 'crisis' approaches," he said. "I now feel more doubtful than ever." The forebodings were justified. Harper Brothers looked at the manuscript and turned it down. (The sinus headaches returned about this time; a doctor suggested Gregg might have syphilis, "but as I never in all my life had the slightest symptoms of that fell disease, it was of course an error.") D. Appleton & Co. agreed to take the book if a ghost writer were allowed to spice it up. Gregg, as his friend-to-be John Bigelow put it, "had no notions of literary art, and he knew it." He humbly accepted a flamboyant sometime actor, author, and translator named Louis Fitzgerald Tasistro to "polish" his manuscript. The two jarred at once. Tasistro, according to Bigelow, "had no difficulty in believing and affirming things that never happened," and he wanted to romanticize a West he had never seen. Gregg, with his western friends always in mind as readers, "would not allow his version of a fact to be expanded or contracted a hair's-breadth, no matter what might be the artistic temptation, nor however unimportant the incident."

The break with Tasistro came quickly and with it the end of the contract with Appleton. Gregg soon after acquired a new publisher, H. G. Langley, and a new editor, John Bigelow, then a young lawyer, later an eminent editor, diplomat, and author.

Bigelow and Gregg got along well (they remained friends until Gregg's death), for Bigelow saw at once that the manuscript needed little revision. "My laundry work added no more value to the washing of it," he later said, "than the washing and ironing adds to the value of a new garment."

Commerce of the Prairies came forth in July 1844, in two slim volumes. Reviewers praised it, and it sold well. The first edition of 2,000 copies was soon exhausted, and Gregg returned East the next year to supervise corrections and additions—all minor—for a second edition. A third printing also followed in 1845, and in the same year an English and a German edition were published.

Gregg's book, like himself, was something of an "odd fish"— part adventure, part travelogue, a blend of anthropology and sociology with a bit of botany and zoology thrown in—all flavored with a patois comprised of strange words like *lazo, stampede, mustang,* and *adobe,* to mention only a few of the Spanish terms Gregg gave his readers. (Spanish has contributed more than any other foreign tongue to the American language, and while Gregg was not the first to use words borrowed from Spanish in print, the popularity of his work suggests he may have had a good deal to do with making them part of the language.) Moreover, the book had the flaws of a self-conscious writer. The lucid, lively style of Gregg's letters and journals tended to become occasionally awkward and stodgy, even pretentious, when he wrote for the public. Maurice G. Fulton, editor of an excellent two-volume edition of the *Diary & Letters of Josiah Gregg* (1941, 1944), has quite correctly observed that an early draft of Gregg's last trip from Santa Fe is much superior to the "rewritten, but less vivid, version of the trip" used in the book.

The public then, as it has since, overlooked the flaws and the oddities of the book. For stay-at-homes Gregg brought alive a world as unknown in that day as the back of the moon is to Americans today. For those going West he offered a superb guidebook to the Santa Fe Trail and what they might find in New Mexico. (One is struck while reading Max L. Moorhead's heavily annotated edition, published in 1954 by the University of Oklahoma Press, how few inaccuracies have turned up in the book, though scholars have had more than a century to ferret out errors.) But perhaps a deeper reason exists for the popularity then, and the

continuing appeal now, of *Commerce of the Prairies*. Gregg wrote
not just of the prairies or of New Mexico but of a way of life,
much as did a contemporary of his, Henry David Thoreau.
Though they lived half a continent apart, their lives, curiously,
shared much in common. Both were bachelors, often in ill health,
and happiest when they cut adrift from society. Each wrote a
single great book. As a literary work *Commerce of the Prairies*
falls far below *Walden*, but the two share certain similarities.
Thoreau went to Walden Pond in 1845, a year after Gregg's
work was published, in order, he said, "to live deliberately, to
front only the the essential facts of life," words Gregg might have
used could he have commanded the language as Thoreau did.
Gregg, with his contempt for the tameness of American civilization, regarded his tour of the prairies as a "a *dangerous* experiment for him who would live a quiet contented life at home,"
words that Thoreau might have used for *his* experiment at Walden. Both men imbued their experiments in living with a passion
—Gregg, less inhibited, dared to speak openly of his "passion for
the Prairies"—that pervades every page of their books. "The best
works of art are the expression of man's struggle to free himself,"
Thoreau wrote. In that sense *Commerce of the Prairies*, for all its
awkwardnesses, survives as a work of art long after the world it
describes has vanished into a civilization even tamer than Gregg
dreamed could ever exist.

4.

After leaving New York behind, Gregg recouped his health
with a "little jaunt" on the prairies—the air "contributed very
much to the strengthening the tone of my stomach and system
generally," he said. The following year he studied medicine at
the University of Louisville, receiving an honorary M.D. in the
spring of 1846. Soon after, though war between the United States
and Mexico had broken out, he headed once again toward Santa
Fe. Independence presented a startling contrast to what it had
been when he last saw it. "The emigration this spring to California or Oregon will be immense," he said, "6,000 souls, with
1,000 wagons, moving westward across the great prairies during
the present summer from this part of our frontier."

Gregg had barely moved into the bracing prairie air when a message arrived urging him to join a body of troops commanded by General John Wool and assigned to take Chihuahua. Gregg abandoned his own plans and headed south to join up with the army. He had been promised an "honorable and profitable" position, but the vaguely worded appointment to General Wool's staff as a "confidential government agent" left him in a limbo between the civilian and military worlds and created what Gregg considered a "humiliating" situation. Though he served more than adequately as guide, interpreter, and cartographer through the strange country, his situation got steadily worse. General Wool resented Gregg's carping reports to western newspapers about the way the campaign was being conducted. The troops, whom Gregg regarded as stupid and vulgar, ridiculed his scientific interests—during the tour of duty he collected some two hundred botanical specimens and large numbers of the skins of Mexican birds—and joshed him for pampering his supposedly delicate health.

At the first chance Gregg and the army parted, to the mutual satisfaction of both. After an abortive trip East—he had hoped for an attractive sinecure with the government, but President Polk failed to offer any encouragement—he returned to settle down in the Mexican city of Saltillo. The urgings of Mexican friends led him to start practicing medicine. A visiting American remarked that he could "make a fortune if he would charge as others do. But you know him," he reported to Gregg's brother. "He won't do it. If a Mexican says to him, 'yo soy probrecito' (I am very poor), he is charged nothing. Even the rich are not charged more than half price."

Never before, except on the prairies, had Gregg been happier—if only he could be as happy, he said, in American society as here among Mexicans—but he soon became restless, for no longer was he his own man. "I shall be compelled to leave here sooner than I intended," he wrote home, for "the Mexicans have come to think I am a wondrous doctor. I have to go night and day—not a moment to spare, except five or seven hours for sleep, for amusements, for social intercourse, for scientific purposes, etc.!"

He left Saltillo in December 1848 on an exploring expedition, collecting botanical specimens and mapping the country as he moved southward. At Mexico City he heard of the discovery of gold in California and decided to "hurry on there." But Gregg could hurry only when he had exhausted his curiosity about the spot he currently occupied. His fascination with Mexico City led to a string of postponements. "He must look into every nook and corner," his brother said. "He must see if any *relic* was to be found to indicate that the place had once been inhabited by another race. More, he must ransack 'musty records.' And then, he must travel the country about." Gregg continued to botanize, and on this trip, his last through Mexico, he collected some seven hundred specimens. (Eventually botanists honored him by naming 23 plants *greggi.*)

At last, after a slow trip across to the western coast of Mexico, then up the California coast by sea, Gregg reached San Francisco in September 1849. A few weeks later he had been hired by a group of miners to search out a coastal bay that would give their settlement on the Trinity River a more direct supply route with San Francisco. Those who accompanied him on the exploring expedition soon became as annoyed with their leader and his precise, deliberate ways, as had those who had traveled with him earlier. A hike across the Coastal Range, which normally took eight days, became a month-long ordeal, partly because of bad weather but mainly because Gregg had to pause to dig for geological specimens, to measure the girth of a gigantic redwood, to study every strange plant and animal he came upon. The "old gentleman," as he was called, though still only forty-three, provoked his edgy companions into quarrels—in memory of one such quarrel the party gave Mad River its name—and even finding the bay they sought did little to heal the wounds of the trip.

On the way back from the expedition, Gregg fell from his horse. A few days later, on February 25, 1850, he died and was buried in an unmarked grave in the wilderness. His geological and botanical collections, as well as the notes he made on this final trip, were lost. He left behind few worldly possessions—some letters, a diary, and *Commerce of the Prairies.*

D.F.H.

Note on the Text

This edition is based on the originally two-volume work published in 1844. Gregg's orthography has been preserved throughout; so has his organization, except in the final two chapters. All headings except those for Chapters 18, 19, and 20 have been added by the editor. Chapters 1 through 14 are drawn from Volume One of the original edition; Chapters 15 through 22 come from Volume Two. For those who might wish to collate this edition with the original, the pagination is as follows. The material in the Preface appears on pages iv–vii in the 1844 work; Chapter 1, pages 32–49; Chapter 2, pages 50–70; Chapter 3, pages 70–85; Chapter 4, pages 87–91, 95–114; Chapter 5, pages 115, 116, 137, 138, 140, 143–161; Chapter 6, pages 166–175; Chapter 7, pages 178–192; Chapter 8, pages 197–198, 199–210; Chapter 9, pages 217–224; Chapter 10, pages 226, 227, 232–244; Chapter 11, pages 245–246, 253–261, 263–266; Chapter 12, pages 267–269, 270, 273–281; Chapter 13, pages 282, 285–287, 290–294, 300–301; Chapter 14, pages 305–320; Chapter 15, Volume Two, pages 9–11, 12–26; Chapter 16, pages 27–34, 36–43, 44–46; Chapter 17, pages 47–49, 53–63; Chapter 18, pages 178–189, 190–193, 195–205; Chapter 19, pages 206–233; Chapter 20, pages 276, 298–318; Chapter 21, pages 64–83, 112–121, 122; Chapter 22, pages 136–158.

Commerce

of

the

Prairies

Preface

In adding another to the list of works which have already been published, appearing to bear more or less directly upon the subject matter of these volumes, I am aware that my labors make their appeal to the public under serious disadvantages. In view of this 'foregone conclusion,' I trust I may be pardoned for prefacing my literary offering with a few words in its justification,—which will afford me an occasion to explain the circumstances that first led to my acquaintance with life upon the Prairies and in Northern Mexico.

For some months preceding the year 1831, my health had been gradually declining under a complication of chronic diseases, which defied every plan of treatment that the sagacity and science of my medical friends could devise. This morbid condition of my system, which originated in the familiar miseries of dyspepsia and its kindred infirmities, had finally reduced me to such a state, that, for nearly a twelve-month, I was not only disqualified for any systematic industry, but so debilitated as rarely to be able to extend my walks beyond the narrow precincts of my chamber. In this hopeless condition, my physicians advised me to take a trip across the Prairies, and, in the change of air and habits which such an adventure would involve, to seek that health which their science had failed to bestow. I accepted their suggestion, and, without hesitation, proceeded at once to make the necessary preparations for joining one of those spring Caravans which were annually starting from the United States, for Santa Fé.

The effects of this journey were in the first place to re-establish my health, and, in the second, to beget a passion for Prairie life which I never expect to survive. At the conclusion of the season which followed my first trip, I became interested as a proprietor in the Santa Fé Trade, and continued to be so, to a greater or less extent, for the eight succeeding years. During the whole of the above periods I crossed the Prairies eight different times; and, with the exception of the time thus spent in travelling to and fro, the greater part of the nine years of which I speak, were passed in Northern Mexico.

Having been actively engaged and largely interested in the commerce of that country and across the Prairies, for so long a period, I feel that I have at least had opportunities for observation, upon the subjects of which I have ventured to treat, superior to those enjoyed by any writers who have preceded me. But not even an attempt has before been made to present any full account of the origin of the Santa Fé Trade and modes of conducting it; nor of the early history and present condition of the people of New Mexico; nor of the Indian tribes by which the wild and unreclaimed regions of that department are inhabited. I think I may also assure my readers that most of the facts presented in my sketch of the natural history of the Prairies, and of the Indian tribes who inhabit them, are now published for the first time. As I have not sought to make a treatise upon these subjects, I have not felt compelled, for the purpose of giving my papers symmetry and completeness, to enter to any extent upon grounds which have already been occupied by other travellers; but have contented myself with presenting such matters and observations as I thought least likely to have come before under the notice of my readers.

I am perfectly sensible, however, that, in the selection of matter, and in the execution of my work, it is very far from being what it should be, and what, in more capable hands, it might have been. I only trust, that, with all its imperfections, it may be found to contain some new and not unimportant facts, which may be thought, in some measure, to justify my appearance for once in the capacity of a bookmaker; for which vocation, in all other respects, I am free to confess myself very poorly qualified.

J.G.

New York, June 12, 1844

BOOK ONE

1. The Departure

People who reside at a distance, and especially at the North, have generally considered St. Louis as the emporium of the Santa Fé Trade; but that city, in truth, has never been a place of rendezvous, nor even of outfit, except for a small portion of the traders who have started from its immediate vicinity. The town of Franklin on the Missouri river, about a hundred and fifty miles further to the westward, seems truly to have been the cradle of our trade; and, in conjunction with several neighboring towns, continued for many years to furnish the greater number of these adventurous traders. Even subsequently to 1831, many wagons have been fitted out and started from this interior section. But as the navigation of the Missouri river had considerably advanced towards the year 1831, and the advantages of some point of debarkation nearer the western frontier were very evident, whereby upwards of a hundred miles of troublesome land-carriage, over unimproved and often miry roads, might be avoided, the new town of Independence, but twelve miles from the Indian border and two or three south of the Missouri river, being the most eligible point, soon began to take the lead as a place of debarkation, outfit and departure, which, in spite of all opposition, it has ever since maintained. It is to this beautiful spot, already grown up to be a thriving town, that the prairie adventurer, whether in search of wealth, health or amusement, is latterly in the habit of repairing, about the first of May, as the caravans usually set out some time during that month. Here they purchase their provisions for the road, and many of their mules, oxen, and even some of their wagons—in short, load all their vehicles, and make their final preparations for a long journey across the prairie wilderness.

As Independence is a point of convenient access (the Missouri river being navigable at all times from March till November), it has become the general 'port of embarkation' for every part of the great western and northern 'prairie ocean.' Besides the Santa Fé caravans, most of the Rocky Mountain traders and trappers, as well as emigrants to Oregon, take this town in their route. During the season of departure, therefore, it is a place of much bustle and active business.

Among the concourse of travellers at this 'starting point,' besides traders and tourists, a number of pale-faced invalids are generally to be met with. The Prairies have, in fact, become very celebrated for their sanative effects—more justly so, no doubt, than the most fashionable watering-places of the North. Most chronic diseases, particularly liver complaints, dyspepsias, and similar affections, are often radically cured; owing, no doubt, to the peculiarities of diet, and the regular exercise incident to prairie life, as well as to the purity of the atmosphere of those elevated unembarrassed regions. An invalid myself, I can answer for the efficacy of the remedy, at least in my own case. Though, like other valetudinarians, I was disposed to provide an ample supply of such commodities as I deemed necessary for my comfort and health, I was not long upon the prairies before I discovered that most of such extra preparations were unnecessary, or at least quite dispensable. A few knick-knacks, as a little tea, rice, fruits, crackers, etc., suffice very well for the first fortnight, after which the invalid is generally able to take the fare of the hunter and teamster. Though I set out myself in a carriage, before the close of the first week I saddled my pony; and when we reached the buffalo range, I was not only as eager for the chase as the sturdiest of my companions, but I enjoyed far more exquisitely my share of the buffalo, than all the delicacies which were ever devised to provoke the most fastidious appetite.

The ordinary supplies for each man's consumption during the journey, are about fifty pounds of flour, as many more of bacon, ten of coffee and twenty of sugar, and a little salt. Beans, crackers, and trifles of that description, are comfortable appendages, but being looked upon as *dispensable* luxuries, are seldom to be found in any of the stores on the road. The buffalo is chiefly depended upon for fresh meat, and great is the joy of the traveller when that noble animal first appears in sight.

The wagons now most in use upon the Prairies are manufactured in Pittsburg; and are usually drawn by eight mules or the same number of oxen. Of late years, however, I have seen much larger vehicles employed, with ten or twelve mules harnessed to each, and a cargo of goods of about five thousand pounds in weight. At an early period the horse was more frequently in use, as mules were not found in great abundance; but as soon as the means for procuring these animals increased, the horse was gradually and finally discarded, except occasionally for riding and the chase.

The supplies being at length procured, and all necessary preliminaries systematically gone through, the trader begins the difficult task of loading his wagons. Those who understand their business take every precaution so to stow away their packages that no jolting on the road can afterwards disturb the order in which they had been disposed. The ingenuity displayed on these occasions has frequently been such, that after a tedious journey of eight hundred miles, the goods have been found to have sustained much less injury, than they would have experienced on a turnpike-road, or from the ordinary handling of property upon our western steam-boats.

The next great difficulty the traders have to encounter is in training those animals that have never before been worked, which is frequently attended by an immensity of trouble. There is nothing, however, in the mode of harnessing and conducting teams in prairie travelling, which differs materially from that practised on the public highways throughout the States,—the representations of certain travelers to the contrary, notwithstanding. From the amusing descriptions which are sometimes given by this class of writers, one would be apt to suppose that they had never seen a wagon or a team of mules before, or that they had just emerged for the first time from the purlieus of a large city. The propensity evinced by these writers for giving an air of romance to everything they have either seen or heard, would seem to imply a conviction on their part, that no statement of unvarnished facts can ever be stamped with the seal of the world's approbation—that a work, in order to prove permanently attractive, should teem with absurdities and abound in exaggerated details. How far such an assumption would be correct, I shall not pause to inquire.

At last all are fairly launched upon the broad prairie—the

miseries of preparation are over—the thousand anxieties occasioned by wearisome consultations and delays are felt no more. The charioteer, as he smacks his whip, feels a bounding elasticity of soul within him, which he finds it impossible to restrain;—even the mules prick up their ears with a peculiarly conceited air, as if in anticipation of that change of scene which will presently follow. Harmony and good feeling prevail everywhere. The hilarious song, the *bon mot* and the witty repartee, go round in quick succession; and before people have had leisure to take cognizance of the fact, the lovely village of Independence, with its multitude of associations, is already lost to the eye.

It was on the 15th of May, 1831, and one of the brightest and most lovely of all the days in the calendar, that our little party set out from Independence. The general rendezvous at Council Grove was our immediate destination. It is usual for the traders to travel thus far in detached parties, and to assemble there for the purpose of entering into some kind of organization, for mutual security and defence during the remainder of the journey. It was from thence that the formation of the *Caravan* was to be dated, and the chief interest of our journey to commence: therefore, to this point we all looked forward with great anxiety. The intermediate travel was marked by very few events of any interest. As the wagons had gone before us, and we were riding in a light carriage, we were able to reach the Round Grove, about thirty-five miles distant, on the first day, where we joined the rear division of the caravan, comprising about thirty wagons.

On the following day we had a foretaste of those protracted, drizzling spells of rain, which, at this season of the year, so much infest the frontier prairies. It began sprinkling about dark, and continued pouring without let or hinderance for forty-eight hours in succession; and as the rain was accompanied by a heavy northwester, and our camp was pitched in the open prairie, without a stick of available timber within a mile of us, it must be allowed that the whole formed a prelude anything but flattering to valetudinarians. For my own part, finding the dearborn carriage in which I had a berth not exactly water-proof, I rolled myself in a blanket and lay snugly coiled upon a tier of boxes and bales, under cover of a wagon, and thus managed to escape a very severe drenching.

The mischief of the storm did not exhaust itself, however, upon our persons. The loose animals sought shelter in the groves at a considerable distance from the encampment, and the wagoners being loth to turn out in search of them during the rain, not a few of course, when applied for, were missing. This, however, is no uncommon occurrence. Travellers generally experience far more annoyance from the straying of cattle during the first hundred miles, than at any time afterwards; because, apprehending no danger from the wild Indians (who rarely approach within two hundred miles of the border), they seldom keep any watch, although that is the very time when a cattle-guard is most needed It is only after some weeks' travel that the animals begin to feel attached to the caravan, which they then consider about as much their home as the stock-yard of a dairy farm.

After leaving this spot the troubles and vicissitudes of our journey began in good earnest; for on reaching the narrow ridge which separates the Osage and Kansas waters (known as 'the Narrows'), we encountered a region of very troublesome quagmires. On such occasions it is quite common for a wagon to sink to the hubs in mud, while the surface of the soil all around would appear perfectly dry and smooth. To extricate each other's wagons we had frequently to employ double and triple teams, with 'all hands to the wheels' in addition—often led by the proprietors themselves up to the waist in mud and water.

Three or four days after this, and while crossing the head branches of the Osage river, we experienced a momentary alarm. Conspicuously elevated upon a rod by the roadside, we found a paper purporting to have been written by the Kansas agent, stating that a band of Pawnees were said to be lurking in the vicinity! The first excitement over, however, the majority of our party came to the conclusion that it was either a hoax of some of the company in advance, or else a stratagem of the Kaws (or Kansas Indians), who, as well as the Osages, prowl about those prairies, and steal from the caravans, during the passage, when they entertain the slightest hope that their maraudings will be laid to others. They seldom venture further, however, than to seize upon an occasional stray animal, which they frequently do with the view alone of obtaining a reward for returning it to its owner. As to the Pawnees, the most experienced traders were well aware that they had not been known to frequent those latitudes since the commencement of the Santa Fé trade. But what contributed as much as anything else to lull the fears of the timid, was an accession to our forces of seventeen wagons which we overtook the same evening.

Early on the 26th of May we reached the long looked-for rendezvous of Council Grove, where we joined the main body of the caravan. Lest this imposing title suggest to the reader a snug and thriving village, it should be observed, that, on the day of our departure from Independence, we passed the last human abode upon our route; therefore, from the borders of Missouri to those of New Mexico not even an Indian settlement greeted our eyes.

This place is about a hundred and fifty miles from Independence, and consists of a continuous stripe of timber nearly half a mile in width, comprising the richest varieties of trees; such as oak, walnut, ash, elm, hickory, etc., and extending all along the valleys of a small stream known as 'Council Grove creek,' the principal branch of the Neosho river. This stream is bordered by the most fertile bottoms and beautiful upland prairies, well adapted to cultivation: such indeed is the general character of the country from thence to Independence. All who have traversed these delightful regions, look forward with anxiety to the day when the Indian title to the land shall be extinguished, and flourishing 'white' settlements dispel the gloom which at present prevails over this uninhabited region. Much of this prolific country now belongs to the Shawnees and other Indians of the border, though some portion of it has never been allotted to any tribe.

The designation of 'Council Grove,' after all, is perhaps the most appropriate that could be given to this place; for we there held a 'grand council,' at which the respective claims of the different 'aspirants to office' were considered, leaders selected, and a system of government agreed upon,—as is the standing custom of these promiscuous caravans. One would have supposed that electioneering and 'party spirit' would hardly have penetrated so far into the wilderness: but so it was. Even in our little community we had our 'office-seekers' and their 'political adherents,' as earnest and as devoted as any of the modern school of politicians in the midst of civilization. After a great deal of bickering and wordy warfare, however, all the 'candidates' found it expedient to decline, and a gentleman by the name of Stanley, without seeking, or even desiring the 'office,' was unanimously proclaimed 'Captain of the Caravan.' The powers of this officer were undefined by any 'constitutional provision,' and consequently vague and uncertain: orders being only viewed as mere requests, they are often obeyed or neglected at the caprice of the subordinates. It is necessary to observe, however, that the captain is expected to direct the order of travel during the day, and to designate the camping-ground at night; with many other functions of a general character, in the exercise of which the company find it convenient to acquiesce. But the little attention that is paid to his commands in cases of emergency, I will leave the reader to become acquainted with, as I did, by observing their manifestations during the progress of the expedition.

But after this comes the principal task of organizing. The proprietors are first notified by 'proclamation' to furnish a list of their men and wagons. The latter are generally apportioned into four 'divisions,' particularly when the company is large—and ours consisted of nearly a hundred wagons,* besides a dozen of dearborns and other small vehicles, and two small cannons (a four and six pounder), each mounted upon a carriage. To each of these divisions, a 'lieutenant' was appointed, whose duty it was to inspect every ravine and creek on the route, select the best crossings, and superintend what is called in prairie parlance, the 'forming' of each encampment.

Upon the calling of the roll, we were found to muster an efficient force of nearly two hundred men without counting invalids or other disabled bodies, who, as a matter of course, are exempt from duty. There is nothing so much dreaded by inexperienced travellers as the ordeal of guard duty. But no matter what the condition or employment of the individual may be, no one has the smallest chance of evading the 'common law of the prairies.' The amateur tourist and the listless loafer are precisely in the same wholesome predicament—they must all take their regular turn at the watch. There is usually a set of genteel idlers attached to every caravan, whose wits are for ever at work in devising schemes for whiling away their irksome hours at the expense of

* About half of these wagons were drawn by ox teams, the rest by mules.— The capital in merchandise of the whole caravan was about $200,000.

others. By embarking in these 'trips of pleasure,' they are enabled
to live without expense; for the hospitable traders seldom refuse
to accommodate even a loafing companion with a berth at their
mess without charge. But then these lounging *attachés* are expected at least to do good service by way of guard duty. None are
ever permitted to furnish a substitute, as is frequently done in
military expeditions, for he that would undertake to stand the
tour of another besides his own, would scarcely be watchful
enough for the dangers of the Prairies. Even the invalid must be
able to produce unequivocal proofs of his inability, or it is a
chance if the plea is admitted. For my own part, although I started
on the 'sick list,' and though the prairie sentinel must stand fast
and brook the severest storm (for then it is that the strictest watch
is necessary), I do not remember ever having missed my post but
once during the whole journey.

The usual number of watches is eight, each standing a fourth of
every alternate night. When the party is small the number is
generally reduced; while in the case of very small bands, they are
sometimes compelled for safety's sake to keep one watch on duty
half the night. With large caravans the captain usually appoints
eight 'sergeants of the guard,' each of whom takes an equal portion of men under his command.

The heterogeneous appearance of our company, consisting of
men from every class and grade of society, with a little sprinkling
of the softer sex, would have formed an excellent subject for an
artist's pencil. It may appear, perhaps, a little extraordinary that
females should have ventured across the Prairies under such forlorn auspices. Those who accompanied us, however, were members of a Spanish family who had been banished in 1829, in
pursuance of a decree of the Mexican congress, and were now
returning to their homes in consequence of a suspension of the
decree. Other females, however, have crossed the prairies to Santa
Fé at different times, among whom I have known two respectable
French ladies, who now reside in Chihuahua.

The wild and motley aspect of the caravan can be but imper-
fectly conceived without an idea of the costumes of its various
members. The most 'fashionable' prairie dress is the fustian frock
of the city-bred merchant furnished with a multitude of pockets
capable of accommodating a variety of 'extra tackling.' Then

there is the backwoodsman with his linsey or leather hunting-shirt—the farmer with his blue jean coat—the wagoner with his flannel-sleeve vest—besides an assortment of other costumes which go to fill up the picture.

In the article of fire-arms there is also an equally interesting medley. The frontier hunter sticks to his rifle, as nothing could induce him to carry what he terms in derision 'the scatter-gun.' The sportsman from the interior flourishes his double-barrelled fowling-piece with equal confidence in its superiority. The latter is certainly the most convenient description of gun that can be carried on this journey; as a charge of buck-shot in night attacks (which are the most common), will of course be more likely to do execution than a single rifle-ball fired at random. The 'repeating' arms have lately been brought into use upon the Prairies, and they are certainly very formidable weapons, particularly when used against an ignorant savage foe. A great many were furnished beside with a bountiful supply of pistols and knives of every description, so that the party made altogether a very brigand-like appearance.

During our delay at the Council Grove, the laborers were employed in procuring timber for axle-trees and other wagon repairs, of which a supply is always laid in before leaving this region of substantial growths; for henceforward there is no wood on the route fit for these purposes; not even in the mountains of Santa Fé do we meet with any serviceable timber. The supply procured here is generally lashed under the wagons, in which way a log is not unfrequently carried to Santa Fé, and even sometimes back again.

2. On the Trail

Owing to the delays of organizing and other preparations, we did not leave the Council Grove camp till May 27th. Although the usual hour of starting with the prairie caravans is after an early breakfast, yet, on this occasion, we were hindered till in the afternoon. The familiar note of preparation, "Catch up! catch up!" was now sounded from the captain's camp, and re-echoed from every division and scattered group along the valley. On such occasions, a scene of confusion ensues, which must be seen to be appreciated. The woods and dales resound with the gleeful yells of the light-hearted wagoners, who, weary of inaction, and filled with joy at the prospect of getting under way, become clamorous in the extreme. Scarcely does the jockey on the race-course ply his whip more promptly at that magic word 'Go,' than do these emulous wagoners fly to harnessing their mules at the spirit-stirring sound of 'Catch up.' Each teamster vies with his fellow who shall be soonest ready; and it is a matter of boastful pride to be the first to cry out—"All's set!"

The uproarious bustle which follows—the hallooing of those in pursuit of animals—the exclamations which the unruly brutes call forth from their wrathful drivers; together with the clatter of bells —the rattle of yokes and harness—the jingle of chains—all conspire to produce an uproarious confusion, which would be altogether incomprehensible without the assistance of the eyes; while these alone would hardly suffice to unravel the labyrinthian manœuvres and hurly-burly of this precipitate breaking up. It is sometimes amusing to observe the athletic wagoner hurrying an animal to its post—to see him 'heave upon' the halter of a stubborn mule, while the brute as obstinately 'sets back,' determined not to 'move a peg' till his own good pleasure thinks it proper to do so—his whole manner seeming to say, "Wait till your hurry's over!" I have more than once seen a driver hitch a harnessed animal to the halter, and by that process haul 'his mulishness' forward, while each of his four projected feet would leave a furrow behind; until at last the perplexed master would wrathfully exclaim, "A mule will be a mule any way you can fix it!"

"All's set!" is finally heard from some teamster—"All's set," is directly responded from every quarter. "Stretch out " immediately vociferates the captain. Then, the 'heps!' of drivers—the cracking of whips—the trampling of feet—the occasional creak of wheels —the rumbling of wagons—form a new scene of exquisite confusion, which I shall not attempt further to describe. "Fall in!" is heard from headquarters, and the wagons are forthwith strung out upon the long inclined plain, which stretches to the heights beyond Council Grove.

After fifteen miles' progress, we arrived at the 'Diamond Spring' (a crystal fountain discharging itself into a small brook), to which, in later years, caravans have sometimes advanced, before 'organizing.' Near twenty-five miles beyond we crossed the Cottonwood fork of the Neosho, a creek still smaller than that of Council Grove, and our camp was pitched immediately in its further valley.

We experienced a temporary alarm during the evening, while we lay encamped at Cottonwood, which was rather more boisterous than serious in its consequences. The wagons had been 'formed' across the neck of a bend in the creek, into which the cattle were turned, mostly in their yokes; for though, when thoroughly trained, teamsters usually unyoke their oxen every night, yet at first they often leave them coupled, to save the trouble of re-yoking them in their unruly state. A little after dark, these animals started simultaneously, with a thundering noise and rattle of the yokes, towards the outlet protected by the wagons, but for which obstacle they might have escaped far into the prairie, and have been irrecoverably lost, or, at least, have occasioned much trouble and delay to recover them. The cause of the fright was not discovered; but oxen are exceedingly whimsical creatures when surrounded by unfamiliar objects. One will sometimes take a fright at the jingle of his own yoke-irons, or the cough of his mate, and, by a sudden flounce, set the whole herd in a flurry. This was probably the case in the present instance; although some of our easily excited companions immediately surmised that the oxen had scented a lurking Pawnee.

Our route lay through uninterrupted prairie for about forty miles—in fact I may say, for five hundred miles, excepting the very narrow fringes of timber along the borders of the streams. The antelope of the high prairies which we now occasionally saw, is sometimes found as far east as Council Grove; and as a few old buffaloes have sometimes been met with about Cottonwood, we now began to look out for this desirable game. Some scattering bulls are generally to be seen first, forming as it would appear the 'van' or 'piquet guards' of the main droves with their cows and calves. The buffalo are usually found much further east early in the spring, than during the rest of the year, on account of the long grass, which shoots up earlier in the season than the short pasturage of the plains.

Our hopes of game were destined soon to be realized; for early on the second day after leaving Cottonwood (a few miles beyond the principal Turkey creek), our eyes were greeted with the sight of a herd amounting to nearly a hundred head of buffalo, quietly grazing in the distance before us. Half of our company had probably never seen a buffalo before (at least in its wild state); and the excitement that the first sight of these 'prairie beeves' occasions among a party of novices, beggars all description. Every horseman was off in a scamper: and some of the wagoners, leaving their teams to take care of themselves, seized their guns and joined the race afoot. Here went one with his rifle or yager—there another with double-barrelled shot-gun—a third with his holster-pistols—a Mexican perhaps with his lance—another with his bow and arrows—and numbers joined without any arms whatever, merely for the 'pleasures of the chase'—all helter-skelter—a regular John Gilpin race, truly 'neck or naught.' The fleetest of the pursuers were soon in the midst of the game, which scattered in all directions, like a flock of birds upon the descent of a hawk.

A few 'beeves' were killed during the chase; and as soon as our camp was pitched, the bustle of kindling fires and preparing for supper commenced. The new adventurers were curious to taste this prairie luxury; while we all had been so long upon salt provisions—now nearly a month—that our appetites were in exquisite condition to relish fresh meat. The fires had scarcely been kindled when the fumes of broiling meat pervaded the surrounding atmosphere; while all huddled about, anxiously watching their cookeries, and regaling their senses in anticipation upon the savory odors which issued from them.

For the edification of the reader, who has no doubt some curiosity on the subject, I will briefly mention, that the 'kitchen and table ware' of the traders usually consists of a skillet, a frying-pan, a sheet-iron camp-kettle, a coffee-pot, and each man with his tin cup and a butcher's knife. The culinary operations being finished, the pan and kettle are set upon the grassy turf, around which all take a 'lowly seat,' and crack their gleesome jokes, while from their greasy hands they swallow their savory viands—all with a relish rarely experienced at the well-spread table of the most fashionable and wealthy citizen.

The insatiable appetite acquired by travellers upon the Prairies is almost incredible, and the quantity of coffee drank is still more so. It is an unfailing and apparently indispensable beverage, served at every meal—even under the broiling noon-day sun, the wagoner will rarely fail to replenish a second time, his huge tin cup.

Early the next day we reached the 'Little Arkansas,' which, although endowed with an imposing name, is only a small creek with a current but five or six yards wide. But, though small, its steep banks and miry bed annoyed us exceedingly in crossing. It is the practice upon the prairies on all such occasions, for several men to go in advance with axes, spades and mattocks, and, by digging the banks and erecting temporary bridges, to have all in readiness by the time the wagons arrive. A bridge over a quagmire is made in a few minutes, by cross-laying it with brush (willows are best, but even long grass is often employed as a substitute), and covering it with earth,—across which a hundred wagons will often pass in safety.

We had now arrived at the point nearest to the border, I believe, where many outrages have been perpetrated upon the traders to Santa Fé. One of the early packing companies lost their animals on this spot, and had to send back for a new supply.

Next day we reached Cow creek, where all the difficulties encountered at Little Arkansas had to be reconquered: but after digging, bridging, shouldering the wheels, with the usual accompaniment of whooping, swearing and cracking of whips, we soon got safely across and encamped in the valley beyond. Alarms now began to accumulate more rapidly upon us. A couple of persons had a few days before been chased to the wagons by a band of ——buffalo; and this evening the encampment was barely formed when two hunters came bolting in with information that a hundred, perhaps of the same 'enemy,' were at hand—at least this was the current opinion afterwards. The hubbub occasioned by this fearful news had scarcely subsided, when another arrived on a panting horse, crying out "Indians! Indians! I've just escaped from a couple, who pursued me to the very camp!" "To arms! to arms!" resounded from every quarter—and just then a wolf, attracted by the fumes of broiling buffalo bones, sent up a most hideous howl across the creek. "Some one in distress!" was instantly shouted: "To his relief!" vociferated the crowd—and off they bolted, one and all, arms in hand, hurly-burly—leaving the camp entirely unprotected; so that had an enemy been at hand indeed, and approached us from the opposite direction, they might easily have taken possession of the wagons. Before they had all returned, however, a couple of hunters came in and laughed very heartily at the expense of the first alarmist, whom they had just chased into the camp.

Half a day's drive after leaving this camp of 'false alarms' brought us to the valley of Arkansas river. This point is about 270 miles from Independence. From the adjacent heights the landscape presents an imposing and picturesque appearance. Beneath a ledge of wave-like yellow sandy ridges and hillocks spreading far beyond, descends the majestic river (averaging at least a quarter of a mile in width), bespeckled with verdant islets, thickly set with cottonwood timber. The banks are very low and barren, with the exception of an occasional grove of stunted trees, hiding behind a swamp or sand-hill, placed there as it were to protect it from the fire of the prairies, which in most parts keeps down every perennial growth. In many places, indeed, where there are no islands, the river is so entirely bare of trees, that the unthinking traveller might approach almost to its very brink, without suspecting its presence.

Thus far, many of the prairies have a fine and productive appearance, though the Neosho river (or Council Grove) seems to form the western boundary of the truly rich and beautiful country of the border. Up to that point the prairies are similar to those of Missouri—the soil equally exuberant and fertile; while all the country that lies beyond is, of a far more barren character —vegetation of every kind is more stinted—the gay flowers more scarce, and the scanty timber of a very inferior quality: indeed, the streams, from Council Grove westward, are lined with very little else than cottonwood, barely interspersed here and there with an occasional elm or hackberry.

Following up the course of this stream for some twenty miles, now along the valley, and again traversing the points of projecting eminences, we reached Walnut creek. I have heard of a surgical operation performed at this point, in the summer of 1826, which, though not done exactly *secundum artem*, might suggest some novel reflections to the man of science. A few days before the caravan had reached this place, a Mr. Broadus, in attempting to draw his rifle from a wagon muzzle foremost, discharged its contents into his arm. The bone being dreadfully shattered, the unfortunate man was advised to submit to an amputation at once; otherwise, it being the month of August, and excessively warm, mortification would soon ensue. But Broadus obstinately refused to consent to this course, till death began to stare him in the face. By this time, however, the whole arm had become gangrened, some spots having already appeared above the place where the operation should have been performed. The invalid's case was therefore considered perfectly hopeless, and he was given up by all his comrades, who thought of little else than to consign him to the grave.

But being unwilling to resign himself to the fate which appeared frowning over him, without a last effort, he obtained the consent of two or three of the party, who undertook to amputate his arm merely to gratify the wishes of the dying man; for in such a light they viewed him. Their only 'case of instruments' consisted of a handsaw, a butcher's knife and a large iron bolt. The teeth of the saw being considered too coarse, they went to work, and soon had a set of fine teeth filed on the back. The knife having been whetted keen, and the iron bolt laid upon the fire, they commenced the operation: and in less time than it takes to tell it, the arm was opened round to the bone, which was almost in an instant sawed off; and with the whizzing hot iron the whole stump was so effectually seared as to close the arteries completely. Bandages were now applied, and the company proceeded on their journey as though nothing had occurred. The arm commenced healing rapidly, and in a few weeks the patient was sound and well, and is perhaps still living, to bear witness to the superiority of the 'hot iron' over ligatures, in 'taking up' arteries.

On the following day our route lay mostly over a level plain, which usually teems with buffalo, and is beautifully adapted to the chase. At the distance of about fifteen miles, the attention of the traveller is directed to the 'Pawnee Rock,' so called, it is said, on account of a battle's having once been fought hard by, between the Pawnees and some other tribe. It is situated at the projecting point of a ridge, and upon its surface are furrowed, in uncouth but legible characters, numerous dates, and the names of various travellers who have chanced to pass that way.

We encamped at Ash creek, where we again experienced sundry alarms in consequence of 'Indian sign,' that was discovered in
the creek valley, such as unextinguished fires, about which were
found some old moccasins,—a sure indication of the recent retreat
of savages from the vicinity. These constant alarms, however,
although too frequently the result of groundless and unmanly
fears, are not without their salutary effects upon the party. They
serve to keep one constantly on the alert, and to sharpen those
faculties of observation which would otherwise become blunted
or inactive. Thus far also we had marched in two lines only; but,
after crossing the Pawnee Fork, each of the four divisions drove
on in a separate file, which became henceforth the order of march
till we reached the border of the mountains. By moving in long
lines as we did before, the march is continually interrupted; for
every accident which delays a wagon ahead stops all those behind.
By marching four abreast, this difficulty is partially obviated, and
the wagons can also be thrown more readily into a condition of
defence in case of attack.

Upon encamping the wagons are formed into a 'hollow square'
(each division to a side), constituting at once an enclosure (or
corral) for the animals when needed, and a fortification against
the Indians. Not to embarrass this cattle-pen, the camp fires are all
lighted outside of the wagons. Outside of the wagons, also, the
travellers spread their beds, which consist, for the most part, of
buffalo-rugs and blankets. Many content themselves with a single
Mackinaw; but a pair constitutes the most regular pallet; and he
that is provided with a buffalo-rug into the bargain, is deemed
luxuriously supplied. It is most usual to sleep out in the open air,
as well to be at hand in case of attack, as indeed for comfort; for
the serene sky of the Prairies affords the most agreeable and
wholesome canopy. That deleterious attribute of night air and
dews, so dangerous in other climates, is but little experienced upon
the high plains: on the contrary, the serene evening air seems to
affect the health rather favorably than otherwise. Tents are so
rare on these expeditions that, in a caravan of two hundred men, I
have not seen a dozen. In time of rain the traveller resorts to his
wagon, which affords a far more secure shelter than a tent; for if
the latter is not beaten down by the storms which so often accompany rain upon the prairies, the ground underneath is at least apt

to be flooded. During dry weather, however, even the invalid prefers the open air.

Prior to the date of our trip it had been customary to secure the horses by hoppling them. The 'fore-hopple' (a leathern strap or rope manacle upon the fore legs) being most convenient, was more frequently used; though the 'side-line' (a hopple connecting a fore and a hind leg) is the most secure; for with this an animal can hardly increase his pace beyond a hobbling walk; whereas, with the fore-hopple, a frightened horse will scamper off with nearly as much velocity as though he were unshackled. But, better than either of these is the practice which the caravans have since adopted of tethering the mules at night around the wagons, at proper intervals, with ropes twenty-five or thirty feet in length, tied to stakes fifteen to twenty inches long, driven into the ground; a supply of which, as well as mallets, the wagoners always carry with them.

It is amusing to witness the disputes which often arise among wagoners about their 'staking ground.' Each teamster is allowed, by our 'common law,' a space of about a hundred yards immediately fronting his wagon, which he is ever ready to defend, if a neighbor shows a disposition to encroach upon his soil. If any animals are found 'staked' beyond the 'chartered limits,' it is the duty of the guard to 'knock them up,' and turn them into the *corral*. Of later years the tethering of oxen has also been resorted to with advantage. It was thought at first that animals thus confined by ropes could not procure a sufficient supply of food; but experience has allayed all apprehension on the subject. In fact, as the camp is always pitched in the most luxuriantly clothed patches of prairie that can be selected, a mule is seldom able to despatch in the course of one night, all the grass within his reach. Again, when animals are permitted to range at liberty, they are apt to mince and nibble at the tenderest blades and spend their time in roaming from point to point, in search of what is most agreeable to their 'epicurean palates;' whereas if they are restricted by a rope, they will at once fall to with earnestness and clip the pasturage as it comes.

Although the buffalo had been scarce for a few days,—frightened off, no doubt, by the Indians whose 'sign' we saw about Ash creek, they soon became exceedingly abundant. The larger droves of these animals are sometimes a source of great annoyance to the caravans as, by running near our loose stock, there is frequent danger of their causing *stampedes* (or general scamper), in which case mules, horses and oxen have been known to run away among the buffalo, as though they had been a gang of their own species. A company of traders, in 1824, lost twenty or thirty of their animals in this way. Hunters have also been deprived of their horses in the same way. Leaping from them in haste, in order to take a more determinate aim at a buffalo, the horse has been known to take fright, and, following the fleeing game, has disappeared with saddle, bridle, pistols, and all—most probably never to be heard of again. In fact, to look for stock upon these prairies, would be emphatically to 'search for a needle in a haystack;' not only because they are virtually boundless, but that being everywhere alive with herds of buffalo, from which horses cannot be distinguished at a distance, one knows not whither to turn in search after the stray animals.

We had lately been visited by frequent showers of rain, and upon observing the Arkansas river, it was found to be rising, which seemed portentous of the troubles which the 'June freshet' might occasion us in crossing it; and, as it was already the 11th of this month, this annual occurrence was now hourly expected. On some occasions caravans have been obliged to construct what is called a buffalo boat, which is done by stretching the hides of these animals over a frame of poles, or, what is still more common, over an empty wagon-body. The 'June freshets,' however, are seldom of long duration; and, during the greatest portion of the year, the channel is very shallow. Still the bed of the river being in many places filled with quicksand, it is requisite to examine and mark out the best ford with stakes, before one undertakes to cross. The wagons are then driven over usually by double teams, which should never be permitted to stop, else animals and wagons are apt to founder, and the loading is liable to be damaged. I have witnessed a whole team down at once, rendering it necessary to unharness and drag each mule out separately: in fact, more than common exertion is sometimes required to prevent these dumpish animals from drowning in their fright and struggles through the water, though the current be but shallow at the place. Hence it is that oxen are much safer for fording streams than mules. As for ourselves, we forded the river without serious difficulty.

Rattlesnakes are proverbially abundant upon all these prairies, and as there is seldom to be found either stick or stone with which to kill them, one hears almost a constant popping of rifles or pistols among the vanguard, to clear the route of these disagreeable occupants, lest they should bite our animals. As we were toiling up through the sandy hillocks which border the southern banks of the Arkansas, the day being exceedingly warm, we came upon a perfect den of these reptiles. I will not say 'thousands,' though this perhaps were nearer the truth— but hundreds at least were coiled or crawling in every direction. They were no sooner discovered than we were upon them with guns and pistols, determined to let none of them escape.

In the midst of this amusing scramble among the snakes, a wild mustang colt, which had, somehow or other, become separated from its dam, came bolting among our relay of loose stock to add to the confusion. One of our mules, evidently impressed with the impertinence of the intruder, sprang forward and attacked it, with the apparent intention of executing summary chastisement; while another mule, with more benignity of temper than its irascible compeer, engaged most lustily in defense of the unfortunate little mustang. As the contest was carried on among the wagons, the teamsters soon became very uproarious; so that the whole, with the snake fracas, made up a capital scene of confusion. When the mule skirmish would have ended, if no one had interfered, is a question which remained undetermined; for some of our company, in view of the consequences that might result from the contest, rather inhumanly took sides with the assailing mule; and soon after they entered the lists, a rifle ball relieved the poor colt from its earthly embarrassments, and the company from further domestic disturbance. Peace once more restored, we soon got under way, and that evening pitched our camp opposite the celebrated 'Caches,' a place where some of the earliest adventurers had been compelled to conceal their merchandise.

Few travellers pass this way without visiting these mossy pits, many of which remain partly unfilled to the present day. In the vicinity, or a few miles to the eastward perhaps, passes the hun-

dredth degree of longitude west from Greenwich, which, from the
Arkansas to Red River, forms the boundary between the United
States and the Mexican, or rather the Texan territory.

The term *cache,* meaning a *place of concealment,* was originally
used by the Canadian French trappers and traders. It is made by
digging a hole in the ground, somewhat in the shape of a jug,
which is lined with dry sticks, grass, or anything else that will
protect its contents from the dampness of the earth. In this place
the goods to be concealed are carefully stowed away; and the
aperture is then so effectually closed as to protect them from the
rains. In *caching,* a great deal of skill is often required, to leave no
signs whereby the cunning savage might discover the place of
deposit. To this end, the excavated earth is carried to some
distance and carefully concealed, or thrown into a stream, if one
be at hand. The place selected for a cache is usually some rolling
point, sufficiently elevated to be secure from inundations. If it be
well set with grass, a solid piece of turf is cut out large enough
for the entrance. The turf is afterward laid back, and taking root,
in a short time no signs remain of its ever having been molested.
However, as every locality does not afford a turfy site, the camp
fire is sometimes built upon the place, or the animals are penned
over it, which effectually destroys all traces of the cache.

This mode of concealing goods seems to have been in use from
the time of the earliest French voyagers in America. Father
Hennepin, during his passage down the Mississippi river, in 1680,
describes an operation of this kind in the following terms: "We
took up the green Sodd, and laid it by, and digg'd a hole in the
Earth where we put our Goods, and cover'd them with pieces of
Timber and Earth, and then put in again the green Turf; so that
'twas impossible to suspect that any Hole had been digg'd under
it, for we flung the Earth into the River." Returning a few weeks
after, they found the cache all safe and sound.

3 . Across the Prairies

Our route had already led us up the course of the Arkansas
river for over a hundred miles, yet the earlier caravans often
passed from fifty to a hundred further up before crossing the

river; therefore nothing like a regular ford had ever been established. Nor was there a road, not even a trail, anywhere across the famous plain, extending between the Arkansas and Cimarron rivers, a distance of over fifty miles, which now lay before us—the scene of such frequent sufferings in former times for want of water. It having been determined upon, however, to strike across this dreaded desert the following morning, the whole party was busy in preparing for the 'water scrape,' as these droughty drives are very appropriately called by prairie travellers. This tract of country may truly be styled the grand 'prairie ocean;' for not a single landmark is to be seen for more than forty miles—scarcely a visible eminence by which to direct one's course. All is as level as the sea, and the compass was our surest, as well as principal guide.

The evening before the embarking of a caravan upon this plain, the captain's voice is usually heard above the din and clatter of the camp, ordering to "fill up the water kegs,"—a precaution which cannot be repeated too often, as new adventurers are usually ignorant of the necessity of providing a supply sufficient to meet every contingency that may befall during two or more days' journey over this arid region. The cooks are equally engrossed by their respective vocations: some are making bread, others preparing viands, and all tasking their ingenuity to lay by such stores as may be deemed expedient for at least two days' consumption. On the following morning (June 14th), the words 'catch up' again resounded through the camp, and the caravan was once more in motion.

The next day we fortunately had a heavy shower, which afforded us abundance of water. Having also swerved considerably toward the south, we fell into a more uneven section of country, where we had to cross a brook swelled by the recent rain, into which one of the wagons was unfortunately overset. This, however, was not a very uncommon occurrence; for unruly oxen, when thirsty, will often rush into a pool in despite of the driver, dragging the wagon over every object in their way, at the imminent risk of turning it topsy-turvy into the water. We were now compelled to make a halt, and all hands flocked to the assistance of the owner of the damaged cargo. In a few minutes about an acre of ground was completely covered with calicoes, and other domestic goods, presenting altogether an interesting spectacle.

All were busily occupied at this work when some objects were seen moving in the distance, which at first were mistaken for buffalo; but were speedily identified as horsemen. Anxiety was depicted in every countenance. Could it be possible that the party of Capt. Sublette, which was nearly a month ahead of us, had been lost in these dreary solitudes? or was it the band of Capt. Bent, who was expected to follow some time after us? This anxious suspense, however, lasted only for a few minutes; and the cry of "Indians!" soon made the welkin ring. Still they appeared to approach too slowly for the western prairie tribes. A little nearer, and we soon perceived that they carried a flag, which turned out to be that of the United States. This welcome sight allayed at once all uneasiness; as it is well known that most savages, when friendly, approach the whites with a hoisted flag, provided they have one. It turned out to be a party of about eighty Sioux, who were on a tour upon the Prairies for the purpose of trading with, stealing from or marauding upon the southwestern nations. Our communications were carried on entirely by signs; yet we understood them perfectly to say, that there were immense numbers of Indians ahead, upon the Cimarron river, whom they described by symbolic language to be Blackfeet and Comanches; a most agreeable prospect for the imagination to dwell upon!

We now moved on slowly and leisurely, for all anxiety on the subject of water had been happily set at rest by frequent falls of rain. But imagine our consternation and dismay, when, upon descending into the valley of the Cimarron, on the morning of the 19th of June, a band of Indian warriors on horseback suddenly appeared before us from behind the ravines—an imposing array of death-dealing savages! There was no merriment in this! It was a genuine alarm—a tangible reality! These warriors, however, as we soon discovered, were only the vanguard of a 'countless host,' who were by this time pouring over the opposite ridge, and galloping directly towards us.

The wagons were soon irregularly 'formed' upon the hill-side: but in accordance with the habitual carelessness of caravan traders, a great portion of the men were unprepared for the emergency. Scores of guns were 'empty,' and as many more had

been wetted by the recent showers, and would not 'go off.' Here
was one calling for balls—another for powder—a third for flints.
Exclamations, such as, "I've broke my ram-rod"—"I've spilt my
caps"—"I've rammed down a ball without powder"—"My gun is
'choked;' give me yours"—were heard from different quarters;
while a timorous 'greenhorn' would perhaps cry out, "Here, take
my gun, you can outshoot me!" The more daring bolted off to
encounter the enemy at once, while the timid and cautious took a
stand with presented rifle behind the wagons. The Indians who
were in advance made a bold attempt to press upon us, which
came near costing them dearly; for some of our fiery backwoodsmen more than once had their rusty but unerring rifles directed
upon the intruders, some of whom would inevitably have fallen
before their deadly aim, had not some of the more prudent traders
interposed. The Indians made demonstrations no less hostile,
rushing, with ready sprung bows, upon a portion of our men who
had gone in search of water, and mischief would, perhaps, have
ensued, had not the impetuosity of the warriors been checked by
the wise men of the nation.

The Indians were collecting around us, however, in such great
numbers, that it was deemed expedient to force them away, so as
to resume our march, or at least to take a more advantageous
position. Our company was therefore mustered and drawn up in
'line of battle;' and, accompanied by the sound of a drum and fife,
we marched towards the main group of the Indians. The latter
seemed far more delighted than frightened with this strange
parade and music, a spectacle they had, no doubt, never witnessed
before; and perhaps looked upon the whole movement rather as
a complimentary salute than a hostile array; for there was no
interpreter through whom any communication could be conveyed
to them. But, whatever may have been their impressions, one
thing is certain,—that the principal chief (who was dressed in a
long red coat of strouding, or coarse cloth) appeared to have full
confidence in the virtues of his calumet; which he lighted, and
came boldly forward to meet our warlike corps, serenely smoking
the 'pipe of peace.' Our captain, now taking a whiff with the
savage chief, directed him by signs to cause his warriors to retire.
This most of them did, to rejoin the long train of squaws and
papooses with the baggage, who followed in the rear, and were

just then seen emerging from beyond the hills. Having slowly descended to the banks of the stream, they pitched their wigwams or lodges; over five hundred of which soon bespeckled the ample valley before us, and at once gave to its recently meagre surface the aspect of an immense Indian village. The entire number of the Indians, when collected together, could not have been less than from two to three thousand—although some of our company insisted that there were at least four thousand souls. In such a case they must have mustered nearly a thousand warriors, while we were but little over two hundred strong. Still, our superior arms and the protection afforded by the wagons, gave us considerably the advantage, even supposing an equality in point of valor. However, the appearance of the squaws and children soon convinced us, that, for the present, at least, they had no hostile intentions; so we also descended into the valley and formed our camp a few hundred yards below them. The 'capitanes,' or head men of the whites and Indians, shortly after met, and, again smoking the calumet, agreed to be friends.

Although we were now on the very banks of the Cimarron, even the most experienced traders of our party, whether through fright or ignorance, seemed utterly unconscious of the fact. Having made our descent, far below the usual point of approach, and there being not a drop of water found in the sandy bed of the river, it was mistaken for Sand creek, and we accordingly proceeded without noticing it. Therefore, after our 'big talk' was concluded, and dinner dispatched, we again set out southward, in search of the Cimarron. As we were starting, warriors, squaws and papooses now commenced flocking about us, gazing at our wagons with amazement; for many of them had never, perhaps, seen such vehicles before. A few chiefs and others followed us to our next encampment; but these were sent away at night.

Our guards were now doubled, as a night attack was apprehended; for although we were well aware that Indians never commit outrages with their families at hand, yet it was feared that they might either send them away or conceal them during the night. A little after dark, these fears seemed about to be realized; as a party of thirty or forty Indians were seen coming up towards the encampment. Immediate preparations were made to attack them, when they turned out to be a band of squaws, with merely a few men as gallants—all of whom were summarily turned adrift, without waiting to speculate upon the objects of their visit. The next morning a few others made their appearance, which we treated in precisely the same manner, as a horse was missing, which it was presumed the Indians had stolen.

We continued our march southward in search of the 'lost river.' After a few miles' travel we encountered a ledge of sand-hills, which obstructed our course, and forced us to turn westward and follow their border for the rest of the day. Finding but little water that night, and none at all the next day, we began by noon to be sadly frightened; for nothing is more alarming to the prairie traveller than a 'water-scrape.' The impression soon became general that we were *lost*—lost on that inhospitable desert, which had been the theatre of so many former scenes of suffering! and our course impeded by sand-hills! A council of the veteran travellers was called to take our emergency into consideration. It was at once resolved to strike in a northwesterly direction in search of the 'dry ravine' we had left behind us, which was now supposed to have been the Cimarron.

We had just set out, when a couple of Indians approached us, bringing the horse we had lost the night before; an apparent demonstration of good faith which could hardly have been anticipated. It was evidently an effort to ingratiate themselves in our favor, and establish an intercourse—perhaps a traffic. But the outrages upon Major Riley, as well as upon a caravan, not two years before, perpetrated probably by the same Indians, were fresh in the memory of all; so that none of us were willing to confide in their friendly professions. On inquiring by means of signs for the nearest water, they pointed to the direction we were travelling: and finally taking the lead, they led us, by the shortest way, to the valley of the long-sought Cimarron, which, with its delightful green-grass glades and flowing torrent (very different in appearance from where we had crossed it below), had all the aspect of an 'elysian vale,' compared with what we had seen for some time past. We pitched our camp in the valley, much rejoiced at having again 'made a port.'

We were not destined to rest long in peace, however. About mid-night we were all aroused by a cry of alarm, the like of which had not been heard since the day Don Quixote had his famous adventure with the fulling-mills; and I am not quite sure but some of our party suffered as much from fright as poor Sancho Panza did on that memorable occasion. But Don Quixote and Sancho only heard the thumping of the mills and the roaring of the waters; while we heard the thumping of the Indian drums, accompanied by occasional yells, which our excited fancies immediately construed into notes of the fearful war-song.

After the whole company had been under arms for an hour or two, finding the cause of alarm approached no nearer, we again retired to rest. But a little before daylight we were again startled by the announcement—"The Indians are coming!—they are upon the very camp!" In a moment every man was up in arms; and several guns were presented to 'salute' the visitors, when, to our extreme mortification, they were found to be but eight or ten in number. They were immediately dispatched, by signs, and directed to remain away till morning—which they did.

On the following day, we had been in motion but a few minutes, when the Indians began flocking around us in large numbers, and by the time we encamped in the evening, we had perhaps a thousand of these pertinacious creatures, males and females, of all ages and descriptions, about us. At night, every means, without resorting to absolute violence, was employed to drive them away, but without entire success. At this time a small band of warriors took the round of our camp, and 'serenaded' us with a monotonous song of *hee-o-hehs*, with the view, I suppose, of gaining permission to remain; hoping, no doubt, to be able to 'drive a fair business' at pilfering during the night. In fact, a few small articles were already missing, and it was now discovered that they had purloined a pig of lead (between fifty and a hundred pounds weight) from one of the cannon-carriages, where it had been carelessly left. This increased the uneasiness which already prevailed to a considerable extent; and many of us would imagine it already moulded into bullets, which we were perhaps destined to receive before morning from the muzzles of their fusils. Some were even so liberal as to express a willingness to pardon the theft, rather than give the Indians the trouble of sending it back in so hasty a manner. After a tedious night of suspense and conjecture, it was no small relief to those whose feelings had been so highly wrought upon, to find, on waking up in the morning, that every man still retained his scalp.

It was generally supposed at the time that there was a great number of Comanches and Arrapahoes among this troop of savages; but they were principally if not altogether Blackfeet and Gros Ventres. We afterward learned that on their return to the northern mountains, they met with a terrible defeat from the Sioux and other neighboring tribes, in which they were said to have lost more than half their number.

We now encountered a great deal of wet weather; in fact this region is famous for cold protracted rains of two or three days' duration. Storms of hail-stones larger than hen's eggs are not uncommon, frequently accompanied by the most tremendous hurricanes. The violence of the wind is sometimes so great that, as I have heard, two road-wagons were once capsized by one of these terrible thunder-gusts; the rain, at the same time, floating the plain to depth of several inches. In short, I doubt if there is any known region out of the tropics, that can 'head' the great prairies in 'getting up' thunder-storms, combining so many of the elements of the awful and sublime.

During these storms the guards were often very careless. This was emphatically the case with us, notwithstanding our knowledge of the proximity of a horde of savages. In fact, the caravan was subject to so little control that the patience of Capt. Stanley underwent some very severe trials; so much so that he threatened more than once to resign. Truly, there is not a better school for testing a man's temper, than the command of a promiscuous caravan of independent traders. The rank of captain is, of course, but little more than nominal. Every proprietor of a two-horse wagon is apt to assume as much authority as the commander himself, and to issue his orders without the least consultation at head-quarters. It is easy then to conceive that the captain has anything but an enviable berth. He is expected to keep order while few are disposed to obey—loaded with execrations for every mishap, whether accidental or otherwise; and when he attempts to remonstrate he only renders himself ridiculous, being entirely without power to enforce his commands. It is to be regretted that some system of 'maritime law' has not been introduced among these traders to secure subordination, which can never be attained while the commander is invested with no legal authority. For my own part, I can see no reason why the captain of a prairie caravan should not have as much power to call his men to account for disobedience or mutiny, as the captain of a ship upon the high seas.

After following the course of the Cimarron for two days longer, we at length reached a place called the 'Willow Bar,' where we took the usual mid-day respite of two or three hours, to afford the animals time to feed, and our cooks to prepare dinner. Our wagons were regularly 'formed,' and the animals turned loose to graze at leisure, with only a 'day-guard' to watch them. Those who had finished their dinners lay stretched upon their blankets, and were just beginning to enjoy the luxury of a siesta—when all of a sudden, the fearful and oft-reiterated cry of "Indians!" turned this scene of repose into one of bustle and confusion.

From the opposite ridge at the distance of a mile, a swarm of savages were seen coming upon us, at full charge, and their hideous whoop and yell soon resounded through the valley. Such a jumbling of promiscuous voices I never expect to hear again. Every one fancied himself a commander, and vociferated his orders accordingly. The air was absolutely rent with the cries of "Let's charge 'em, boys!"—"Fire upon 'em, boys!"—"Reserve! don't fire till they come nearer!"—while the voice of our captain was scarcely distinguishable in his attempts to prevent such rash proceedings. As the prairie Indians often approach their friends as well as enemies in this way, Captain Stanley was unwilling to proceed to extremities, lest they might be peacefully inclined. But a 'popping salute,' and the whizzing of fusil balls over our heads, soon explained their intentions. We returned them several rifle shots by way of compliment, but without effect, as they were at too great a distance.

The novices were not a little discouraged at these frequent inroads of the enemy, although it is very seldom that any lives are lost in encounters with them. In the course of twenty years since the commencement of this trade, I do not believe there have been a dozen deaths upon the Santa Fé route, even including those who have been killed off by disease, as well as by the Indians.

4. Santa Fé

It was on the last day of June that we arrived at the 'Upper Spring,' which is a small fountain breaking into a ravine that declines towards the Cimarron some three or four miles to the north. The scarcity of water in these desert regions, gives to every little spring an importance which, of course, in more favored countries it would not enjoy. We halted at noon on the brook below, and then branched off towards the waters of the Canadian, in an average direction of about thirty degrees south of west. As the wagon-road passes upon the adjacent ridge a quarter of a mile to the south of this spring, some of us, to procure a draught of its refreshing water, pursued a path along the ravine, winding through dense thickets of underbrush, matted with green-briers and grape-vines, which, with the wild-currant and plum-bushes, were all bent under their unripe fruit. The wildness of this place, with its towering cliffs, craggy spurs, and deep-cut crevices, became doubly impressive to us, as we reflected that we were in the very midst of the most savage haunts. Often will the lonely traveller, as he plods his weary way in silence, imagine in each click of a pebble, the snap of a firelock, and in every rebound of a twig, the whisk of an arrow. After regaling ourselves with a draught of the delicious beverage which gushed from the pure fountain, we ascended the rugged heights and rejoined the caravan half a mile beyond.

We had now a plain and perfectly distinguishable track before us, and a party of *avant-couriers*, known in the technical parlance of the Prairies as 'runners,' soon began to make preparations for pushing forward in advance of the caravan into Santa Fé, though we were yet more than two hundred miles from that city. It is customary for these runners to take their departure from the caravans in the night, in order to evade the vigilance of any enemy that might be lurking around the encampment. They are generally proprietors or agents; and their principal purpose is to procure and send back a supply of provisions, to secure good store-houses, and what is no less important, to obtain an agreeable understanding with the officers of the custom-house.

The second day after the departure of the runners, as we lay encamped at McNees's creek, the Fourth of July dawned upon us. Scarce had gray twilight brushed his dusky brow, when our patriotic camp gave lively demonstrations of that joy which plays around the heart of every American on the anniversary of this triumphant day. The roar of our artillery and rifle platoons resounded from every hill, while the rumbling of the drum and the

shrill whistle of the fife, imparted a degree of martial interest to
the scene which was well calculated to stir the souls of men. There
was no limit to the huzzas and enthusiastic ejaculations of our
people; and at every new shout the dales around sent forth a
gladsome response. This anniversary is always hailed with heart-
felt joy by the wayfarer in the remote desert; for here the strifes
and intrigues of party-spirit are unknown: nothing intrudes, in
these wild solitudes, to mar that harmony of feeling, and almost
pious exultation, which every true-hearted American experiences
on this great day.

The next day's march brought us in front of the Rabbit-Ear
Mound, which might now be seen at a distance of eight or ten
miles south of us, and which before the present track was established, served as a guide to travellers. The first caravan of wagons
that crossed these plains, passed on the south side of these
mounds, having abandoned our present route at the 'Cold Spring,'
where we encamped on the night of the 1st of July. Although the
route we were travelling swerves somewhat too much to the north,
that pursued by the early caravans as stated above, made still a
greater circuit to the south, and was by far the most inconvenient.

As we were proceeding on our march, we observed a horseman
approaching, who excited at first considerable curiosity. His picturesque costume, and peculiarity of deportment, however, soon
showed him to be a Mexican *Cibolero* or Buffalo-hunter. These
hardy devotees of the chase usually wear leathern trousers and
jackets, and flat straw hats; while, swung upon the shoulder of
each hangs his *carcage* or quiver of bow and arrows. The long
handle of their lance being set in a case, and suspended by the
side with a strap from the pommel of the saddle, leaves the point
waving high over the head, with a tassel of gay parti-colored stuffs
dangling at the tip of the scabbard. Their fusil, if they happen to
have one, is suspended in like manner at the other side, with a
stopper in the muzzle fantastically tasselled.

The *Cibolero* saluted us with demonstrations of joy; nor were
we less delighted at meeting with him; for we were now able to
obtain information from Santa Fé, whence no news had been
received since the return of the caravan the preceding fall. Traders
and idlers, with equal curiosity, clustered around the new visitor;
every one who could speak a word of Spanish having some ques-

tion to ask:—"What prospects?"—"How are goods?"—"What news from the South?"—while the more experienced traders interested themselves chiefly to ascertain the condition of the custom-house, and who were the present revenue officers; for unpropitious changes sometimes occur during the absence of the caravans.

Our *Cibolero* was desirous to sell us some provisions, which, by the by, were welcome enough; for most of the company were out of bread, and meat was becoming very scarce, having seen but few buffalo since our first encounter with the Indians on the Cimarron. Our visitor soon retired to his camp hard by, and, with several of his comrades, afterwards brought us an abundance of dry buffalo beef, and some bags of coarse oven-toasted loaves, a kind of hard bread, much used by Mexican travellers. It is prepared by opening the ordinary leavened rolls, and toasting them brown in an oven. Though exceedingly hard and insipid while dry, it becomes not only soft but palatable when soaked in water —or better still in 'hot coffee.' But what we procured on this occasion was unusually stale and coarse, prepared expressly for barter with the Comanches, in case they should meet any: yet bread was bread, emphatically, with us just then.

A word concerning the *Ciboleros* may not be altogether uninteresting. Every year, large parties of New-Mexicans, some provided with mules and asses, others with *carretas* or truckle-carts and oxen, drive out into these prairies to procure a supply of buffalo beef for their families. They hunt, like the wild Indians, chiefly on horseback, and with bow and arrow, or lance, with which they soon load their carts and mules. They find no difficulty in curing their meat even in mid-summer, by slicing it thin and spreading or suspending it in the sun; or, if in haste, it is slightly barbecued. During the curing operation they often follow the Indian practice of beating or kneading the slices with their feet, which they contend contributes to its preservation.

Here the extraordinary purity of the atmosphere is remarkably exemplified. The caravans cure meat in the same simple manner, except the process of kneading. A line is stretched from corner to corner on each side of a wagon-body, and strung with slices of beef, which remains from day to day till it is sufficiently cured to be stacked away. This is done without salt, and yet it very rarely

putrifies. In truth, as blow-flies are unknown here, there is nothing to favor putrefaction.

But I have not yet done with the meat-curing operations. While
in the midst of the buffalo range, travellers usually take the precaution of laying up a supply of beef for exigencies in the absence
of the 'prairie cattle.' We had somewhat neglected this provision
in time of abundance, by which we had come near being reduced
to extremities. Caravans sometimes lie by a day or two to provide
a supply of meat; when numbers of buffalo are slaughtered, and
the flesh 'jerked,' or slightly barbecued, by placing it upon a scaf-
fold over a fire. The same method is resorted to by Mexicans when
the weather is too damp or cloudy for the meat to dry in the open
air.

We were now approaching the 'Round Mound,' a beautiful
round-topped cone, rising nearly a thousand feet above the level
of the plain by which it is for the most part surrounded. We were
yet at least three miles from this mound, when a party set out on
foot to ascend it, in order to get a view of the surrounding country.
They felt confident it was but half a mile off—at most, three-
quarters; but finding the distance so much greater than they had
anticipated, many began to lag behind, and soon rejoined the
wagons. The optical illusions occasioned by the rarified and transparent atmosphere of these elevated plains, are often truly
remarkable, affording another exemplification of its purity. One
would almost fancy himself looking through a spy-glass, for objects frequently appear at scarce one-fourth of their real distance
—frequently much magnified, and more especially elevated. I
have often seen flocks of antelopes mistaken for droves of elks or
wild horses, and when at a great distance, even for horsemen;
whereby frequent alarms are occasioned. I have also known tufts
of grass or weeds, or mere buffalo bones scattered on the prairies,
to stretch upward to the height of several feet, so as to present
the appearance of so many human beings. Ravens in the same way
are not unfrequently taken for Indians, as well as for buffalo; and
a herd of the latter upon a distant plain often appear so increased
in bulk that they would be mistaken by the inexperienced for a
grove of trees. This is usually attended with a continual waving
and looming, which often so writhe and distort distant objects as
to render them too indistinct to be discriminated. The illusion

seems to be occasioned by gaseous vapors rising from the ground while the beaming rays of the sun are darting upon it.

But the most curious, and at the same time the most perplexing phenomenon, occasioned by optical deception, is the *mirage*, or, as familiarly called upon the Prairies, the 'false ponds.' Even the experienced traveller is often deceived by these upon the arid plains, where a disappointment is most severely felt. The thirsty wayfarer, after jogging for hours under a burning sky, at length espies a pond—yes, it must be water—it looks too natural for him to be mistaken. He quickens his pace, enjoying in anticipation the pleasure of a refreshing draught: but lo! as he approaches, it recedes or entirely disappears; and when upon its apparent site, he is ready to doubt his own vision—he finds but a parched plain under his feet. It is not until he has been thus a dozen times deceived, that he is willing to relinquish the pursuit: and then, perhaps, when he really does see a pond, he will pass it unexamined, for fear of another disappointment.

The philosophy of these 'false ponds' seems generally not well understood. They have usually been attributed to *refraction*, by which a section of the bordering sky would appear below the horizon: but there can be no doubt that they are the effect of *reflection*, upon a gas emanating perhaps from the sun-scorched earth and vegetable matter. Or it may be that a surcharge of carbonic acid, precipitated upon the flats and sinks of those plains, by the action of the sun, produces the effect. At least, it appears of sufficient density, when viewed very obliquely, to reflect the objects beyond: and thus the opposite sky being reflected in the *pond of gas*, gives the appearance of water. As a proof that it is the effect of reflection, I have often observed the distant trees and hilly protuberances which project above the horizon beyond, distinctly inverted in the 'pond;' whereas, were it the result of refraction, these would appear erect, only cast below the surface. Indeed, many are the singular atmospheric phenomena observable upon the plains, which would afford a field of interesting research for the curious natural philosopher.

At last, some of the most persevering of our adventurers succeeded in ascending the summit of the Round Mound, which commands a full and advantageous view of the surrounding country, in some directions to the distance of a hundred miles or more.

Looking southward a varied country is seen, of hills, plains, mounds, and sandy undulations; but on the whole northern side, extensive plains spread out, studded occasionally with variegated peaks and ridges. Far beyond these, to the northwestward, and low in the horizon a silvery stripe appears upon an azure base, resembling a list of chalk-white clouds. This is the perennially snow-capped summit of the eastern spur of the Rocky Mountains.

These immense bordering plains, and even the hills with which they are interspersed, are wholly destitute of timber, except a chance scattering tree upon the margins of the bluffs and ravines, which but scantily serves to variegate the landscape. Not even a buffalo was now to be seen to relieve the dull monotony of the scene; although at some seasons (and particularly in the fall) these prairies are literally strewed with herds of this animal. Then, 'thousands and tens of thousands' might at times be seen from this eminence. But the buffalo is a migratory animal, and even in the midst of the Prairies where they are generally so very abundant, we sometimes travel for days without seeing a single one; though no signs of hunter or Indian can be discovered. To say the truth, however, I have never seen them anywhere upon the Prairies so abundant as some travellers have represented—in dense masses, darkening the whole prairies. I have only found them in scattered herds, of a few scores, hundreds, or sometimes thousands in each, and where in the greatest numbers, dispersed far and wide; but with large intervals between. Yet they are very sensibly and rapidly decreasing. There is a current notion that the whites frighten them away; but I would ask, where do they go to? To be sure, to use a hunter's phrase, they 'frighten a few out of their skins;' yet for every one killed by the whites, more than a hundred, perhaps a thousand, fall by the hands of the savages. From these, however, there is truly 'nowhere to flee;' for they follow them wheresoever they go: while the poor brutes instinctively learn to avoid the fixed establishments, and, to some degree, the regular travelling routes of the whites.

As the caravan was passing under the northern base of the Round Mound, it presented a very fine and imposing spectacle to those who were upon its summit. The wagons marched slowly in four parallel columns, but in broken lines, often at intervals of many rods between. The unceasing 'crack, crack,' of the wagoners'

whips, resembling the frequent reports of distant guns, almost
made one believe that a skirmish was actually taking place between two hostile parties: and a hostile engagement it virtually
was to the poor brutes, at least; for the merciless application of the
whip would sometimes make the blood spirt from their sides—and
that often without any apparent motive of the wanton *carrettieri*,
other than to amuse themselves with the flourishing and loud
popping of their lashes!

The rear wagons are usually left without a guard; for all the
loose horsemen incline to be ahead, where they are to be seen
moving in scattered groups, sometimes a mile or more in advance.
As our camp was pitched but a mile west of the Round Mound,
those who lingered upon its summit could have an interesting
view of the evolutions of 'forming' the wagons, in which the
drivers by this time had become very expert. When marching four
abreast, the two exterior lines spread out and then meet at the
the front angle; while the two inner lines keep close together until
they reach the point of the rear angle, when they wheel suddenly
out and close with the hinder ends of the other two; thus systematically concluding a right-lined quadrangle, with a gap left at the
rear corner for the introduction of the animals.

Our encampment was in a beautiful plain, but without water,
of which, however, we had had a good supply at noon. Our cattle,
as was the usual custom, after having grazed without for a few
hours, were now shut up in the pen of the wagons. Our men were
all wrapt in peaceful slumber, except the guard, who kept their
silent watch around the encampment; when all of a sudden, about
the ominous hour of mid-night, a tremendous uproar was heard,
which caused every man to start in terror from his blanket couch,
with arms in hand. Some animal, it appeared, had taken fright at
a dog, and by a sudden start, set all around him in violent motion;
the panic spread simultaneously throughout the pen; and a scene
of rattle, clash, and 'lumbering,' ensued, which far surpassed
everything we had yet witnessed. A general 'stampede' (*estam-
pida*, as the Mexicans say) was the result. Notwithstanding the
wagons were tightly bound together, wheel to wheel, with ropes
or chains, and several stretched across the gaps at the corners of
the *corral*, the oxen soon burst their way out; and though mostly
yoked in pairs, they went scampering over the plains, as though

Tam O'Shanter's 'cutty-sark' Nannie had been at their tails. All attempts to stop them were vain; for it would require 'Auld Clootie' himself to check the head-way of a drove of oxen, when once thoroughly frightened. Early the following morning we made active exertions to get up a sufficient quantity of teams to start the caravan. At Rock Creek, a distance of six or seven miles, we were joined by those who had gone in pursuit of the stock. All the oxen were found, except some half a dozen, which were never recovered. No mules were lost: a few that had broken loose were speedily retaken. The fact is, that though mules are generally easiest scared, oxen are decidedly the worst when once started. The principal advantage of the latter in this respect is, that Indians have but little inducement to steal them, and therefore few attempts would be made upon a caravan of oxen.

We were now entering a region of rough, and in some places, rocky road, as the streams which intervene from this to the mountains are all bordered with fine sandstone. These rugged passes acted very severely upon our wagons, as the wheels were by this time becoming loose and 'shackling,' from the shrink of the wood, occasioned by the extreme dryness and rarity of this elevated atmosphere. The spokes of some were beginning to reel in the hubs, so that it became necessary to brace them with 'false spokes,' firmly bound with 'buffalo tug.' On some occasions, the wagon tires have become so loose upon the felloes as to tumble off while travelling. The most effective mode of tightening slackened tires (at least that most practised on the plains, as there is rarely a portable forge in company), is by driving strips of hoop-iron around between the tire and felloe—simple wedges of wood are sometimes made to supply the place of iron. During halts I have seen a dozen wheels being repaired at the same time, occasioning such a clitter-clatter of hammers, that one would almost fancy himself in a ship-yard.

Emerging from this region of asperities, we soon passed the 'Point of Rocks,' as a diminutive 'spur' projecting from the north is called, at the foot of which springs a charming little fount of water. This is but thirty or forty miles from the principal mountains, along whose border, similar detached ridges and hills are frequently to be seen. The next day, having descended from the table plain, we reached the principal branch of the Canadian river, which is here but a rippling brook, hardly a dozen paces in width, though eighty miles from its source in the mountains to the north. The bottom being of solid rock, this ford is appropriately called by the ciboleros, *el Vado de Piedras*. The banks are very low and easy to ascend. The stream is called *Rio Colorado* by the Mexicans, and is known among Americans by its literal translation of *Red River*. This circumstance perhaps gave rise to the belief that it was the head branch of our main stream of this name: but the nearest waters of the legitimate 'Red River of Natchitoches,' are still a hundred miles to the south of this road.

In descending to the Rio Colorado, we met a dozen or more of our countrymen from Taos, to which town (sixty or seventy miles distant) there is a direct but rugged route across the mountains. It was a joyous encounter, for among them we found some of our old acquaintances whom we had not seen for many years. During our boyhood we had 'spelt' together in the same country school, and roamed the wild woods with many a childish glee. They turned about with us, and the remainder of our march was passed in answering their inquiries after their relatives and friends in the United States.

Before reaching the stream, we encountered another party of visitors, being chiefly custom-house agents or clerks, who, accompanied by a military escort, had come out to guard the caravan to the Capital. The ostensible purpose of this escort was to prevent smuggling,—a company of troops being thus dispatched every year, with strict injunctions to watch the caravans. This custom appears since to have nearly grown out of use: and well might it be discontinued altogether, for any one disposed to smuggle would find no difficulty in securing the services of these preventive guards, who, for a trifling *douceur*, would prove very efficient auxiliaries, rather than obstacles to the success of any such designs. As we were forming in the valley opposite where the escort was encamped, Col. Vizcarra, the commandant, honored us with a salute from his artillery, which was promptly responded to by our little cannon.

Considering ourselves at last out of danger of Indian hostilities (although still nearly a hundred and forty miles from Santa Fé); and not unwilling to give our 'guard' as much trouble as possible, we abandoned the organization of our caravan a few miles beyond the Colorado; its members wending their way to the Capital in almost as many detached parties as there were proprietors. The road from this to San Miguel (a town nearly a hundred miles distant), leads in a southwestern direction along the base of, and almost parallel with, that spur of snow-clad mountains, which has already been mentioned, bearing down east of the Rio del Norte.

This region is particularly celebrated for violent showers, hail-storms, and frightful thunder-gusts. The sudden cooling and contraction of the atmosphere which follows these falls of rain, very often reverses the current of the lower stratum of air; so that a cloud which has just ceased pouring its contents and been wafted away, is in a few minutes brought back, and drenches the traveller with another torrent. I was deeply impressed with a scene I witnessed in the summer of 1832, about two days' journey beyond the Colorado, which I may be excused for alluding to in this connection. We were encamped at noon, when a murky cloud issued from behind the mountains, and, after hovering over us for a few minutes, gave vent to one of those tremendous peals of thunder which seem peculiar to those regions, making the elements tremble, and leaving us so stunned and confounded that some seconds elapsed before each man was able to convince himself that he had not been struck by lightning. A sulphureous stench filled the atmosphere; but the thunderbolt had skipped over the wagons and lighted upon the *caballada*, which was grazing hard by; some of which were afterward seen stretched upon the plain. It was not a little singular to find an ox lying lifeless from the stroke, while his mate stood uninjured by his side, and under the same yoke.

Some distance beyond the Colorado, a party of about a dozen (which I joined) left the wagons to go ahead to Santa Fé. Fifty miles beyond the main branch of this stream we passed the last of the Canadian waters, known to foreigners as the *Mora*. From thence to the *Gallinas*, the first of the Rio del Norte waters, the road stretches over an elevated plain, unobstructed by any mountainous ridge. At Gallinas creek, we found a large flock of sheep grazing upon the adjacent plain; while a little hovel at the foot of a cliff showed it to be a *rancho*. A swarthy *ranchero* soon made his appearance, from whom we procured a treat of goat's milk, with some dirty ewe's milk 'curdle cheese' to supply the place of bread.

Some twenty miles from this place we entered San Miguel, the first settlement of any note upon our route. This consists of irregular clusters of mud-wall huts, and is situated in the fertile valley of Rio Pecos, a silvery little river which ripples from the snowy mountains of Santa Fé—from which city this frontier village is nearly fifty miles to the southeast. The road makes this great southern bend, to find a passway through the broken extremity of the spur of mountains before alluded to, which from this point south is cut up into detached ridges and table plains. This mountain section of the road, even in its present unimproved condition, presents but few difficult passes, and might, with little labor, be put in good order.

A few miles before reaching the city, the road again emerges into an open plain. Ascending a table ridge, we spied in an extended valley to the northwest, occasional groups of trees, skirted with verdant corn and wheat fields, with here and there a square block-like protuberance reared in the midst. A little further, and just ahead of us to the north, irregular clusters of the same opened to our view. "Oh, we are approaching the suburbs!" thought I, on perceiving the cornfields, and what I supposed to be brick-kilns scattered in every direction. These and other observations of the same nature becoming audible, a friend at my elbow said, "It is true those are heaps of unburnt bricks, nevertheless they are *houses*—this is the city of Santa Fé."

Five or six days after our arrival, the caravan at last hove in sight, and wagon after wagon was seen pouring down the last declivity at about a mile distance from the city. To judge from the clamorous rejoicings of the men, and the state of agreeable excitement which the muleteers seemed to be laboring under, the spectacle must have been as new to them as it had been to me. It was truly a scene for the artist's pencil to revel in. Even the animals seemed to participate in the humor of their riders, who grew more and more merry and obstreperous as they descended towards the city. I doubt, in short, whether the first sight of the walls of Jerusalem were beheld by the crusaders with much more tumultuous and soul-enrapturing joy.

The arrival produced a great deal of bustle and excitement among the natives. *"Los Americanos!"*—*"Los carros!"*—*"La entrada de la caravana!"* were to be heard in every direction; and crowds of women and boys flocked around to see the new-comers; while crowds of *léperos* hung about as usual to see what they could pilfer. The wagoners were by no means free from excitement on this occasion. Informed of the 'ordeal' they had to pass, they had spent the previous morning in 'rubbing up;' and now they were prepared, with clean faces, sleek combed hair, and their choicest Sunday suit, to meet the 'fair eyes' of glistening black that were sure to stare at them as they passed. There was yet another preparation to be made in order to 'show off' to ad-vantage. Each wagoner must tie a bran new 'cracker' to the lash of his whip; for, on driving through the streets and the *plaza publica*, every one strives to outvie his comrades in the dexterity with which he flourishes this favorite badge of his authority.

Our wagons were soon discharged in the ware-rooms of the custom-house; and a few days' leisure being now at our disposal, we had time to take that recreation which a fatiguing journey of ten weeks had rendered so necessary. The wagoners, and many of the traders, particularly the novices, flocked to the numerous fandangoes, which are regularly kept up after the arrival of a caravan. But the merchants generally were anxiously and actively engaged in their affairs—striving who should first get his goods out of the custom-house, and obtain a chance at the 'hard chink' of the numerous country dealers, who annually resort to the Capital on these occasions.

Now comes the harvest for those idle interpreters, who make a business of 'passing goods,' as they term it; for as but a small portion of the traders are able to write the Spanish language, they are obliged to employ these legal go-betweens, who pledge them-selves, for a stipulated fee, to make the 'arrangements,' and translate the *manifiestos* (that is, bills of merchandise to be *mani-fested* at the custom-house), and to act the part of interpreters throughout.

The inspection ensues, but this is rarely carried on with rigid adherence to rules; for an 'actuated sympathy' for the merchants, and a 'specific desire' to promote the trade, cause the inspector to open a few of such packages only, as will exhibit the least dis-crepancy with the manifest.

The *derechos de arancel* (tariff imposts) of Mexico are extremely oppressive, averaging about a hundred per cent. upon the United States' cost of an ordinary 'Santa Fé assortment.' Those on cotton textures are particularly so. But it is scarcely necessary to add that there are believed to be very few ports in the Republic at which these rigid exactions are strictly executed. An 'arrangement'—a compromise is expected, in which the officers are sure at least to provide for themselves. At some ports, a custom has been said to prevail, of dividing the legal duties into three equal parts: one for the officers—a second for the merchants—the other for the government.

The arrival of a caravan at Santa Fé changes the aspect of the place at once. Instead of the idleness and stagnation which its streets exhibited before, one now sees everywhere the bustle, noise and activity of a lively market town. As the Mexicans very rarely speak English, the negotiations are mostly conducted in Spanish.

5 . New Mexico

Having resided for nearly nine years in Northern Mexico, and enjoyed opportunities for observation which do not always fall to the lot of a trader, it has occurred to me that a few sketches of the country—the first settlements—the early, as well as more recent struggles with the aboriginal inhabitants—their traditions and antiquities—together with some account of the manners and customs of the people, etc., would not be altogether unacceptable to the reader. The dearth of information which has hitherto prevailed on this subject, is my best apology for travelling out of my immediate track, and trespassing as it were upon the department of the regular historian.

New Mexico possesses but few of those natural advantages, which are necessary to anything like a rapid progress in civilization. Though bounded north and east by the territory of the United States, south by that of Texas and Chihuahua, and west by Upper California, it is surrounded by chains of mountains and prairie wilds, extending to a distance of 500 miles or more, except in the direction of Chihuahua, from which its settlements are

separated by an unpeopled desert of nearly two hundred miles—
and without a single means of communication by water with any
other part of the world.

There is not a single navigable stream to be found in New
Mexico. The famous Rio del Norte is so shallow, for the most part
of the year, that Indian canoes can scarcely float in it. Its navigation is also obstructed by frequent shoals and rippling sections for
a distance of more than a thousand miles below Santa Fé. This
river is only known to the inhabitants of Northern Mexico as
Rio del Norte, or North river, because it descends from that direction; yet in its passage southward, it is in some places called *Rio
Grande,* on account of its extent; but the name of *Rio Bravo* (Bold
or Rapid river), so often given to it on maps, is seldom if ever
heard among the people. Though its entire length, following its
meanders from its source in the Rocky Mountains to the Gulf of
Mexico, must be considerably over two thousand miles, it is
hardly navigable to the extent of two hundred miles above its
mouth.

Santa Fé, the capital of New Mexico, is the only town of any
importance in the province. We sometimes find it written *Santa
Fé de San Francisco* (Holy Faith of St. Francis), the latter being the
patron, or tutelary saint. Like most of the towns in this section of
country it occupies the site of an ancient Pueblo or Indian village,
whose race has been extinct for a great many years. Its situation
is twelve or fifteen miles east of the Rio del Norte, at the western
base of a snow-clad mountain, upon a beautiful stream of small
mill-power size, which ripples down in icy cascades, and joins the
river some twenty miles to the southwestward. The population of
the city itself but little exceeds 3000; yet, including several surrounding villages which are embraced in its corporate jurisdiction,
it amounts to nearly 6,000 souls.

The town is very irregularly laid out, and most of the streets
are little better than common highways traversing scattered settlements which are interspersed with corn-fields nearly sufficient
to supply the inhabitants with grain. The only attempt at anything
like architectural compactness and precision, consists in four tiers
of buildings, whose fronts are shaded with a fringe of *portales* or
corredores of the rudest possible description. They stand around
the public square, and comprise the *Palacio,* or Governor's house,

the Custom-house, the Barracks (with which is connected the fearful *Calabozo*), the *Casa Consistorial* of the *Alcaldes*, the *Capilla de los Soldados* or Military Chapel, besides several private residences, as well as most of the shops of the American traders.

The population of New Mexico is almost exclusively confined to towns and villages, the suburbs of which are generally farms. Even most of the individual *ranchos* and *haciendas* have grown into villages,—a result almost indispensable for protection against the marauding savages of the surrounding wilderness. The principal of these settlements are located in the valley of the Rio del Norte, extending from nearly one hundred miles north to about one hundred and forty south of Santa Fé. The most important of these, next to the capital, is *El Valle de Taos,* so called in honor of the *Taosa* tribe of Indians, a remnant of whom still forms a *Pueblo* in the north of the valley. No part of New Mexico equals this valley in amenity of soil, richness of produce and beauty of appearance. Whatever is thrown into its prolific bosom, which the early frosts of autumn will permit to ripen, grows to a wonderful degree of perfection.

Salubrity of climate is decidedly the most interesting feature in the character of New Mexico. Nowhere—not even under the much boasted Sicilian skies can a purer or a more wholesome atmosphere be found. Bilious diseases—the great scourge of the valley of the Mississippi—are here almost unknown. Persons withered almost to mummies, are to be encountered occasionally, whose extraordinary age is only to be inferred from their recollection of certain notable events which have taken place in times far remote.

A sultry day, from Santa Fé north, is of very rare occurrence. The summer nights are usually so cool and pleasant that a pair of blankets constitutes an article of comfort seldom dispensed with. The winters are long but not so subject to sudden changes as in damper climates; the general range of the thermometer, throughout the year, being from 10° to 75° above zero, of Fahrenheit.

The great elevation of all the plains about the Rocky Mountains, is perhaps the principal cause of the extraordinary dryness of the atmosphere. There is but little rain throughout the year, except from July to October—known as the *rainy season;* and as the Missouri traders usually arrive about its commencement, the coincidence has given rise to a superstition, quite prevalent among the vulgar, that the Americans bring the rain with them. During seasons of drought, especially, they look for the arrival of the annual caravans as the harbinger of speedy relief.

If we exclude the unsubjugated savages, the entire population of New Mexico, including the Pueblo Indians, cannot be set down, according to the best estimates I have been able to obtain, at more than 70,000 souls. These may be divided as follows: white creoles, say 1,000; Mestizos, or mixed creoles, 59,000; and Pueblos, 10,000. Of naturalized citizens, the number is inconsiderable— scarcely twenty; and if we except transient traders, there are not over double as many alien residents. There are no negroes in New Mexico, and consequently neither mulattoes nor *zambos*.

Agriculture, like almost everything else in New Mexico, is in a very primitive and unimproved state. A great portion of the peasantry cultivate with the hoe alone—their plows (when they have any) being only used for mellow grounds, as they are too rudely constructed to be fit for any other service. Those I have seen in use are mostly fashioned in this manner:—a section of the trunk of a tree, eight or ten inches in diameter, is cut about two feet long, with a small branch left projecting upwards, of convenient length for a handle. With this a beam is connected to which oxen are yoked. The block, with its fore end sloped downwards to a point, runs flat, and opens a furrow similar to that of the common shovel plow. What is equally worthy of remark is, that these plows are often made exclusively of wood, without one particle of iron, or even a nail to increase their durability.

The *labores* and *milpas* (cultivated fields) are often, indeed most usually, without any enclosure. The owners of cattle are obliged to keep herdsmen constantly with them, else graze them at a considerable distance from the farms; for if any trespass is committed upon the fields by stock, the proprietor of the latter is bound to pay damages: therefore, instead of the cultivator's having to guard his crop from the cattle as with us, the owners of these are bound to guard them from the crops. Only a chance farm is seen fenced with poles scattered along on forks, or a loose hedge of brush. Mud-fences, or walls of very large *adobes*, are also occasionally to be met with.

The necessity of irrigation has confined, and no doubt will continue to confine agriculture principally to the valleys of the

constant and flowing streams. In some places the crops are frequently cut short by the drying up of the streams. Where water is
abundant, however, art has so far superseded the offices of nature
in watering the farms, that it is almost a question whether the in-
terference of nature in the matter would not be a disadvantage. On
the one hand the husbandman need not have his grounds overflowed if he administers the water himself, much less need he
permit them to suffer from drought. He is therefore more sure of
his crop than if it were subject to the caprices of the weather in
more favored agricultural regions.

The staple productions of the country are emphatically Indian
corn and wheat. The former grain is most extensively employed
for making *tortillas*—an article of food greatly in demand among
the people, the use of which has been transmitted to them by the
aborigines. The corn is boiled in water with a little lime: and when
it has been sufficiently softened, so as to strip it of its skin, it is
ground into paste upon the *metate*, and formed into a thin cake.
This is afterwards spread on a small sheet of iron or copper, called
comal (*comalli*, by the Indians), and placed over the fire, where, in
less than three minutes, it is baked and ready for use. The thinness
of the tortilla is always a great test of skill in the maker, and much
rivalry ensues in the art of preparation. The office of making tortillas has, from the earliest times, pertained chiefly to the women,
who appear to be better adapted to this employ than the other
sex, both as regards skill and dexterity, in preparing this particular
food for the table. I perfectly agree with the historian Clavigero,
however, in the opinion that "although this species of corn-bread
may be very wholesome and substantial, and well-flavored when
newly made, it is unpleasant when cold."

A sort of thin mush, called *atole*, made of Indian meal, is
another article of diet, the preparation of which is from the aborigines; and such is its nationality, that in the North it is frequently
called *el café de los Mexicanos* (the coffee of the Mexicans). How
general soever the use of coffee among Americans may appear,
that of *atole* is still more so among the lower classes of Mexicans.
They virtually 'breakfast, dine and sup' upon it. Of this, indeed,
with *frijoles* and *chile* (beans and red pepper), consists their principal food. The extravagant use of red pepper among the Mexicans
has become truly proverbial. It enters into nearly every dish at

every meal, and often so predominates as entirely to conceal the character of the viands. It is likewise ground into a sauce, and thus used even more abundantly than butter. *Chile verde* (green pepper), not as a mere condiment, but as a salad, served up in different ways, is reckoned by them one of the greatest luxuries. But however much we may be disposed to question their taste in this particular, no one can hesitate to do homage to their incomparable chocolate, in the preparation of which the Mexicans surely excel every other people.

The rancheros, and all the humbler classes of people, very seldom use any table for their meals, an inconvenience which is very little felt, as the dishes are generally served out from the kitchen in courses of a single plate to each guest, who usually takes it upon his knees. Knives and forks are equally dispensed with, the viands being mostly hashed or boiled so very soft as to be eaten with a spoon. This is frequently supplied by the *tortilla*, a piece of which is ingeniously doubled between the fingers, so as to assist in the disposal of anything, be it ever so rare or liquid. Thus it may well be said, as in the story of the Oriental monarch, that these rancheros employ a new spoon for every mouthful: for each fold of the tortilla is devoured with the substance it conveys to the mouth.

The very singular custom of abstaining from all sorts of beverage during meals, has frequently afforded me a great deal of amusement. Although a large cup of water is set before each guest, it is not customary to drink it off till the repast is finished. Should any one take it up in his hand while in the act of eating, the host is apt to cry out, "Hold, hold! there is yet more to come." I have never been able to ascertain definitely the meaning of this peculiarity; but from the strictness with which it is observed, it is natural to suppose, that the use of any kind of drink whilst eating, is held extremely unwholesome.* The New Mexicans use but little wine at meals, and that exclusively of the produce of the Paso del Norte.

But to return to the productions of the soil. *Cotton* is cultivated to no extent, although it has always been considered as indigenous

---

* What also strikes the stranger as a singularity in that country, is that the females rarely ever eat with the males—at least in the presence of strangers —but usually take their food in the kitchen by themselves.

to the country; while the ancient manufactures of the aborigines prove it to have been especially so in this province. *Flax* is entirely neglected, and yet a plant resembling in every respect that of the *linum usitatissimum*, is to be found in great abundance in many of the mountain valleys. The potato (*la papa*), although not cultivated in this country till very lately, is unquestionably an indigenous plant, being still found in a state of nature in many of the mountain valleys—though of small size, seldom larger than filberts: whence it appears that this luxury had not its exclusive origin in South America, as is the current opinion of the present day. Universal as the use of tobacco is among these people, there is very little of it grown, and that chiefly of a light and weak species, called by the natives *punche*, which is also indigenous, and still to be met with growing wild in some places.

There is but little timber in New Mexico, except in the mountains and along the water-courses; the table-plains and valleys are generally all open prairie. The forest growths, moreover, of all the north of Mexico, present quite a limited variety of timber, among which the common pitch-pine mostly predominates. The tree which appears to be most peculiar to the country, is a kind of scrub pine called *piñon*, which grows generally to the height of twenty or thirty feet, with leaves ever-green and pine-like, but scarcely an inch long. From the surface of this tree exudes a species of turpentine resembling that of the pitch-pine, but perhaps less resinous. The wood is white and firm, and much used for fuel. The most remarkable appendage of this tree is the fruit it bears, which is also known by the same name. This is a little nut about the size of a kidney-bean, with a rich oily kernel in a thin shell, enclosed in a chestnut-like bur. It is of pleasant flavor and much eaten by the natives, and considerable quantities are exported annually to the southern cities. It is sometimes used for the manufacture of a certain kind of oil, said to be very good for lamps.

The *mezquite* tree, vulgarly called *muskeet* in Texas, where it has attained some celebrity, grows in some of the fertile valleys of Chihuahua to the height of thirty and forty feet, with a trunk of one to two feet in diameter. The wood makes excellent fuel, but it is seldom used for other purposes, as it is crooked, knotty, and very coarse and brittle, more resembling the honey locust (of which it might be considered a scrubby species) than the mahogany, as some people have asserted. The fruit is but a diminutive honey-locust in appearance and flavor, of the size and shape of a flattened bean-pod, with the seeds disposed in like manner. This pod, which, like that of the honey locust, encloses a glutinous substance, the Apaches and other tribes of Indians grind into flour to make their favorite *pinole*. The mezquite seems undoubtedly of the *Acacia Arabica* species; as some physicians who have examined the gum which exudes from the tree, pronounce it genuine Arabic.

But by far the most important indigenous product of the soil of New Mexico is its pasturage. Most of the high table-plains afford the finest grazing in the world, while, for want of water, they are utterly useless for most other purposes. The scanty moisture which suffices to bring forth the natural vegetation is insufficient for agricultural productions, without the aid of irrigation. The high prairies of all Northern Mexico differ greatly from those of our border in the general character of their vegetation. They are remarkably destitute of the gay flowering plants for which the former are so celebrated, being mostly clothed with different species of a highly nutritious grass called *grama*, which is of a very short and curly quality. The highlands, upon which alone this sort of grass is produced, being seldom verdant till after the rainy season sets in, the *grama* is only in perfection from August to October. But being rarely nipt by the frost until the rains are over, it cures upon the ground and remains excellent hay—equal if not superior to that which is cut and stacked from our western prairies. Although the winters are rigorous, the feeding of stock is almost entirely unknown in New Mexico; nevertheless, the extensive herds of the country, not only of cattle and sheep, but of mules and horses, generally maintain themselves in excellent condition upon the dry pasturage alone through the cold season, and until the rains start up the green grass again the following summer.

6 . Mining

The only successful mines known in New Mexico at the present day, are those of gold, the most important one of which is that originally incorporated as *El Real de Dolores*, but generally known by the significant name of *El Placer*. This mine lies in a low detached spur of mountains, at a distance of twenty-seven miles south of the capital. In 1828, a *Sonoreño* who was in the habit of herding his mules in that vicinity, being one day in pursuit of some that had strayed into the mountains, happened to pick up a stone, which he soon identified as being of the same class that was to be found in the gold regions of Sonora. Upon a little further examination, he detected sundry particles of gold, which did not fail to occasion some degree of excitement in the country. Although the amount procured from these mines, was, for the first two or three years, very insignificant, yet it answered the purpose of testing the quality of the metal, which was found to be of uncommon purity. A market was therefore very soon opened with foreign merchants.

The quantity of gold extracted between the years 1832 and '35 could not have amounted to less than from $60,000 to $80,000 per annum. Since this time, however, there has been a considerable falling off, some seasons producing but $30,000 or $40,000. It is believed, notwithstanding, that the entire aggregate yield since the first discovery has exceeded half a million of dollars. The reduction in profit during the last few years has been caused more by want of energy and enterprise, than by exhaustion of the precious metal, as only a very small portion of the 'gold region' has as yet been dug; and experience has shown that the 'dust' is about as likely to be found in one part of it as in another. All the best 'diggings' in the immediate vicinity of the water, however, seem pretty well excavated: in some places the hills and valleys are literally cut up like a honey-comb.

The dust and grains obtained at this mine, are virgin gold, and, as before remarked, of very fine quality, producing at the United States Mint an average of at least $19.70 to the ounce troy after melting, or about $19.30 gross. It was at first bought by the traders at the rate of fifteen dollars per ounce, but in consequence of the competition which was afterwards excited among the dealers, its price was raised for a short time above its maximum at the Mint, although it has since settled down at about $17.30 per ounce troy.

During the process of these excavations, when such a depth has been reached as to render a ladder indispensable, a pole ten or fifteen feet long is cut full of notches for that purpose, and set diagonally in the orifice. In proportion as the pit becomes deeper, others are added, forming a somewhat precarious zigzag staircase, by which the agile miner descends and ascends without even using his hands to assist himself, although with a large load of earth upon his shoulders. It is in this way that most of the rubbish is extracted from these mines, as windlasses or machinery of any kind are rarely used.

The winter season is generally preferred by the miners, for the facilities it affords of supplying the gold-washers with water in the immediate neighborhood of their operations; for the great scarcity of water about the mining regions is a very serious obstacle at other seasons to successful enterprise. Water in winter is obtained by melting a quantity of snow thrown into a sink, with heated stones. Those employed as washers are very frequently the wives and children of the miners. A round wooden bowl called *batea*, about eighteen inches in diameter, is the washing vessel, which they fill with the earth, and then immerse it in the pool, and stir it with their hands; by which operation the loose dirt floats off, and the gold settles to the bottom. In this manner they continue till nothing remains in the bottom of the *batea* but a little heavy black sand mixed with a few grains of gold, the value of which (to the trayful) varies from one to twelve cents, and sometimes, in very rich soils, to twenty-five or more. Some attempts have been made to wash with machinery, but as yet without success; partly owing to the scarcity of water, but as much perhaps to a lack of perseverance, and to the arbitrary restrictions imposed upon foreigners, who, after all, are the only persons that have ever attempted any improvements of the kind.

When the Placer was in its greatest *bonanza*—yielding very large profits to those engaged in the business—the 'mining fever' rose to such a tremendous pitch among the New Mexicans, particularly the government officers, that every one fancied he saw a door opened for the accumulation of a princely fortune. Could any dependence be placed in the integrity of the government, I have no doubt that, with sufficient capital and the aid of machinery (such as is used in the mines of Georgia and Carolina), the old mines of this province might be reopened, and a great number of the *placeres* very extensively and profitably worked. But as New Mexico is governed at present, there is no security in an enterprise of the kind. The progress of a foreign adventurer is always liable to be arrested by the jealousy of the government, upon the first flattering *bonanza*. Americans in particular would have little to hope for in the way of redress; for our government has shown itself so tardy in redressing or revenging injuries done its citizens by foreign states, that they would be oppressed, as they have been, with less scruple because with more impunity than the subjects of any other nation.

The gold regions are, for the most part, a kind of common property, and have been wrought chiefly by an indigent class of people, known familiarly as *gambucinos*, a name applied to petty miners who work 'on their own hook.' Among these one very seldom finds any foreigners; for according to the present simple method of working, the profit is too small and too precarious to entice the independent American laborer, who is seldom willing to work for less than a dollar a day clear of all expenses; while the Mexican *gambucino* is content with two or three *reales*, most of which is required to furnish him food. Therefore these poor miners lead a miserable life after all. When short of means they often support themselves upon only a *real* each per day, their usual food consisting of bread and a kind of coarse cake-sugar called *piloncillo*, to which is sometimes added a little crude ranchero cheese; yet they seem perfectly satisfied.

To prevent collisions among such heterogeneous multitudes as are to be found at the mining places, some municipal provisions have been established, in pursuance of which any person may open a *labor* or pit on unoccupied ground not nearer than ten paces to another, and is entitled to the same extent in every direction, not interfering with prior claims—his *labor* being confirmed for a small fee by application to the alcalde. But if the proprietor abandon his *labor* for a certain time, any one that chooses may take possession.

Besides the Placer of which I have already spoken, others have lately been discovered in the same ledge of mountains towards the south, one of which is now extensively worked, being already filled with retail shops of every description, where all the gold that is extracted, is either sold or bartered. The *gambucinos* being generally destitute of all other resources, are often obliged to dispose of their gold daily—and very frequently in driblets of but a few cents value. *Placeres* of gold have also been discovered in the mountains of Abiquiú, Taos and elsewhere, which have been worked to some extent. In truth, as some of the natives have justly remarked, New Mexico is almost one continued *placer;* traces of gold being discoverable over nearly the whole surface of the country. The opinion formerly entertained that gold is only to be found in southern climates, seems fully confuted here; for at a point called Sangre de Cristo, considerably north of Taos, (above the 37th degree of latitude), and which from its location among the snowy mountains of that region, is ice-bound over half the year, a very rich *placer* has been discovered; yet owing to the peculiarly exposed situation in which it lies, it has been very little worked.

For the last century no *silver* mines have been in successful operation in New Mexico. A few years ago there was discovered near the village of Manzano, in the mountains of Tomé, a vein of silver which bid fair to prove profitable; but when the ore came to be tested, the rock was found to be so hard that the pursuit has been entirely abandoned.

In addition to gold and silver, there are also to be found, in many isolated spots, ores of copper, zinc, and lead; although the latter is so mixed up with copper and other hard metals, as to be almost unfit for ordinary purposes. The copper obtained in the province has frequently been found to contain a slight mixture of the precious metals, well worth extracting. Iron is also abundant.

7 . Domestic Animals

Nothing that has come within my sphere of observation in New Mexico, has astonished me more than the little attention that is paid to the improvement of domestic animals. While other nations have absolutely gone mad in their endeavors to better their breeds of horses, and have ransacked the four quarters of the world for the best blood and purest pedigrees, the New Mexicans, so justly celebrated for skilful horsemanship, and so much devoted to equestrian exercise, that they have been styled a race of centaurs, leave the propagation of their horses exclusively to chance; converting their best and handsomest steeds into saddle-horses.

Their race of *horses* is identical with that which is found running wild on the Prairies, familiarly known by the name of *mustang*. Although generally very small, they are quick, active and spirited: and were they not commonly so much injured in the breaking, they would perhaps be as hardy and long-lived as any other race in existence. Some of their *caballos de silla* or saddle-horses are so remarkably well trained, that they will stop suddenly upon the slightest check, charge against a wall without shrinking, and even attempt to clamber up its sides. In addition to this, a complete riding horse should have a peculiar up-and-down gait, affording all the exercise of the most violent trotter, while he gets over the ground so slowly as to enable the *caballero* to enjoy the 'pleasures' of a fatiguing ride of hours, without losing sight of his mistress's balcony.

The little attention paid to the breeding of horses in New Mexico, may perhaps be accounted for from the fact that, until lately, when the continued depredations of the hostile Indians discouraged them from their favorite pursuit, the people of the country had bestowed all their care in the raising of *mules*. This animal is in fact to the Mexican, what the camel has always been to the Arab—invaluable for the transportation of freight over sandy deserts and mountainous roads, where no other means of conveyance could be used to such advantage. These mules will travel for hundreds of miles with a load of the most bulky and unwieldy articles, weighing frequently three or four hundred pounds.

The *Aparejo* (or pack-saddle, if it can be so styled), is a large pad, consisting of a leathern case stuffed with hay, which covers the back of the mule and extends half way down on both sides. This is secured with a wide sea-grass bandage, with which the poor brute is so tightly laced as to reduce the middle of its body to half its natural size. During the operation of lacing, the corseted quadruped stands trembling in perfect agony, not an inapt emblem of some fashionable exquisites who are to be met with lounging on tip-toe, in all the principal thoroughfares of large cities.

The muleteers contend that a tightly laced beast will travel, or at least support burdens, with greater ease; and though they carry this to an extreme, still we can hardly doubt that a reasonable tension supports and braces the muscles. It is necessary too for the *aparejo* to be firmly bound on to prevent its slipping and chafing the mule's back; indeed, with all these precautions, the back, withers and sides of the poor brute are often horribly mangled— so much so that I have seen the rib-bones bare, from day to day, while carrying a usual load of three hundred pounds! The *aparejo* is also furnished with a huge crupper, which often lacerates the tail most shockingly. It is this packing that leaves most of the lasting cicatrices and marks so common upon Mexican mules.

The *carga*, if a single package, is laid across the mule's back, but when composed of two, they are placed lengthwise, side by side; and being coupled with a cord, they are bound upon the aparejo with a long rope of sea-grass or raw-hide, which is so skilfully and tensely twined about the packages as effectually to secure them upon the animal. The mule is at first so tightly bound that it seems scarcely able to move; but the weight of the pack soon settles the aparejo, and so loosens the girths and cords as frequently to render it necessary to tighten them again soon after getting under way. It keeps most of the muleteers actively employed during the day, to maintain the packs in condition; for they often lose their balance and sometimes fall off. This is done without detaining the *atajo* (drove of pack-mules), the rest of which travel on while one is stopped to adjust its disordered pack.

It is truly remarkable to observe with what dexterity and skill the *Arrieros*, or muleteers, harness and adjust the packs of merchandise upon their beasts. Half a dozen usually suffice for forty or fifty mules. Two men are always engaged at a time in the dispatch of each animal, and rarely occupy five minutes in the complete adjustment of his *aparejo* and *carga*. In this operation they frequently demonstrate a wonderful degree of skill in the application of their strength. A single man will often seize a package which, on a 'dead lift,' he could hardly have raised from the ground, and making a fulcrum of his knees and a lever of his arms and body, throw it upon the mule's back with as much apparent ease as if the effort cost him but little exertion. At stopping-places the task of unpacking is executed with still greater expedition. The packages are piled in a row upon the ground, and in case of rain the *aparejos* are laid upon them, over which is stretched a covering of *mantas de guangoche* (sheets of sea-grass texture), which protects the goods against the severest storms; a ditch also being cut around the pile, to prevent the water from running underneath. In this way freights are carried from point to point, and over the most rugged mountain passes at a much cheaper rate than foreigners can transport their merchandise in wagons, even through a level country. The cheapness of this mode of transportation arises from the very low wages paid to the *arrieros,* and the little expense incurred to feed both them and the mules. The salary of the muleteer ranges from two to five dollars per month; and as their food seldom consists of anything else except corn and *frijoles,* it can be procured at very little cost. When the *arrieros* get any meat at all, it is generally at their own expense.

An *atajo* is conducted in a very systematic manner, each *arriero* having his appropriate sphere of action allotted to him. They have also their regulations and technicalities, which, if not as numerous, are about as unintelligible to the uninitiated as sailors' terms. One person, called the *savanero,* has the charge of the mules at night, which are all turned loose without tether or hopple, with the *mulera* or bell-mare, to prevent them from straying abroad. Although the attachment of the mules to the *mulera* appears very great, it seems to be about as much for the bell as for the animal. What the queen-bee is to a hive, so is the *mulera* to an *atajo.* No matter what may be the temper of a mule, it can seldom be driven away from her; and if she happen to be taken from among her associates, the latter immediately become depressed and melancholy, and ramble and whinny in every direction, as if they were completely lost. In addition to preparing food for the party, it is the office of the *madre* (or mother, as the cook of the company is facetiously called) to lead the *mulera* ahead, during the journey, after which the whole pack follows in orderly procession.

The muleteers, as well as the *vaqueros* (cow-herds), are generally mounted upon swift and well-trained horses, and in their management of the animals will often perform many surprising feats, which would grace an equestrian circus in any country; such, for instance, as picking up a dollar from the ground at every pass with the horse at full gallop. But the greatest display of skill and agility consists in their dextrous use of the *lazo* or *lareat*,* which is usually made of horse-hair, or sea-grass tightly twisted together, with a convenient noose at one end. Their aim is always more sure when the animal to be caught is running at full speed, for then it has no time to dodge the *lareat*. As soon as the noose is cast, the *lazador* fetches the end of his *lazo* a turn round the high pommel of his saddle, and by a quick manœuvre the wildest horse is brought up to a stand or topsy-turvy at his pleasure. By this process, the head of the animal is turned towards his subduer, who, in order to obtain the mastery over him more completely, seldom fails to throw a *bozal* (or half-hitch, as boatmen would say) around the nose, though at full rope's length.

If the object of pursuit happens to be a cow or an ox, the *lazo* is usually thrown about the horns instead of the neck. Two *vaqueros*, each with his rope to the horns, will thus subject the wildest and most savage bull, provided they are mounted upon well-trained steeds. While the infuriated animal makes a lunge at one of his pursuers, the other wheels round and pulls upon his rope, which always brings the beast about in the midst of his career; so that between the two he is jerked to and fro till he becomes exhausted and ceases to make any further resistance. The use of the lazo is not confined to the *arrieros* and *vaqueros*, although these generally acquire most skill in that exercise: it prevails in every rank of life; and no man, especially among the rancheros, would consider his education complete until he had learned this national accomplishment. They acquire it in fact from infancy; for it forms one of the principal rural sports of children, who may daily be seen with their *lazitos*, noosing the dogs and chickens about the yards, in every direction.

The lazo is often employed also as a 'weapon' both offensive and defensive. In skirmishes with the Indians, the mounted *vaquero*, if haplessly without arms, will throw this formidable object round the neck or the body of his enemy, who, before he has time to disencumber himself, is jerked to the ground and dragged away at full speed; when, if his brains are not beaten

---

* *Lasso* and *lariat*, as most usually written, are evidently corruptions of the Spanish *lazo* and *la reata* (the latter with the article *la* compounded), both meaning kinds of rope. I have therefore preferred retaining the orthography indicated by their etymology.

out against the stones, roots, or trees, he becomes at least so stunned and disabled that the *lazador* can dispatch him at his leisure. The panther, the bear, and other ferocious animals of the mountains and prairies, are also successfully attacked in this manner.

The laws and customs of the country with regard to the ownership of animals are very annoying to the inexperienced foreign traveller. No matter how many proprietors a horse or mule may have had, every one marks him with a huge hieroglyphic brand, which is called the *fierro*, and again, upon selling him, with his *venta*, or sale-brand; until at last these scars become so multiplied as to render it impossible for persons not versed in this species of 'heraldry,' to determine whether the animal has been properly *vented* or not; yet any *fierro* without its corresponding *venta* lays the beast liable to the claim of the brander. Foreigners are the most frequently subjected to this kind of imposition; and when a party of *estrangeros* enters any of the southern towns, they are immediately surrounded by a troop of loungers, who carefully examine every horse and mule; when, should they by chance discover any *unvented* brand, they immediately set to work to find some one with a branding-iron of the same shape, by which the beast is at once claimed and taken; for in all legal processes the only proof required of the claimant is his *fierro*, or branding-iron, which, if found to assimilate in shape with the mark on the animal, decides the suit in his favor.

But while I fully acknowledge the pretensions of the mule, as an animal of general usefulness, I must not forget paying a passing tribute to that meek and unostentatious member of the brute family, the 'patient ass;' or, as it is familiarly called by the natives, *el burro*. This docile creature is here emphatically the 'poor man's friend,' being turned to an infinite variety of uses, and always submissive under the heaviest burdens. He is not only made to carry his master's grain, his fuel, his water, and his luggage, but his wife and his children. Frequently the whole family is stowed away together upon one diminutive donkey. In fact, the chief riding animal of the peasant is the *burro*, upon which saddle, bridle, or halter, is seldom used. The rider, seated astride his haunches instead of his back, guides the docile beast with a bludgeon which he carries in his hand.

Nothing, perhaps, has been more systematically attended to

in New Mexico than the raising of *sheep*. When the territory was at the zenith of its prosperity, *ranchos* were to be met with upon the borders of every stream, and in the vicinity of every mountain where water was to be had. Even upon the arid and desert plains, and many miles away from brook or pond, immense flocks were driven out to pasture; and only taken to water once in two or three days. On these occasions it is customary for the shepherds to load their burros with *guages* filled with water, and return again with their folds to the plains. The *guage* is a kind of gourd, of which there are some beautiful specimens with two bulbs; the intervening neck serving to retain the cord by which it is carried.

These itinerent herds of sheep generally pass the night wherever the evening finds them, without cot or enclosure. Before nightfall the principal shepherd sallies forth in search of a suitable site for his *hato*, or temporary sheep-fold; and building a fire on the most convenient spot, the sheep generally draw near it of their own accord. Should they incline to scatter, the shepherd then seizes a torch and performs a circuit or two around the entire fold, by which manœuvre, in their efforts to avoid him, the heads of the sheep are all turned inwards; and in that condition they generally remain till morning, without once attempting to stray. It is unnecessary to add that the flock is well guarded during the night by watchful and sagacious dogs against prowling wolves or other animals of prey. The well-trained shepherd's dog of this country is indeed a prodigy: two or three of them will follow a flock of sheep for a distance of several miles as orderly as a shepherd, and drive them back to the pen again at night, without other guidance than their own extraordinary instincts.

Sheep may be reckoned the staple production of New Mexico, and the principal article of exportation. Between ten and twenty years ago, about 200,000 head were annually driven to the southern markets; indeed, it is asserted, that, during the most flourishing times, as many as 500,000 were exported in one year. This trade has constituted a profitable business to some of the *ricos* of the country. They would buy sheep of the poor rancheros at from fifty to seventy-five cents per head, and sell them at from one to two hundred per cent advance in the southern markets. A large quantity of wool is of course produced, but of an inferior quality. Inconsiderable amounts have been introduced into the United

States *via* Missouri, which have sometimes been sold as low as fifteen cents per pound. It is bought, however, at the New Mexican ranchos at a very low rate—three or four cents per pound, or (as more generally sold) per fleece, which will average, perhaps, but little over a pound. Yet, from the superiority of the pasturage and climate, New Mexico might doubtless grow the finest wool in the world. In conformity with their characteristic tardiness in improvement, however, the natives have retained their original stocks, which are wretchedly degenerate. They formerly sheared their flocks chiefly for their health, and rarely preserved the fleece, as their domestic manufactures consumed but a comparatively small quantity.

But the *ganado menor*, or small beasts of pasture (that is, sheep and goats in general), have of late been very much reduced in quantity; having suffered to a deplorable extent from the frequent inroads of the aboriginal 'lords of the soil,' who, every now and then, whenever hunger or caprice prompts them, attack the ranchos, murder the shepherds, and drive the sheep away in flocks of thousands. Indeed, the Indians have been heard to observe, that they would long before this have destroyed every sheep in the country, but that they prefer leaving a few behind for breeding purposes, in order that their Mexican shepherds may raise them new supplies!

The sheep of New Mexico are exceedingly small, with very coarse wool, and scarcely fit for anything else than mutton, for which, indeed, they are justly celebrated. Their flesh has a peculiarly delicious flavor, and is reckoned by epicures to be far superior to our best venison; owing probably in part to the excellence of the grass upon which they feed. The flesh of the sheep is to the New Mexican what that of the hog is to the people of our Western States,—while pork is but seldom met with in Northern Mexico. The sheep there are also remarkable for horny appendages, which frequently branch out in double or triple pairs, giving the head a very whimsical and grotesque appearance. I have seen some of them with at least six separate horns, each pointing in a different direction.

Although the raising of *goats* has not been made so much of a business as the raising of sheep, the former are nevertheless to be found in great abundance. Their milk is much more generally used that than of the cow, not only because it is sweeter and richer, but because the goat, like the *burro*, sustains itself upon the mere rubbish that grows in the mountain passes, and on the most barren hills, where cows could not exist without being regularly fed. The flesh of the goat is coarse, but wholesome, and being cheaper than mutton or beef, it is very freely used by the poor. That of the kid is hardly surpassed for delicacy and sweetness.

With regard to domestic *fowls*, it may be worthy of remark, that there is not to be found, as I believe, in all New Mexico, a single species (saving half a dozen turkeys perhaps, and a few pigeons), except the common hen, of which, however, there is a sufficient abundance. The goose, the duck, the peacock, etc., are altogether unknown.

8 . Arts and Crafts

There is no part of the civilized globe, perhaps, where the Arts have been so much neglected, and the progress of Science so successfully impeded as in New Mexico. Reading and writing may fairly be set down as the highest branches of education that are taught in the schools; for those pedants who occasionally pretend to teach arithmetic, very seldom understand even the primary rules of the science of numbers. I should perhaps make an exception in favor of those ecclesiastics, who have acquired their education abroad; and who, from their vocation, are necessarily obliged to possess a smattering of Latin. Yet it is a well known fact that the majority of this privileged class, even, are lamentably deficient in the more important branches of familiar science. I have been assured by a highly respectable foreigner, who has long resided in the country, that the questions were once deliberately put to him by a curate—whether Napoleon and Washington were not *one* and the *same* person, and whether Europe was not a province of Spain!

Yet, notwithstanding this dreadful state of ignorance on all those subjects which it behooves man to be acquainted with, it is truly astonishing to notice the correctness with which the common people speak their mother tongue, the Spanish. The application of words out of their classical sense may occasionally occur, but a violation of the simple grammatical rules (which is so common among the illiterate who use the English language), is extremely rare. In pronunciation, the only material difference between them and the Castilian race, consists in the adoption of certain provincialisms, which can hardly be ranked as defects. They have also adopted many significant Indian words from their aboriginal predecessors and neighbors, which serve to embellish and amplify this already beautiful and copious language.

In nothing is the deplorable state of things already noticed made more clearly manifest, than in the absence of a public press. There has never been a single newspaper or periodical of any kind published in New Mexico, except in the year 1834, when a little foolscap sheet (entitled *El Crepúsculo*) was issued weekly, for about a month, to the tune of fifty subscribers, and was then abandoned, partially for want of patronage and partially because the editor had accomplished his object of procuring his election to Congress. Indeed, the only printing press in the country is a small affair which was brought the same year across the prairies from the United States, and is now employed occasionally in printing billets, primers and Catholics catechisms. This literary negligence is to be attributed, not more to the limited number of reading people, than to those injudicious restrictions upon that freedom of the press, which is so essential to its prosperity. An editor attempting to arraign the conduct of public functionaries, or to oppose 'the powers that be,' is sure to subject himself to persecution, and most probably suspension, a tyrannical course of proceeding which has checked the career of two or three papers even among the more enlightened inhabitants of Chihuahua, where a miserable organ of the Government is still occasionally issued from the office of the *Imprenta del Gobierno,* or Government Press. No wonder then that the people of Northern Mexico are so much behind their neighbors of the United States in intelligence, and that the pulse of national industry and liberty beats so low!

Medical science is laboring under similar disadvantages; there being not a single native physician in the province*; although a great multitude of singular cures are daily performed with in-

---

* Neither is there a professed lawyer in New Mexico: a fact which at least speaks favorably of the state of litigation in the country.

digenous roots and herbs that grow in abundance all over the country. But lest a knowledge of this scarcity of doctors should induce some of the Esculapian faculty to strike for Santa Fé in quest of fortune, I would remark that the country affords very poor patronage. Foreign physicians who have visited New Mexico, have found the practice quite unprofitable; not more for the want of patients, than on account of the poverty of the people. Nine-tenths of those who are most subject to disease, are generally so destitute of means, that the only return they can make, is, *"Dios se lo pague"* (May God pay you!). Even the more affluent classes do not hesitate sometimes to liquidate their bills in the same currency.

The mechanical arts have scarcely risen above the condition they were found in among the aborigines. Gold and silversmiths are perhaps better skilled in their respective trades than any other class of artisans whatever; as the abundance of precious metals in former days, and the ruling passion of the people for ostenta-tious show, gave a very early stimulus to the exercise of this pe-culiar talent. Some mechanics of this class have produced such singular specimens of ingenious workmanship, that on examin-ing them, we are almost unwilling to believe that rude art could accomplish so much. Even a bridle-bit or a pair of spurs it would no doubt puzzle the 'cutest' Yankee to fashion after a Mexican model—such as I have seen manufactured by the commonest blacksmiths of the country.

In carpentry and cabinet-work the mechanic has to labor to great disadvantage, on account of a want of tools and scarcity of suitable timber. Their boards have to be hewed out with the axe —sawed lumber being absolutely unknown throughout New Mexico, except what is occasionally cut by foreigners. The axe commonly used for splitting and hewing is formed after the model of those clumsy hatchets known as 'squaw-axes' among Indian traders. Yet this is not unfrequently the only tool of the worker in wood: a cart or a plow is often manufactured without even an auger, a chisel, or a drawing-knife.

In architecture, the people do not seem to have arrived at any great perfection, but rather to have conformed themselves to the clumsy style which prevailed among the aborigines, than to waste their time in studying modern masonry and the use of lime. The materials generally used for building are of the crudest possible description; consisting of unburnt, sun-dried bricks, cemented together with a species of mortar made of simple clay and sand. These bricks are called *adobes,* and every edifice, from the church to the *palacio,* is constructed of the same stuff. In fact, I should remark, perhaps, that though all Southern Mexico is celebrated for the magnificence and wealth of its churches, New Mexico deserves equal fame for poverty-stricken and shabby-looking houses of public worship.

The general plan of the Mexican dwellings is nearly the same everywhere. Whether from motives of pride, or fear of the savages, the wealthier classes have adopted the style of Moorish castles; so that all the larger buildings have more the appearance of so many diminutive fortifications, than of private family residences. Let me add, however, that whatever may be the roughness of their exterior, they are extremely comfortable inside. A tier of rooms on each side of a square, comprising as many as the convenience of the occupant may require, encompass an open *patio* or court, with but one door opening into the street,—a huge gate, called *la puerta del zaguan,* usually large enough to admit the family coach. The back tier is generally occupied with the *cocina, dispensa, granero* (kitchen, provision-store, and granary), and other offices of the same kind. Most of the apartments, except the winter rooms, open into the *patio;* but the latter are most frequently entered through the *sala* or hall, which, added to the thickness of their walls and roofs, renders them delightfully warm during the cold season, while they are perfectly cool and agreeable in summer. In fact, hemmed in as these apartments are with nearly three feet of earth, they may be said to possess all the pleasant properties of cellars, with a freer circulation of air, and nothing of the dampness which is apt to pervade those subterranean regions.

The floors are all constructed of beaten earth 'slicked over' with soft mortar, and covered generally with a coarse carpet of domestic manufacture. The interior of each apartment is roughly plastered over with a clay mortar unmixed with lime, by females who supply the place of trowels with their hands. It is then whitewashed with calcined *yeso* or gypsum, a deleterious stuff, that is always sure to engraft its affections upon the clothing of those who come in contact with it. To obviate this, the parlors and family rooms are usually lined with wall-paper or calico, to the height of five or six feet. The front of the house is commonly plastered in a similar manner, although not always white-washed. In the suburbs of the towns, and particularly in the villages and ranchos, a fantastic custom prevails of painting only a portion of the fronts of the houses, in the shape of stripes, which imparts to the landscape a very striking and picturesque appearance.

The houses of the villages and ranchos are rarely so spacious as those of the capital, yet their construction is much the same. Some very singular subterrene dwellings are to be found in a few places. I was once passing through the village of Casa Colorada, when I observed some noisy urchins just before me, who very suddenly and mysteriously disappeared. Upon resorting to the spot, I perceived an aperture under a hillock, which, albeit considerably larger, was not very unlike the habitations of the little prairie dogs.

The immense expense attending the purchase of suitable furniture and kitchen-ware, indeed, the frequent impossibility of obtaining these articles at any price, caused the early settlers of Northern Mexico to resort to inventions of necessity, or to adopt Indian customs altogether, many of which have been found so comfortable and convenient, that most of those who are now able to indulge in luxuries, feel but little inclination to introduce any change. Even the few pine-board chairs and settees that are to be found about the houses are seldom used; the prevailing fashion being to fold mattresses against the walls, which, being covered over with blankets, are thus converted into sofas. Females, indeed, most usually prefer accommodating themselves, *à l'Indienne*, upon a mere blanket spread simply upon the floor.

Wagons of Mexican manufacture are not to be found; although a small number of American-built vehicles, of those introduced by the trading caravans, have grown into use among the people. Nothing is more calculated to attract the curiosity of strangers than the unwieldy *carretas* or carts of domestic construction, the massive wheels of which are generally hewed out of a large cottonwood. This, however, being rarely of sufficient size to form the usual diameter, which is about five feet, an additional segment or

felloe is pinned upon each edge, when the whole is fashioned into
an irregular circle. A crude pine or cottonwood pole serves for the
axle-tree, upon which is tied a rough frame of the same material
for a body. To this huge truckle it is necessary to hitch at least
three or four yokes of oxen; for even a team of six would find it
difficult to draw the load of a single pair with an ordinary cart. The
labor of the oxen is much increased by the Mexican mode of
harnessing, which appears peculiarly odd to a Yankee. A rough
pole serves for a yoke, and, with the middle tied to the cart-tongue,
the extremities are placed across the heads of the oxen behind the
horns, to which they are firmly lashed with a stout rawhide thong.
Thus the head is maintained in a fixed position, and they pull, or
rather push by the force of the neck, which, of course, is kept
continually strained upwards.

Rough and uncouth as these *carretas* always are, they constitute
nevertheless the 'pleasure-carriages' of the rancheros, whose families are conveyed in them to the towns, whether to market, or to
fiestas, or on other joyful occasions. It is truly amusing to see these
rude vehicles bouncing along upon their irregularly rounded
wheels, like a limping bullock, and making the hills and valleys
around vocal with the echo of their creaking and frightful sounds.

The New Mexicans are celebrated for the manufacture of
coarse blankets, which is an article of considerable traffic between
them and the southern provinces, as also with the neighboring
Indians, and on some occasions with the United States. The finer
articles are curiously woven in handsome figures of various colors.
These are of different qualities, the most ordinary being valued at
about two dollars apiece, while those of the finest texture, especially their imitations of the *Sarape Navajó,* will sell for twenty
dollars or more. There have also been made in New Mexico a few
imitations of the *Sarape Saltillero,*—the blanket of Saltillo, a city
of the south celebrated for the manufacture of the most splendid
fancy blankets, singularly figured with all the colors of the rain-
bow. These are often sold for more than fifty dollars each. What
renders the weaving of the fancy blankets extremely tedious, is,
that the variegation of colors is all effected with the shuttle, the
texture in other respects being perfectly plain, without even a
twill. An additional value is set upon the fine *sarape* on account

of its being a fashionable substitute for a cloak. Indeed, the inferior sarape is the only over-dress used by the peasantry in the winter.

Besides blankets, the New Mexicans manufacture a kind of coarse twilled woollen stuff, called *gerga,* which is checkered with black and white, and is used for carpets, and also by the peasantry for clothing, which, in fact, with some other similar domestic stuffs, together with buckskin, constituted almost the only article of wear they were possessed of, till the trade from Missouri furnished them with foreign fabrics at more reasonable prices than they had been in the habit of paying to the traders of the southern provinces. Their domestic textures are nearly all of wool, there being no flax or hemp and but little cotton spun. The manufacture even of these articles is greatly embarrassed for want of good spinning and weaving machinery. Much of the spinning is done with the *huso* or *malacate* (the whirligig spindle), which is kept whirling in a bowl with the fingers while the thread is drawn. The dexterity with which the females spin with this simple apparatus is truly astonishing.

9 . The People

The stature of both sexes in New Mexico is commonly below medium: but they are mostly well proportioned, of athletic make, and sound, healthy constitutions. Their complexion is generally dark; but every variety of shade is found among them, from the lightest European tint to the swarthiest hue. Their darkness has resulted partly from their original Moorish blood, but more from intermarriages with the aborigines. An occasional Indian, and sometimes an entire village, have abandoned their wonted seclusion, and become identified with their conquerors. In the North, the system of Indian slavery has contributed still more to the same result. They buy the captive children of both sexes of the wild tribes, taken prisoners among each other, or by the Pueblos in their petty wars with the former—and indeed by the Mexicans themselves—who are generally held in bondage to the age of twenty-one years, and some, from ignorance, their whole lives. Such as resume their liberty intermarry with the race of their masters, becoming Mexican citizens, often undistinguishable from many of the already dark-hued natives. The present race of New Mexicans has thus become an amalgam, averaging about equal parts of the European and aboriginal blood. The peasantry, as well from a more general intermixture with the Indian, as from exposure, are the darkest; yet the tawny complexion pervades all classes—the rich as well as the poor.

The females, although many of them are about as broad-featured as the veriest Indian, not unfrequently possess striking traits of beauty. They are remarkable for small feet and handsome figures, notwithstanding their profound ignorance of the 'refined art' of lacing. The belles of the ranchos and villages have a disgusting habit of besmearing their faces with the crimson juice of a plant or fruit called *alegría*, which is not unlike blood; as also with clay and starch. This is not intended, as some travellers have supposed, as a beautifying appendage, but for the purpose of protecting the skin from the sun. A country beauty will often remain in this filthy condition for a whole fortnight, in order to appear to advantage at some favorite feast or ball; when, by washing off the paint, the cheeks look as fresh and ruddy as the natural darkness of their skin will permit.

The New Mexicans appear to have inherited much of the cruelty and intolerance of their ancestors, and no small portion of their bigotry and fanaticism. Being of a highly imaginative temperament and of rather accommodating moral principles—cunning, loquacious, quick of perception and sycophantic, their conversation frequently exhibits a degree of tact—a false glare of talent eminently calculated to mislead and impose. They have no stability except in artifice; no profundity except for intrigue: qualities for which they have acquired an unenviable celebrity. Systematically cringing and subservient while out of power, as soon as the august mantle of authority falls upon their shoulders, there are but little bounds to their arrogance and vindictiveness of spirit. While such are the general features of the character of the Northern Mexicans, however, I am fain to believe and acknowledge, that there are to be found among them numerous instances of uncompromising virtue, good faith and religious forbearance.

But taking the Northern Mexicans without distinction of class or degree, there is scarcely a race of people on the face of the earth more alive to the dictates of charity—that is, alms-giving; which is more owing perhaps to the force of religious instruction than to real sympathy for the sufferings of the indigent and the helpless. The law making no provision for paupers, there is no country perhaps more infested with beggars, especially from Chihuahua south. In the large cities, Saturday is the alms-giving day by custom; and on such occasions the *limosneros* (as the mendicant race is called), may be seen promenading the streets in gangs of thirty or forty, or in smaller numbers, performing genuflections at every nook and corner of the town, each croaking aloud his favorite set of orisons and inviting the blessings of heaven upon every man, woman or child, who may have been so fortunate as to propitiate the benison by casting a few *clacos* into his outstretched hand. In some sections of the country, this system of begging has proved so successful that parents have actually been known to maim and deform their children, during the earliest stages of infancy, in order to fit them for the trade, and thereby secure to themselves a constant source of emolument for the remainder of their lives. Persons affecting disease and frequently malformation for the purpose of exciting the commiseration of the wayfarer, are also extremely numerous. I had often observed in Chihuahua a robust-looking fellow, who, to all appearance, had partially lost the use of his lower extremities, sliding about the streets from door to door upon a sort of cushion, asking alms. One fine day, a furious bull, pursued by some *vaqueros*, came plunging down in the direction where he sat, moaning and grieving most piteously; when, forgetting his physical disabilities, he sprang to his feet with the agility of a dancing master, and incontinently betook himself to his heels.

The Northern Mexicans have often been branded with cowardice: a stigma which may well be allowed to rest upon the wealthier classes, and the city-bred caballeros, from whose ranks are selected the military leaders who decide the fate of battles. But the rancheros, or as they might be still more appropriately styled —the yeomanry of the country, inured as they are from their peculiar mode of life to every kind of fatigue and danger, possess a much higher calibre of moral courage. Their want of firmness in the field, is partially the result of their want of confidence in their commanders; while the inefficacy and worthlessness of their weapons are alone sufficient to inspire even a valiant heart with dismal forebodings. I have seen persons of the lower class do things, however, which would really seem to indicate a superlative degree of courage. Some of them will often perform journeys alone through wildernesses teeming with murderous savages; but as they not unfrequently embark upon these perilous jaunts un-armed, it is evident they depend greatly upon good luck and swiftness of limbs, and still more upon the protection of their favorite saint, *La Virgen de Guadalupe.*

The Mexicans, like the French, are remarkable for their polite-ness and suavity of manners. You cannot visit a friend but he assures you that, *"Está V. en su casa, y puede mandar,"* etc. (You are in your own house, and can command, etc.), or, *"Estoy entera-mente á su disposicion"* (I am wholly at your disposal), without, however, meaning more than an expression of ordinary courtesy. Nor can you speak in commendation of any article, let its value be what it may, but the polite owner immediately replies, *"Tómelo, V. Señor; es suyo"* (Take it, sir; it is yours), without the slightest intention or expectation that you should take him at his word. In epistolary correspondence, the ratio of respect is generally indi-cated by the width of the left margin. If the letter is addressed to an equal, about one-fourth of the page is occupied for that pur-pose; but when extraordinary respect is intended to be shown to a superior, nearly one-half of the page is left a blank. There are other marks of civility and respect peculiar to the country, which among us would be accounted absolute servility.

In their salutations, the ancient custom of close embrace, not only between individuals of the same sex, but between those of different sexes, is almost universal. It is quite a luxury to meet a pretty señorita after some absence. The parties approach, shake hands in a cordial manner, and without loosening the grasp, the left arm of each is brought about the other's waist; and while a gentle embrace brings their persons closer to each other, the contact of the cheeks becomes inevitable—without admitting a kiss, however, which would be held as decidedly indelicate. In short, it is worth while absenting oneself, for the gratification of a first meeting with the prettier of one's female friends upon the return.

Among the least unpleasant customs of this country is that of the *siesta* or afternoon nap; a species of indulgence in which all classes are prone to share. The stores, private and public offices, are, by common consent, generally closed at one o'clock (that being the usual dinner hour), and not re-opened till three. During that interval nearly every kind of business and labor is suspended. The streets are comparatively deserted; the rich and the poor retire to their respective couches, and remain wrapped in slumber, or 'thinking o' nothing,' till the loud peal of the three o'clock bell warns them to resume their occupations.

10 . The Administration of Justice

The administration of the laws in Northern Mexico constitutes one of the most painful features of her institutions. Justice, or rather judgments, are a common article of traffic; and the hapless litigant who has not the means to soften the claws of the alcalde with a 'silver unction,' is almost sure to get severely scratched in the contest, no matter what may be the justice of his cause, or the uprightness of his character. It is easy to perceive, then, that the poor and the humble stand no chance in a judicial contest with the wealthy and consequential, whose influence, even apart from their facilities for corrupting the court and suborning witnesses, is sufficient to neutralize any amount of plebeian testimony that might be brought against them.

The evil consequences arising from maladministration of justice in New Mexico are most severely felt by foreigners, against whom a strong prejudice prevails throughout the South. Of these, the citizens of the United States are by far the most constant sufferers; an inevitable result of that sinister feeling with which the 'rival republic' views the advancement and superiority of her more industrious neighbors. It is a notorious fact, that while the English are universally treated with comparative consideration and respect, the Americans residing in the southern parts of the republic are frequently taunted with the effeminacy of their government and its want of decision. So openly has this preference for British subjects been manifested, and so thoroughly conscious have the Americans become of the humiliating fact, that when a mercantile

firm, consisting of an American and an Englishman, has occasion
to present a memorial of any description, or to sue either for an act
of favor or of justice from the nation, the application is sure to be
made in the name of the latter, knowing it will thus be more likely
to command proper attention.

The only tribunals of 'justice' in New Mexico are those of the
ordinary *alcaldes* or justices of the peace; and an appeal from
them is carried to the Supreme Court in the department of Chihuahua. The course of litigation is exceedingly simple and summary. The plaintiff makes his verbal complaint or demand before
the alcalde, who orders him to summon the defendant, which is
done by simply saying, *"Le llama el alcalde"* (the alcalde calls you)
into his presence, the applicant acting thus in the double capacity
of constable and complainant. The summons is always verbal, and
rarely for a future time—instant attendance being expected.
Should the defendant refuse to obey this simple mandate (which,
by the bye, is a very rare occurrence), the alcalde sends his *baston
de justicia*, his staff of justice, an ordinary walking-cane, distinguished only by a peculiar black silk tassel. This never fails to
enforce compliance, for a refusal to attend after being shown the
staff, would be construed into a contempt of court, and punished
accordingly. The witnesses are sometimes sworn upon a cross cut
on the *baston de justicia*, or more frequently, perhaps, upon a
cross formed with the finger and thumb. Generally speaking, however, the process of examination is gone through without a single
oath being administered; and in the absence of witnesses, the
alcalde often proceeds to sentence upon the simple statements of
the contending parties. By a species of mutual agreement, the
issue of a suit is sometimes referred to *hombres buenos* (arbi-
trators), which is the nearest approximation that is made to trial
by jury. In judicial proceedings, however, but little, or rather no
attention is paid to any code of laws; in fact, there is scarcely one
alcalde in a dozen who knows what a law is, or who ever saw a
law-book. Their decisions, when not influenced by corrupt agen-
cies, are controlled by the prevailing customs of the country.

In the administration of justice, there are three distinct and
privileged jurisdictions, known as *fueros*: the *eclesiástico*, which
provides that no member of the clergy, at least of the rank of
curate and upwards, shall ever be arraigned before a civil tribunal,

but shall be tried by their superiors in the order; the *militar,* which makes a similar provision in favor not only of commissioned officers, but of every common soldier from the ranks; and the *civil* or ordinary courts, for all cases in which the defendants are laymen. These *fuerors* have hitherto maintained the ecclesiastical and military classes in perfect independence of the civil authorities. It is no wonder, then, that the cause of freedom in Mexico has made so little progress.

Imprisonment is almost the only sort of punishment resorted to in the North. For debt, petit larceny, highway robbery, and murder, the usual sentence is *"A la cárcel"* (to jail), where a person is likely to remain about as long for inability to pay *dos reales,* as for the worst of crimes: always provided he has not the means to pacify the offended majesty of the law. I never heard of but one execution for murder in New Mexico, since the declaration of independence. The most desperate and blood-stained criminals escape with impunity, after a few weeks of incarceration, unless the prosecutor happens to be a person of great influence; in which case, the prisoner is detained in the *calabozo* at will, even when the offence committed has been of a trivial character. Notwithstanding this laxity in the execution of the laws, there are few murders of any kind committed.

In case of debt, as before remarked, the delinquent is sent to jail—provided the creditor will not accept his services. If he will, however, the debtor becomes *nolens volens* the servant of the creditor till the debt is satisfied; and, serving, as he does, at very reduced wages, his expenses for clothing, and other necessaries, but too often retain him in perpetual servitude. Now, according to the usages, if not the laws of the country, he is bound to serve his master until all arrearages are liquidated; and is only enabled to effect an exchange of masters, by engaging another to pay his debt, to whom he becomes in like manner bound.

As I have already remarked, capital crimes and highway robberies are of comparatively rare occurrence in the North, but in smaller delinquencies, such as pilfering and petty rogueries of every shade and description, the common classes can very successfully compete with any other people. Nothing indeed can be left exposed or unguarded without great danger of its being immediately stolen. No husbandman would think of leaving his axe or his hoe, or anything else of the slightest value lying out over night. Empty wagons are often pillaged of every movable piece of iron, and even the wheels have been carried away. Pieces of merchandise are frequently purloined from the shelves, when they happen to be in reach. In Chihuahua, goods have actually been snatched from the counter while being exposed to the inspection of a pretended purchaser.

The impunity with which delinquencies of this description are every day committed is perhaps in some degree, the consequence of those severe enactments, such as the *Leyes de las Indias* (the laws of the Indies), which rendered many thefts and robberies punichablo with death. The magiotracy contracted the habit of frequently winking at crime, rather than resort to the barbarous expedients prescribed by the letter of the law. The utmost that can be gained now by public prosecution, is the recovery of the stolen property, if that be anywhere to be found, and occasionally a short period of imprisonment for the culprit.

The love of gambling also deserves to be noticed as a distinguishing propensity of these people. Indeed it may well be said, without any undue stretch of imagination, that shop-lifting, pocket-picking, and other elegant pastimes of the same kindred, are the legitimate offspring, especially among the lower classes, of that passion for gaming, which in Mexico more than anywhere else—to use Madame Calderon's language—"is impregnated with the constitution—in man, woman, and child." It prevails in the lowly hut, as well as in the glittering saloon; nor is the sanctity of the gown nor the dignity of station sufficient proof against the fascinations of this exciting vice. No one considers it a degradation to be seen frequenting a *monte bank:* the governor himself and his lady, the grave magistrate and the priestly dignity, the gay caballero and the titled señora may all be seen staking their doubloons upon the turn of a card; while the humbler ranchero, the hired domestic and the ragged pauper, all press with equal avidity to test their fortune at the same shrine. There are other games at cards practised among these people, depending more upon skill; but that of *el monte*, being one exclusively of chance, seems to possess an all-absorbing attraction, difficult to be conceived by the uninitiated spectator.

The following will not only serve to show the light in which gambling is held by all classes of society, but to illustrate the purifying effects of wealth upon character. Some twelve or fifteen years ago there lived (or rather roamed) in Taos a certain female of very loose habits, known as *La Tules*. Finding it difficult to obtain the means of living in that district, she finally extended her wanderings to the capital. She there became a constant attendant on one of those pandemoniums where the favorite game of *monte* was dealt *pro bono publico*. Fortune, at first, did not seem inclined to smile upon her efforts, and for some years she spent her days in lowliness and misery. At last her luck turned, as gamblers would say, and on one occasion she left the bank with a spoil of several hundred dollars! This enabled her to open a bank of her own, and being favored by a continuous run of good fortune, she gradually rose higher and higher in the scale of affluence, until she found herself in possession of a very handsome fortune. In 1842, she sent to the United States some ten thousand dollars to be invested in goods. She still continues her favorite 'amusement,' being now considered the most expert 'monte dealer' in all Santa Fé. She is openly received in the first circles of society: I doubt, in truth, whether there is to be found in the city a lady of more fashionable reputation than this same Tules, now known as Señora Doña Gertrudes Barceló.

Bull-baiting and cock-fighting, about which so much has been said by every traveller in Mexico, are also very popular 'amusements' in the North, and generally lead to the same excesses and the same results as gaming. The cock-pit rarely fails to be crowded on Sundays and other feast days; on which occasions the church, the ball-room, the gambling-house, and the cock-pit look like so many opposite establishments; for nothing is more common than to see people going from one place to another by alternate fits, just as devotional feeling or love of pleasure happens to prompt them.

One of the most attractive sports of the rancheros and the peasantry, and that which, more than any other, calls for the exercise of skill and dexterity, is that called *correr el gallo*, practised generally on St. John's day. A common cock or hen is tied by the feet to some swinging limb of a tree, so as to be barely within the reach of a man on horseback: or the fowl is buried alive in a small pit in the ground leaving only the head above the surface. In either case, the racers, passing at full speed, grapple the head of the fowl, which being well greased generally slips out of their fingers. As soon as some one, more dextrous than the rest, has succeeded in tearing it lose, he claps spurs to his steed and endeavors to escape with the prize. He is hotly pursued, however, by the whole sporting crew, and the first who overtakes him tries to get possession of the fowl, when a strife ensues, during which the poor chicken is torn into atoms. Should the holder of the trophy be able to outstrip his pursuers, he carries it to a crowd of fair spectators and presents it to his mistress, who takes it to the fandango which usually follows, as a testimony of the prowess of her lover.

Among the vaqueros, and even among persons of distinction, *el coleo* (tailing) is a much nobler exercise than the preceding, and is also generally reserved for days of festivity. For this sport the most untractable ox or bull is turned loose upon a level common, when all the parties who propose to join in the amusement, being already mounted, start off in pursuit of him. The most successful rider, as soon as he gets near enough to the bull, seizes him by the tail, and with a sudden manœuvre, whirls him topsy-turvy upon the plain—to the no little risk of breaking his own neck, should his horse stumble or be tripped by the legs of the falling bull.

Respecting *fandangos*, I will observe that this term, as it is used in New Mexico, is never applied to any particular dance, but is the usual designation for those ordinary assemblies where dancing and frolicking are carried on; *baile* (or ball) being generally applied to those of a higher grade. The former especially are very frequent; for nothing is more general, throughout the country, and with all classes than dancing. From the gravest priest to the buffoon—from the richest nabob to the beggar—from the governor to the ranchero—from the soberest matron to the flippant belle—from the grandest *señora* to the *cocinera*—all partake of this exhilarating amusement. To judge from the quantity of tuned instruments which salute the ear almost every night in the week, one would suppose that a perpetual carnival prevailed everywhere. The musical instruments used at the *bailes* and *fandangos* are usually the fiddle and *bandolin*, or *guitarra*, accompanied in some villages by the *tombé* or little Indian drum. The musicians occasionally acquire considerable proficiency in the use of these instruments. But what most oddly greets, and really outrages most Protestant ears, is the accompaniment of divine service with the very same instruments, and often with the same tunes.

Of all the petty vices practised by the New Mexicans, the *vicio inocente* of smoking among ladies, is the most intolerable; and yet it is a habit of which the loveliest and the most refined equally partake. The *puro* or *cigarro** is seen in the mouths of all: it is handed round in the parlor, and introduced at the dinner table— even in the ball-room it is presented to ladies as regularly as any other species of 'refreshment;' and in the dance the señorita may often be seen whirling round with a lighted *cigarrito* in her mouth. The belles of the Southern cities are very frequently furnished with *tenazitas de oro* (little golden tongs), to hold the cigar with, so as to prevent their delicate fingers from being polluted either with the stain or scent of tobacco; forgetting at the same time its disagreeable effects upon the lips and breath.

Notwithstanding their numerous vices, however, I should do the New Mexicans the justice to say that they are but little addicted to inebriety and its attendant dissipations. Yet this doubtlessly results to a considerable degree from the dearness of spirituous liquors, which virtually places them beyond the reach of the lower classes.

11 . Religion

The Mexicans seem the legitimate descendants of the subjects of 'His Most Catholic Majesty;' for the Romish faith is not only the religion established by law, but the only one tolerated by the constitution: a system of republican liberty wholly incompre-

---

* The *puro* is a common cigar of *pure* tobacco; but the term *cigarro* or *cigarrito* is applied to those made of cut tobacco rolled up in a strip of paper or corn-husk. The latter are by far in the most general use in New Mexico, even among the men, and are those only smoked by the females. In this province cigarros are rarely sold in the shops, being generally manufactured by every one just as they are needed. Their expertness in this 'accomplishment' is often remarkable. The mounted vaquero will take out his *guagito* (his little tobacco-flask), his packet of *hojas* (or prepared husks), and his flint, steel, etc.,—make his cigarrito, strike fire and commence smoking in a minute's time—all while at full speed: and the next minute will perhaps lazo the wildest bull without interrupting his smoke.

hensible to the independent and tolerant spirits of the United States. Foreigners only of other creeds, in accordance with treaty stipulations, can worship privately within their own houses.

In the variety and grossness of popular superstitions, Northern Mexico can probably compete with any civilized country in the world. Others may have their extravagant traditions, their fanatical prejudices, their priestly impostures, but here the popular creed seems to be the embodiment of as much that is fantastic and improbable in idolatrous worship, as it is possible to clothe in the garb of a religious faith.

It is a part of the superstitious blindness of these people to believe that every one of their legion of canonized saints possesses the power of performing certain miracles; and their aid is generally invoked on all occasions of sickness and distress. The kindest office, therefore, that the friends of a sick person can perform, is to bring forward the image of some of those saints whose healing powers have been satisfactorily tested. The efficacy of these superstitious remedies will not be difficult to account for, when the powerful influence of the imagination upon disease is taken into consideration.

The images of patron saints are never put in such general requisition, however, as in seasons of severe drought. The priests, being generally expert at guessing the approach of a pluvial period, take good care not to make confident promises till they have substantial reason to anticipate a speedy fulfilment of their prophecies. When the fitting season draws nigh, they carry out the image of Nuestra Señora de Guadalupe, or that of some other favorite saint, and parade about the streets, the fields and the meadows, followed by all the men, women, and children of the neighborhood, in solemn procession. Should the clouds condescend to vouchsafe a supply of rain within a week or two of this general humiliation, no one ever thinks of begrudging the scores of dollars that have been paid to the priests for bringing about so happy a result.

Speaking of processions, I am reminded of another peculiar custom so prevalent in Mexico, that it never fails to attract the attention of strangers. This is the passage of the Sacred Host to the residence of persons dangerously ill, for the purpose of administering to them the Extreme Unction. In New Mexico, however, this procession is not attended with so much ostentatious display as it is in the South, the paradise of ecclesiastics, where it is conveyed in a black coach drawn by a pair of black mules, accompanied by armed soldiers and followed by crowds of *léperos* of all sexes and ages. During the procession of the Host, two church-bells of different tones are kept sounding by alternate strokes. Also the carriage is always preceded by a bell-man tinkling a little bell in regular time, to notify all within hearing of its approach, that they may be prepared to pay it due homage. When this bell is heard, all those that happen to be within sight of the procession, though at ever so great a distance, instantly kneel and remain in that position till it has passed out of sight. On these occasions, if an American happens to be within hearing, he endeavors to avoid the *cortége*, by turning the corner of a street or entering a shop or the house of a friend; for although it may be expedient, and even rational, to conform with the customs and ceremonies of those countries we are sojourning in, very few Protestants would feel disposed to fall on their knees before a coach freighted with frail mortals pretending to represent the Godhead! I am sorry to say that non-compliants are frequently insulted and sometimes pelted with stones by the rabble. Even a foreign artisan was once massacred in the Mexican metropolis because he refused to come out of his shop, where he was kneeling, and perform the act of genuflexion in the street!

This abject idolatry sometimes takes a still more humiliating aspect, and descends to the worship of men in the capacity of religious rulers. On the occasion of the Bishop of Durango's visit to Santa Fé in 1833, an event which had not taken place for a great many years, the infatuated population hailed his arrival with as much devotional enthusiasm as if it had been the second advent of the Messiah. Magnificent preparations were made everywhere for his reception: the streets were swept, the roads and bridges on his route repaired and decorated; and from every window in the city there hung such a profusion of fancy curtains and rich cloths that the imagination was carried back to those glowing descriptions of enchanted worlds which one reads of in the fables of necromancers. I must observe, however, that there is a custom in all the towns of Mexico (which it would not be safe to neglect), providing that whenever a religious procession takes place, all the doors and windows facing the street along which it is to pass, shall be decorated with shawls, carpets, or fancy cloths, according to the means and capabilities of the proprietor. During the bishop's sojourn in Santa Fé, which, to the great joy of the inhabitants, lasted for several weeks, he never appeared in the streets but that 'all true Catholics' who were so fortunate as to obtain a glimpse of his *Señoría Ilustrísima* immediately dropped upon their knees, and never moved from that position till the mitred priest had either vouchsafed his benediction or had disappeared. Even the principal personages of the city would not venture to address him till they had first knelt at his feet and kissed his 'pastoral ring.' This, however, is only a heightened picture of what occurs every day in the intercourse between the rancheros and the common padres of the country. The slavish obsequiousness of the lower classes towards these pampered priests is almost incredible.

No people are more punctual in their attendance upon public worship, or more exact in the performance of the external rites of religion, than the New Mexicans. A man would about as soon think of venturing in twenty fathoms of water without being able to swim, as of undertaking a journey without hearing mass first. These religious exercises, however, partake but seldom of the character of true devotion; for people may be seen chattering or tittering while in the act of crossing themselves, or muttering some formal prayer. Indeed, it is the common remark of strangers, that they are wont to wear much graver countenances while dancing at a fandango than during their devotional exercises at the foot of the altar. In nothing, however, is their observance of the outward forms of religion more remarkable than in their deportment every day towards the close of twilight, when the large bell of the *Parroquia* peals for *la oracion,* or vespers. All conversation is instantly suspended—all labor ceases—people of all classes, whether on foot or on horseback, make a sudden halt—even the laden porter, groaning under the weight of an insupportable burden, stops in the midst of his career and stands still. An almost breathless silence reigns throughout the town, disturbed only by the occasional sibilations of the devout multitude: all of which, accompanied by the slow heavy peals of a large sonorous bell, afford a scene truly solemn and appropriate. At the expiration of about two minutes the charm is suddenly broken by the clatter of livelier-toned bells; when, *presto,* all is bustle and confusion again—the colloquial chit-chat is resumed—the smith plies upon his anvil with redoubled energy—the clink of the hammer simultaneously resounds in every direction—the wayfarers are again in motion, and both pleasure and business, in short, assume their respective sway; and a *buenas tardes* (good evening) to those present closes the ceremony.

Although the Catholics have a saint for each day in the year, the number of canonized *fiestas* in which labor is prohibited has been somewhat reduced in Mexico. *La Semana Santa,* or Passion Week, is perhaps the period when the religious feeling, such as it is, is mostly fully excited: *Viernes Santo* (Good Friday), especially, is observed with great pomp and splendor. An image of Christ large as life, nailed to a huge wooden cross, is paraded through the streets, in the midst of an immense procession, accompanied by a glittering array of carved images, representing the Virgin Mary, Mary Magdalene, and several others; while the most notorious personages of antiquity, who figured at that great era of the world's history,—the centurion with a band of guards, armed with lances, and apparelled in the costume supposed to have been worn in those days,—may be seen bestriding splendidly caparisoned horses, in the breathing reality of flesh and blood. Taking it all in all, this spectacle,—the ceremonies and manœuvres which attend its career through the densely crowded and ornamented streets,—are calculated to produce impressions of a most confused description, in which regret and melancholy may be said to form no inconsiderable share.

In New Mexico, the institution of marriage changes the legal rights of the parties, but it scarcely affects their moral obligations. It is usually looked upon as a convenient cloak for irregularities, which society less willingly tolerates in the lives of unmarried women. Yet when it is considered that the majority of matches are forced and ill-assorted, some idea may be formed of the little incitement that is given to virtue. There are very few parents who would stoop to consult a young lady's wishes before concluding a marriage contract, nor would maidens, generally, ever dream of a matrimonial connection unless proposed first by the father. The lover's proposals are, upon the same principle, made in writing direct to the parents themselves, and without the least deference to the wishes or inclinations of the young lady whose hand is thus sought in marriage. The tender emotions engendered between lovers during walks and rambles along the banks of silent streams, are never experienced in this country; for the sexes are seldom permitted to converse or be together alone. In short, instances have actually occurred when the betrothed couple have never seen each other till brought to the altar to be joined in wedlock.

Among the humbler classes, there are still more powerful causes calculated to produce irregularity of life; not the least of which is the enormous fee that must be paid to the curate for tying the matrimonial knot. This system of extortion is carried so far as to amount very frequently to absolute prohibition: for the means of the bridegroom are often insufficient for the exigency of the occasion; and the priests seldom consent to join people in wedlock until the money has been secured to them. The curates being without control, the marriage rates are somewhat irregular, but they usually increase in proportion to the character of the ceremonies and to the circumstances of the parties. The lowest are adapted to the simplest form, solemnized in church during attendance at mass; but with the excuse of any extra service and ceremonies, particularly if performed at a private house, the fees are increased often as high as several hundred dollars: I have heard of $500 being paid for a marriage ceremony.

The baptismal and burial fees (neither of which can be avoided without incurring the charge of heresy) are also a great terror to the candidates for married life. "If I marry," says the poor yeoman, "my family must go unclad to baptize my children; and if any of them should die, we must starve ourselves to pay the burial charges." The fee for baptism, it is true, is not so exorbitant, and in accordance to custom, is often paid by the *padrino* or sponsor; but the burial costs are almost equally extravagant with those of marriage, varying in proportion to the age and circumstances of the deceased. A faithful Mexican servant in my employ at Chihuahua, once solicited forty dollars to bury his mother. Upon my expressing some surprise at the exorbitancy of the amount, he replied—"That is what the cura demands, sir, and if I do not pay it my poor mother will remain unburied!" Thus this man was obliged to sacrifice several months' wages, to pamper the avarice of a vicious and mercenary priest. On another occasion, a poor

widow in Santa Fé, begged a little medicine for her sick child:
"Not," said the disconsolate mother, "that the life of the babe
imports me much, for I know the *angelito* will go directly to
heaven; but what shall I do to pay the priest for burying it? He
will take my house and all from me—and I shall be turned desolate
into the streets"—and so saying, she commenced weeping
bitterly.

Indigent parents are thus frequently under the painful necessity
of abandoning and disowning their deceased children, to avoid the
responsibility of burial expenses. To this end the corpse is sometimes deposited in some niche or corner of the church during the
night; and upon being found in the morning, the priest is bound to
inter it gratis, unless the parent can be discovered, in which case
the latter would be liable to severe castigation, besides being
bound to pay the expenses.

Children that have not been baptized are destined, according to
the popular faith, to a kind of negative existence in the world of
spirits, called *Limbo*, where they remain for ever without either
suffering punishment or enjoying happiness. Baptized infants, on
the other hand, being considered without sin, are supposed to
enter at once into the joys of heaven. The deceased child is then
denominated an *angelito* (a little angel), and is interred with joy
and mirth instead of grief and wailing. It is gaudily bedecked with
fanciful attire and ornaments of tinsel and flowers; and being
placed upon a small bier, it is carried to the grave by four children
as gaily dressed as their circumstances will allow; accompanied
by musicians using the instruments and playing the tunes of the
fandangos; and the little procession is nothing but glee and merriment.

12. The Pueblos

Allusion has so frequently been made to the aboriginal tribes of
New Mexico, known as *Los Pueblos*, that I think I shall not be
trespassing too much upon the patience of the reader, in glancing
rapidly at some of the more conspicuous features of their national
habits and character.

Although the term *Pueblo* in Spanish literally means the

people, and their *towns*, it is here specifically applied to the
Christianized Indians (as well as their villages)—to those aborigines whom the Spaniards not only subjected to their laws, but to
an acknowledgment of the Romish faith, and upon whom they
forced baptism and the cross in exchange for the vast possessions
of which they robbed them. All that was left them was, to each
Pueblo a league or two of land situated around their villages, the
conquerors reserving to themselves at least ninety-nine hun-
dredths of the whole domain as a requital for their generosity.

When these regions were first discovered it appears that the
inhabitants lived in comfortable houses and cultivated the soil, as
they have continued to do up to the present time. Indeed, they
are now considered the best horticulturists in the country, furnish-
ing most of the fruits and a large portion of the vegetable supplies
that are to be found in the markets. They were until very lately
the only people in New Mexico who cultivated the grape. They
also maintain at the present time considerable herds of cattle,
horses, etc. They are, in short, a remarkably sober and industrious
race, conspicuous for morality and honesty, and very little given
to quarrelling or dissipation, except when they have had much
familiar intercourse with the Hispano-Mexican population.

Most of these Pueblos call themselves the descendants of Mon-
tezuma, although it would appear that they could only have been
made acquainted with the history of that monarch, by the Spaniards; as this province is nearly two thousand miles from the
ancient kingdom of Mexico. At the time of the conquest they must
have been a very powerful people—numbering near a hundred
villages, as existing ruins would seem to indicate; but they are
now reduced to about twenty, which are scattered in various parts
of the territory.

The population of these Pueblos will average nearly five hundred souls each(though some hardly exceed one hundred), making
an aggregate of nine or ten thousand. At the time of the original
conquest, at the close of the sixteenth century, they were, as has
been mentioned, much, perhaps ten-fold, more numerous. Ancient
ruins are now to be seen scattered in every quarter of the territory:
of some, entire stone walls are yet standing, while others are
nearly or quite obliterated, many of them being now only known
by their names which history or tradition has preserved to us.

Numbers were no doubt destroyed during the insurrection of 1680, and the petty internal strifes which followed.

Several of these Pueblos have been converted into Mexican villages, of which that of *Pecos* is perhaps the most remarkable instance. What with the massacres of the second conquest, and the inroads of the Comanches, they gradually dwindled away, till they found themselves reduced to about a dozen, comprising all ages and sexes; and it was only a few years ago that they abandoned the home of their fathers and joined the Pueblo of Jemez.

Although nominally under the jurisdiction of the federal government, as Mexican citizens, many features of their ancient customs are still retained, as well in their civil rule as in their religion. Each Pueblo is under the control of a *cacique* or *gobernadorcillo*, chosen from among their own sages, and commissioned by the governor of New Mexico. The cacique, when any public business is to be transacted, collects together the principal chiefs of the Pueblo in an *estufa*, or cell, usually under ground, and there lays before them the subjects of debate, which are generally settled by the opinion of the majority. No Mexican is admitted to these councils, nor do the subjects of discussion ever transpire beyond the precincts of the cavern. The council has also charge of the interior police and tranquillity of the village. One of their regulations is to appoint a secret watch for the purpose of keeping down disorders and vices of every description, and especially to keep an eye over the young men and women of the village. When any improper intercourse among them is detected, the parties are immediately carried to the council, and the cacique intimates to them that they must be wedded forthwith. Should the girl be of bad character, and the man, therefore, unwilling to marry her, they are ordered to keep separate under penalty of the lash. Hence it is, that the females of these Pueblos are almost universally noted for their chastity and modest deportment.

They also elect a *capitan de guerra,* a kind of commander-in-chief of the warriors, whose office it is to defend their homes and their interests both in the field and in the council chamber. Though not very warlike, these Pueblos are generally valiant, and well skilled in the strategies of Indian warfare; and although they have been branded with cruelty and ferocity, yet they can hardly be said to surpass the Mexicans in this respect: both, in times of war, pay but little regard either to age or sex. I have been told that when the Pueblos return from their belligerent expeditions, instead of going directly to their homes, they always visit their council cell first. Here they undress, dance, and carouse, frequently for two days in succession before seeing their families.

Although the Pueblos are famous for hospitality and industry, they still continue in the rudest state of ignorance, having neither books nor schools among them, as none of their languages have been reduced to rules, and very few of their children are ever taught Spanish. A degree of primitiveness characterizes all their amusements, which bear a strong similarity to those of the wilder tribes. Before the New Mexican government had become so much impoverished, there was wont to be held in the capital on the 16th of September of every year, a national celebration of the declaration of Independence, to which the Pueblos were invited. The warriors and youths of each nation with a proportionate array of dusky damsels would appear on these occasions, painted and ornamented in accordance with their aboriginal customs, and amuse the inhabitants with all sorts of grotesque feats and native dances. Each Pueblo generally had its particular uniform dress and its particular dance. The men of one village would sometimes disguise themselves as elks, with horns on their heads, moving on all-fours, and mimicking the animal they were attempting to personate. Others would appear in the garb of a turkey, with large heavy wings, and strut about in imitation of that bird. But the Pecos tribe, already reduced to seven men, always occasioned most diversion. Their favorite exploit was, each to put on the skin of a buffalo, horns, tail, and all, and thus accoutred scamper about through the crowd, to the real or affected terror of all the ladies present, and to the great delight of the boys.

The Pueblo villages are generally built with more regularity than those of the Mexicans, and are constructed of the same materials as were used by them in the most primitive ages. Their dwelling-houses, it is true, are not so spacious as those of the Mexicans, containing very seldom more than two or three small apartments upon the ground floor, without any court-yard, but they have generally a much loftier appearance, being frequently two stories high and sometimes more. A very curious feature in these buildings, is, that there is most generally no direct communication between the street and the lower rooms, into which they descend by a trap-door from the upper story, the latter being accessible by means of ladders. Even the entrance to the upper stories is frequently at the roof. This style of building seems to have been adopted for security against their marauding neighbors of the wilder tribes, with whom they were often at war. When the family had all been housed at night, the ladder was drawn up, and the inmates were thus shut up in a kind of fortress, which bid defiance to the scanty implements of warfare used by the wild Indians.

Some of these villages were built upon rocky eminences deemed almost inaccessible: witness for instance the ruins of the ancient Pueblo of San Felipe, which may be seen towering upon the very verge of a precipice several hundred feet high, whose base is washed by the swift current of the Rio del Norte. The still existing Pueblo of Acoma also stands upon an isolated mound whose whole area is occupied by the village, being fringed all around by a precipitous *ceja* or cliff. The inhabitants enter the village by means of ladders, and by steps cut into the solid rock upon which it is based.

At the time of the conquest, many of these Pueblos manufactured some singular textures of cotton and other materials; but with the loss of their liberty, they seem to have lost most of their arts and ingenuity; so that the finer specimens of native fabrics are now only to be met with among the Moquis and Navajoes, who still retain their independence. The Pueblos, however, make some of the ordinary classes of blankets and *tilmas*,* as well as other woollen stuffs. They also manufacture, according to their aboriginal art, both for their own consumption, and for the purposes of traffic, a species of earthenware not much inferior to the coarse crockery of our common potters. The pots made of this material stand fire remarkably well, and are the universal substitutes for all the purposes of cookery, even among the Mexicans, for the iron castings of this country, which are utterly unknown there. Rude as this kind of crockery is, it nevertheless evinces a great deal of skill, considering that it is made entirely without

---

* The *tilma* is a sort of small but durable blanket, worn by the Indians as a mantle.

lathe or any kind of machinery. It is often fancifully painted with colored earths and the juice of a plant called *guaco,* which brightens by burning. They also work a singular kind of wicker-ware, of which some bowls (if they may be so called) are so closely platted, that, once swollen by dampness, they serve to hold liquids, and are therefore light and convenient vessels for the purposes of travellers.

The dress of many of the Pueblos has become assimilated in some respects to that of the common Mexicans; but by far the greatest portion still retain most of their aboriginal costume. The Taosas and others of the north somewhat resemble the prairie tribes in this respect; but the Pueblos to the south and west of Santa Fé dress in a different style, which is said to be similar in many respects to that of the aboriginal inhabitants of the city of Mexico. The moccasin is the only part of the prairie suit that appears common to them all, and of both sexes. They mostly wear a kind of short breeches and long stockings, the use of which they most probably acquired from the Spaniards. The *saco,* a species of woollen jacket without sleeves, completes their exterior garment; except during inclement seasons, when they make use of the tilma. Very few of them have hats or head-dress of any kind; and they generally wear their hair long—commonly fashioned into a *queue* wrapped with some colored stuff. The squaws of the northern tribes dress pretty much like those of the Prairies; but the usual costume of the females of the southern and western Pueblos is a handsome kind of small blanket of dark color, which is drawn under one arm and tacked over the other shoulder, leaving both arms free and naked. It is generally worn with a cotton chemise underneath and is bound about the waist with a girdle. We rarely if ever see a thorough-bred Pueblo woman in Mexican dress.

The weapons most in use among the Pueblos are the bow and arrow, with a long-handled lance and occasionally a fusil. The rawhide shield is also much used, which, though of but little service against fire-arms, serves to ward off the arrow and lance.

The aliment of these Indians is, in most respects, similar to that of the Mexicans; in fact, as has been elsewhere remarked, the latter adopted with their utensils numerous items of aboriginal

diet. The *tortilla*, the *atole*, the *pinole*,* and many others, together
with the use of *chile*, are from the Indians. Some of the wilder
tribes make a peculiar kind of *pinole*, by grinding the bean of the
mezquite tree into flour, which is then used as that of corn. And
besides the tortilla they make another singular kind of bread, if
we may so style it, called *guayave*, a roll of which so much resembles a 'hornets' nest,' that by strangers it is often designated by
this title. It is usually made of Indian corn prepared and ground
as for tortillas, and diluted into a thin paste. I once happened to
enter an Indian hut where a young girl of the family was baking
guayaves. She was sitting by a fire, over which a large flat stone
was heating, with a crock of prepared paste by her side. She thrust
her hand into the paste, and then wiped it over the heated stone.
What adhered to it was instantly baked and peeled off. She
repeated this process at the rate of a dozen times or more per
minute. Observing my curiosity, the girl handed me one of the
'sheets,' silently; for she seemed to understand but her native
tongue. I found it pleasant enough to the taste; though when cold,
as I have learned by experience, it is, like the cold tortilla, rather
tough and insipid. They are even thinner than wafers; and some
dozens, being folded in a roll, constitute the laminate composition
before mentioned. Being thus preserved, they serve the natives
for months upon their journeys.

13 . The Wild Tribes

All the Indians of New Mexico not denominated Pueblos—not
professing the Christian religion—are ranked as *wild tribes*, although these include some who have made great advances in arts,
manufactures and agriculture.

The principal wild tribes which inhabit or extend their incur-

---

* *Pinole* is in effect the *cold-flour* of our hunters. It is the meal of parched
Indian corn, prepared for use by stirring it up with a little cold water. This
food seems also to have been of ancient use among the aborigines of other
parts of America. Father Charlevoix, in 1721, says of the savages about the
northern lakes, that they "reduce [the maize] to Flour which they call *Farine
froide* (cold Flour), and this is the best Provision that can be made for
Travellers."

sions or peregrinations upon the territory of New Mexico, are the *Navajóes*, the *Apaches*, the *Yutas*, the *Caiguas* or Kiawas, and the *Comanches*. Of the latter I will speak in another place. The two first are from one and the same original stock, there being, even at the present day, no very important difference in their language. The Apaches are divided into numerous petty tribes, of one of which an insignificant band, called Jicarillas, inhabiting the mountains north of Taos, is an isolated and miserable remnant.

The *Navajóes* are supposed to number about 10,000 souls, and though not the most numerous, they are certainly the most important, at least in a historical point of view, of all the northern tribes of Mexico. They reside in the main range of Cordilleras, 150 to 200 miles west of Santa Fé, on the waters of Rio Colorado of California, not far from the region, according to historians, from whence the Azteques emigrated to Mexico; and there are many reasons to suppose them direct descendants from the remnant, which remained in the North, of this celebrated nation of antiquity. Although they mostly live in rude *jacales*, somewhat resembling the wigwams of the Pawnees, yet, from time immemorial, they have excelled all others in their original manufactures: and, as well as the Moquis, they are still distinguished for some exquisite styles of cotton textures, and display considerable ingenuity in embroidering with feathers the skins of animals, according to their primitive practice. They now also manufacture a singular species of blanket, known as the *Sarape Navajó*, which is of so close and dense a texture that it will frequently hold water almost equal to gum-elastic cloth. It is therefore highly prized for protection against the rains. Some of the finer qualities are often sold among the Mexicans as high as fifty or sixty dollars each.

Notwithstanding the present predatory and somewhat unsettled habits of the Navajoes, they cultivate all the different grains and vegetables to be found in New Mexico. They also possess extensive herds of horses, mules, cattle, sheep and goats of their own raising, which are generally celebrated as being much superior to those of the Mexicans; owing, no doubt, to greater attention to the improvement of their stocks.

Though Baron Humbolt tells us that some missionaries were established among this tribe prior to the general massacre of 1680, but few attempts to christianize them have since been made. They now remain in a state of primitive paganism—and not only independent of the Mexicans, but their most formidable enemies.

I come now to speak of the *Apaches,* the most extensive and powerful, yet the most vagrant of all the savage nations that inhabit the interior of Northern Mexico. They are supposed to number some fifteen thousand souls, although they are subdivided into various petty bands, and scattered over an immense tract of country. Those that are found east of the Rio del Norte are generally known as *Mezcaleros,* on account of an article of food much in use among them, called *mezcal,** but by far the greatest portion of the nation is located in the west, and is mostly known by the sobriquet of *Coyoteros,* in consequence, it is said, of their eating the *coyote* or prairie wolf. The Apaches are perhaps more given to itinerant habits than any other tribe in Mexico. They never construct houses, but live in the ordinary wigwam, or tent of skins and blankets. They manufacture nothing—cultivate nothing: they seldom resort to the chase, as their country is destitute of game—but seem to depend entirely upon pillage for the support of their immense population, at least two thousand of which are warriors.

For their food, the Apaches rely chiefly upon the flesh of the cattle and sheep they can steal from the Mexican ranchos and haciendas. They are said, however, to be more fond of the meat of the mule than that of any other animal. I have seen about encampments which they had recently left, the remains of mules that had been slaughtered for their consumption. Yet on one occasion I saw their whole trail, for many miles, literally strewed with the carcasses of these animals, which, it was evident, had not been killed for this purpose. It is the practice of the Apache chiefs, as I have understood, whenever a dispute arises betwixt their warriors relative to the ownership of any particular animal, to kill the brute at once, though it be the most valuable of the drove; and so check all further cavil. It was to be inferred from the number of dead mules they left behind them, that the most harmonious relations could not have existed between the members of the tribe, at least

---

* *Mezcal* is the baked root of the *maguey* (*agave Americana*) and of another somewhat similar plant.

during this period of their journeyings. Like most of the savage tribes of North America, the *Apaches* are passionately fond of spirituous liquors, and may frequently be seen, in times of peace, lounging about the Mexican villages, in a state of helpless inebriety.

The range of this marauding tribe extends over some portions of California, most of Sonora, the frontiers of Durango, and at certain seasons it even reaches Coahuila: Chihuahua, however, has been the mournful theatre of their most constant depredations. Every nook and corner of this once flourishing state has been subjected to their inroads. Such is the imbecility of the local governments, that the savages, in order to dispose of their stolen property without even a shadow of molestation, frequently enter into partial treaties of peace with one department, while they continue to wage a war of extermination against the neighboring states. This arrangement supplies them with an ever-ready market, for the disposal of their booty and the purchase of munitions wherewith to prosecute their work of destruction. In 1840, I witnessed the departure from Santa Fé of a large trading party freighted with engines of war and a great quantity of whisky, intended for the Apaches in exchange for mules and other articles of plunder which they had stolen from the people of the south. This traffic was not only tolerated but openly encouraged by the civil authorities, as the highest public functionaries were interested in its success—the governor himself not excepted.

The Apaches, now and then, propose a truce to the government of Chihuahua, which is generally accepted very nearly upon their own terms. It has on some occasions been included that the marauders should have a *bona fide* right to all their stolen property. A *venta* or quit-claim brand, has actually been marked by the government upon large numbers of mules and horses which the Indians had robbed from the citizens. It is hardly necessary to add that these truces have rarely been observed by the wily savages longer than the time necessary for the disposal of their plunder. As soon as more mules were needed for service or for traffic—more cattle for beef—more scalps for the war-dance—they would invariably return to their deeds of ravage and murder.

The depredations of the Apaches have been of such long duration, that, beyond the immediate purlieus of the towns, the whole country from New Mexico to the borders of Durango is almost entirely depopulated. The haciendas and ranchos have been mostly abandoned, and the people chiefly confined to towns and cities. To such a pitch has the temerity of those savages reached, that small bands of three or four warriors have been known to make their appearance within a mile of the city of Chihuahua in open day, killing the laborers and driving off whole herds of mules and horses without the slightest opposition. Occasionally a detachment of troops is sent in pursuit of the marauders, but for no other purpose, it would seem, than to illustrate the imbecility of the former, as they are always sure to make a precipitate retreat, generally without even obtaining a glimpse of the enemy. And yet the columns of a little weekly sheet published in Chihuahua always teem with flaming accounts of prodigious feats of valor performed by the 'army of operations' against *los bárbaros*: showing how "the enemy was pursued with all possible vigor"—how the soldiers "displayed the greatest bravery, and the most unrestrainable desire to overhaul the dastards," and by what extraordinary combinations of adverse circumstances they were "compelled to relinquish the pursuit." Indeed it would be difficult to find a braver race of people than the *Chihuahueños* contrive to make themselves appear upon paper.

The *Yutas* (or *Eutaws*, as they are generally styled by Americans) are one of the most extensive nations of the West, being scattered from the north of New Mexico to the borders of Snake river and Rio Colorado, and numbering at least ten thousand souls. The habits of the tribe are altogether itinerant. A band of about a thousand spend their winters mostly in the mountain valleys northward of Taos, and the summer season generally in the prairie plains to the east, hunting buffalo. The vernacular language of the Yutas is said to be distantly allied to that of the Navajoes, but it has appeared to me much more guttural, having a deep sepulchral sound resembling ventriloquism. Although these Indians are nominally at peace with the New Mexican government, they do not hesitate to lay the hunters and traders who happen to fall in with their scouting parties under severe contributions; and on some occasions they have been known to proceed even to personal violence. A prominent Mexican officer was scourged not long ago by a party of Yutas, and yet the government has never dared to resent the outrage.

14 . The Return Trip

I do not propose to detain the reader with an account of my journeyings between Mexico and the United States, during the seven years subsequent to my first arrival at Santa Fé. I will here merely remark, that I crossed the plains to the United States in the falls of 1833 and 1836, and returned to Santa Fé with goods each succeeding spring. It was only in 1838, however, that I eventually closed up my affairs in Northern Mexico, and prepared to take my leave of the country, as I then supposed, for ever. But in this I was mistaken, as will appear in the sequel.

The most usual season for the return of the caravans to the United States is the autumn, and not one has elapsed since the commencement of the trade which has not witnessed some departure from Santa Fé with that destination. They have also crossed occasionally in the spring, but without any regularity or frequency, and generally in very small parties. Even the 'fall companies,' in fact, are small when compared with the outward-bound caravans; for besides the numbers who remain permanently in the country, many of those who trade southward return to the United States *via* Matamoros or some other Southern port. The return parties of autumn are therefore comparatively small, varying in number from fifty to a hundred men. They leave Santa Fé some four or five weeks after their arrival—generally about the first of September. In these companies there are rarely over thirty or forty wagons; for a large portion of those taken out by the annual caravans are disposed of in the country.

Some of the traders who go out in the spring, return the ensuing fall, because they have the good fortune to sell off their stock promptly and to advantage: others are compelled to return in the fall to save their credit; nay, to preserve their homes, which, especially in the earlier periods, have sometimes been mortgaged to secure the payment of the merchandise they carried out with them. In such cases, their goods were not unfrequently sold at great sacrifice, to avoid the penalties which the breaking of their engagements at home would involve. New adventurers, too, are apt to become discouraged with an unanticipated dullness of times, and not unfrequently sell off at wholesale for the best price they can get, though often at a serious loss. But those who are regularly engaged in this trade usually calculate upon employing a season—perhaps a year in closing an enterprise—in selling off their goods and making their returns.

The wagons of the return caravans are generally but lightly laden: one to two thousand pounds constitute the regular return cargo for a single wagon; for not only are the teams unable to haul heavy loads, on account of the decay of pasturage at this season, but the approaching winter compels the traders to travel in greater haste; so that this trip is usually made in about forty days. The amount of freight, too, from that direction is comparatively small. The remittances, as has already been mentioned, are chiefly in specie or gold and silver bullion. The gold is mostly *dust*, from the Placer or gold mine near Santa Fé: the silver bullion is all from the mines of the South—chiefly from those of Chihuahua. To these returns may be added a considerable number of mules and asses— some buffalo rugs, furs, and wool,—which last barely pays a return freight for the wagons that would otherwise be empty.

On the 4th of April, 1838, we departed from Santa Fé. Our little party was found to consist of twenty-three Americans, with twelve Mexican servants. We had seven wagons, one dearborn, and two small field-pieces, besides a large assortment of small-arms. The principal proprietors carried between them about $150,000 in specie and bullion, being for the most part the proceeds of the previous year's adventure.

We moved on at a brisk and joyous pace until we reached Ocaté creek, a tributary of the Colorado, a distance of a hundred and thirty miles from Santa Fé, where we encountered a very sudden bereavement in the death of Mr. Langham, one of our most respected proprietors. This gentleman was known to be in weak health, but no fears were entertained for his safety. We were all actively engaged in assisting the more heavily laden wagons over the miry stream, when he was seized with a fit of apoplexy and expired instantly. The deceased was from St. Louis, though he had passed the last eleven years of his life in Santa Fé, during the whole of which period he had seen neither his home nor his relatives.

The melancholy rites being concluded, we resumed our line of march. We now continued for several days without the occurrence

of any important accident or adventure. On the 19th we encamped
in the Cimarron valley, about twelve miles below the Willow Bar.
The very sight of this desolate region, frequented as it is by the
most savage tribes of Indians, was sufficient to strike dismay into
the hearts of our party; but as we had not as yet encountered any
of them, we felt comparatively at ease. Our mules and horses were
'staked' as usual around the wagons, and every man, except the
watch, betook himself to his blanket, in anticipation of a good
night's rest. The hour of mid-night had passed away, and nothing
had been heard except the tramping of the men on guard, and the
peculiar grating of the mules' teeth, nibbling the short grass of
the valley. Ere long, however, one of our sentinels got a glimpse
of some object moving stealthily along, and as he was straining
his eyes to ascertain what sort of apparition it could be, a loud
Indian yell suddenly revealed the mystery. This was quickly followed by a discharge of fire-arms, and the shrill note of the 'Pawnee whistle,' which at once made known the character of our
visitors. As usual, the utmost confusion prevailed in our camp:
some, who had been snatched from the land of dreams, ran their
heads against the wagons—others called out for their guns while
they had them in their hands. During the height of the bustle and
uproar, a Mexican servant was observed leaning with his back
against a wagon, and his fusil elevated at an angle of forty-five
degrees, cocking and pulling the trigger without ceasing, and
exclaiming at every snap, *"Carajo, no sirve!"*—Curse it, it's good
for nothing.

The firing still continued—the yells grew fiercer and more frequent; and everything betokened the approach of a terrible conflict. Meanwhile a number of persons were engaged in securing
the mules and horses which were staked around the encampment;
and in a few minutes they were all shut up in the *corral*—a hundred head or more in a pen formed by seven wagons. The enemy
failing in their principal object—to frighten off our stock, they
soon began to retreat; and in a few minutes nothing more was to
be heard of them. All that we could discover the next morning
was, that none of our party had sustained any injury, and that we
had not lost a single animal.

On our passage this time across the 'prairie ocean' which lay
before us, we ran no risk of getting bewildered or lost, for there

was now a plain wagon trail across the entire stretch of our route, from the Cimarron to Arkansas river.

This track, which has since remained permanent, was made in the year 1834. Owing to continuous rains during the passage of the caravan of that year, a plain trail was then cut in the softened turf, on the most direct route across this arid desert, leaving the Arkansas about twenty miles above the 'Caches.' This has ever since been the regular route of the caravans; and thus a recurrence of those distressing sufferings from thirst, so frequently experienced by early travellers in that inhospitable region, has been prevented.

We forded the Arkansas without difficulty, and pursued our journey to the Missouri border with comparative ease; being only now and then disturbed at night by the hideous howlings of wolves, a pack of which had constituted themselves into a kind of 'guard of honor,' and followed in our wake for several hundred miles—in fact to the very border of the settlements. They were at first attracted no doubt by the remains of buffalo which were killed by us upon the high plains, and afterwards enticed on by an occasional fagged animal, which we were compelled to leave behind, as well as by the bones and scraps of food, which they picked up about our camps. Not a few of them paid the penalty of their lives for their temerity.

Upon reaching the settlements, I had an opportunity of experiencing a delusion which had been the frequent subject of remark by travellers on the Prairies before. Accustomed as we had been for some months to our little mules, and the equally small-sized Mexican ponies, our sight became so adjusted to their proportions, that when we came to look upon the commonest hackney of our frontier horses, it appeared to be almost a monster. I have frequently heard exclamations of this kind from the new arrivals:— "How the Missourians have improved their breed of horses!"— "What a huge gelding!"—"Did you ever see such an animal!" This delusion is frequently availed of by the frontiersmen to put off their meanest horses to these deluded travellers for the most enormous prices.

On the 11th of May we arrived at Independence, after a propitious journey of only thirty-eight days.

BOOK TWO

15. A Return to the Prairies

An unconquerable propensity to return to prairie life inclined me to embark in a fresh enterprise. The blockade of the Mexican ports by the French also offered strong inducements for undertaking such an expedition in the spring of 1839; for as Chihuahua is supplied principally through the sea-ports, it was now evident that the place must be suffering from great scarcity of goods. Being anxious to reach the market before the ports of the Gulf were re-opened, we deemed it expedient to abandon the regular route from Missouri for one wholly untried, from the borders of Arkansas, where the pasturage springs up nearly a month earlier. It is true, that such an attempt to convey heavily laden wagons through an unexplored region was attended with considerable risk; but as I was familiar with the general character of the plains contiguous to the north, I felt little or no apprehension of serious difficulties, except from what might be occasioned by regions of sandy soil. I have often been asked since, why we did not steer directly for Chihuahua, as our trade was chiefly destined for that place, instead of taking the circuitous route *via* Santa Fé. I answer, that we dreaded a journey across the southern prairies on account of the reputed aridity of the country in that direction, and I had no great desire to venture directly into a southern port in the present state of uncertainty as to the conditions of entry.

Suitable arrangements having been made, and a choice stock of about $25,000 worth of goods shipped to Van Buren on the Arkansas river, we started on the evening of the 21st of April, but made very little progress for the first eight days. On the 28th of April we crossed the Arkansas river a few miles above the mouth of the Canadian fork.

On the 2d of May we crossed the North Fork of the Canadian about a mile from its confluence with the main stream. A little westward of this there is a small village of Creek Indians, and a

shop or two kept by American traders. An Indian who had quar-
relled with his wife, came out and proposed to join us, and, to our
great surprise, carried his proposal into execution. The next morning his repentant consort came to our camp, and set up a most
dismal weeping and howling after her truant husband, who, notwithstanding, was neither to be caught by tears nor softened by
entreaties, but persisted in his determination to see foreign countries. His name was Echú-eleh-hadjó (or *Crazy-deer-foot*), but,
for brevity's sake, we always called him *Chuly*. He was industrious, and possessed many clever qualities, though somewhat disposed to commit excesses whenever he could procure liquor, which
fortunately did not occur until our arrival at Santa Fé. He proved
to be a good and willing hand on the way, but as he spoke no
English, our communication with him was somewhat troublesome.
I may as well add here, that, while in Santa Fé, he took another
freak and joined a volunteer corps, chiefly of Americans, orga-
nized under one James Kirker to fight the Navajó and Apache
Indians; the government of Chihuahua having guaranteed to them
all the spoils they should take. With these our Creek found a few
of his 'red brethren'—Shawnees and Delawares, who had wan-
dered thus far from the frontier of Missouri. After this little army
was disbanded, Chuly returned home, as I have been informed,
with a small party who crossed the plains directly from
Chihuahua.

We had never considered ourselves as perfectly *en chemin* till
after crossing the Arkansas river; and as our little party experienced no further change, I may now be permitted to introduce
them collectively to the reader. It consisted of thirty-four men,
including my brother John Gregg and myself. These men had all
been hired by us except three, two of whom were Eastern-bred
boys—a tailor and a silversmith—good-natured, clever little fel-
lows, who had thought themselves at the 'jumping-off place'
when they reached Van Buren, but now seemed nothing loth to
extend their peregrinations a thousand miles or so further, in the
hope of 'doing' the 'Spaniards,' as the Mexicans are generally
styled in the West, out of a little surplus of specie. The other was
a German peddler, who somewhat resembled the Dutchman's
horse, "put him as you vant, and he ish alvays tere;" for he did
nothing during the whole journey but descant on the value of a

chest of trumperies which he carried, and with which he calculated, as he expressed it, to "py a plenty of te Shpanish tollar." The
trip across the Prairies cost these men absolutely nothing, inasmuch as we furnished them with all the necessaries for the journey, in consideration of the additional strength they brought to
our company.

It is seldom that such a variety of ingredients are found mixed
up in so small a compass. Here were the representatives of seven
distinct nations, each speaking his own native language, which
produced at times a very respectable jumble of discordant sounds.
There was one Frenchman whose volubility of tongue and curious
gesticulations, contrasted very strangely with the frigidity of two
phlegmatic wanderers from Germany; while the calm eccentricity
of two Polish exiles, the stoical look of two sons of the desert
(the Creek already spoken of, and a Chickasaw), and the panto-
mimic gestures of sundry loquacious Mexicans, contributed in no
small degree to heighten the effects of the picture. The Americans
were mostly backwoodsmen, who could handle the rifle far better
than the whip, but who nevertheless officiated as wagoners.

We had fourteen road wagons, half drawn by mules, the others
by oxen (eight of each to the team); besides a carriage and a
Jersey wagon. Then we had two swivels mounted upon one pair
of wheels; but one of them was attached to a movable truckle, so
that, upon stopping, it could be transferred to the other side of
the wagons. One of these was a long brass piece made to order,
with a calibre of but an inch and a quarter, yet of sufficient metal
to throw a leaden ball to the distance of a mile with surprising
accuracy. The other was of iron, and a little larger. Besides these,
our party was well supplied with small arms. The Americans
mostly had their rifles and a musket in addition, which they
carried in their wagons, always well charged with ball and buck-
shot. Then my brother and myself were each provided with one of
Colt's repeating rifles, and a pair of pistols of the same, so that we
could, if necessary, carry thirty-six ready-loaded shots apiece;
which alone constituted a capacity of defence rarely matched even
on the Prairies.

Previous to our departure we had received a promise from the
war department of an escort of U. S. Dragoons, as far as the
borders of the Mexican territory; but, upon sending an express to

Gen. Arbuckle at Fort Gibson to that effect, we were informed
that in consequence of some fresh troubles among the Cherokees,
it was doubtful whether the force could be spared in time. This
was certainly no very agreeable news, inasmuch as the escort
would have been very serviceable in assisting to search out a
track over the unexplored wilderness we had to pass. It was too
late, however, to recede; and so we resolved at all hazards to
pursue our journey.

We had advanced beyond the furthest settlements of the
Creeks and Seminoles, and pitched our camp on a bright balmy
evening, in the border of a delightful prairie, when some of the
young men, attracted by the prospect of game, shouldered their
rifles and wended their steps through the dense forest which lay
contiguous to our encampment. Among those that went forth,
there was one of the 'down-easters' already mentioned, who was
much more familiar with the interior of a city than of a wilderness
forest. As the shades of evening were beginning to descend and
all the hunters had returned except him, several muskets and even
our little field-pieces were fired, but without effect. The night
passed away, and the morning dawned upon the encampment,
and still he was absent. The firing was then renewed; but soon
after he was seen approaching, very sullen and dejected. He came
with a tale of perilous adventures and 'hair-breadth 'scapes' upon
his lips, which somewhat abated the storm of ridicule by which
he was at first assailed. It seemed that he had heard our firing on
the previous evening, but believed it to proceed from a contrary
direction—a very common mistake with persons who have become bewildered and lost. Thus deceived and stimulated by the
fear of Indians (from a party of whom he supposed the firing to
proceed), he continued his pathless wanderings till dark, when, to
render his situation still more critical, he was attacked by a
'painter'—*anglice*, panther—which he actually succeeded in beating off with the breech of his gun, and then betook himself to the
topmost extremity of a tree, where, in order to avoid a similar
intrusion, he passed the remainder of the night. From a peculiar
odor with which the shattered gun was still redolent, however, it
was strongly suspected that the 'terrific painter' was not many
degrees removed, in affinity, from a—polecat.

We had just reached the extreme edge of the far famed 'Cross-

Timbers' when we were gratified by the arrival of forty dragoons, under the command of Lieut. Bowman, who had orders to accompany us to the supposed boundary of the United States. On the same evening we had the pleasure of encamping together at a place known as Camp Holmes, a wild romantic spot in latitude 35° 5', and but a mile north of the Canadian river.

From the Arkansas river to Chouteau's Fort, our route presented an unbroken succession of grassy plains and fertile glades, intersected here and there with woody belts and numerous rivulets, most of which, however, are generally dry except during the rainy season. As far as Camp Holmes, we had a passable wagon road, which was opened upon the occasion of the Indian treaty, and was afterwards kept open by the Indian traders. Yet, notwithstanding the road, this stretch gave us more trouble—presented more rugged passes, miry ravines and steep ascents—than all the rest of our journey put together.

We had not been long at the Fort, before we received a visit from a party of Comanches, who having heard of our approach came to greet us a welcome, on the supposition that it was their friend Chouteau returning to the fort with fresh supplies of merchandise. Great was their grief when we informed them that their favorite trader had died at Fort Gibson, the previous winter. On visiting their wigwams and inquiring for their *capitan,** we were introduced to a corpulent, squint-eyed old fellow, who certainly had nothing in his personal appearance indicative of rank or dignity. This was Tábba-quena (or the Big Eagle), a name familiar to all the Comanche traders. As we had frequently heard that he spoke Spanish fluently, we at once prepared ourselves for a social chit-chat; but, on accosting him in that tongue and inquiring whether he could talk Spanish, he merely replied 'Poquito,' putting at the same time his forefinger to his ear, to signify that he merely understood a little—which proved true to a degree, for our communication was chiefly by signs. We were now about to launch upon an unknown region—our route lay henceforth across that unexplored wilderness, of which I have so frequently spoken, without either pilot or trail to guide us for nearly 500 miles. We

---

* Most of the prairie Indians seem to have learned this Spanish word, by which, when talking with the whites, all their chiefs are designated.

had to depend entirely upon our knowledge of the geographical position of the country for which we were steering, and the indications of a compass and sextant. This was emphatically a pioneer trip; such a one also as had, perhaps, never before been undertaken—to convey heavily laden wagons through a country almost wholly untrod by civilized man, and of which *we*, at least, knew nothing. We were therefore extremely anxious to acquire any information our visitors might be able to give us; but Tábba-quena being by no means experienced in wagon tactics, could only make us understand, by gestures, mixed with a little wretched Spanish, that the route up the Canadian presented no obstacles according to *his* mode of travelling. He appeared, however, very well acquainted with the whole Mexican frontier, from Santa Fé to Chihuahua, and even to the Gulf, as well as with all the Prairies. During the consultation he seemed occasionally to ask the opinions of other chiefs who had huddled around him. Finally, we handed him a sheet of paper and a pencil, signifying at the same time a desire that he would draw us a map of the Prairies. This he very promptly executed; and although the draft was somewhat rough, it bore, much to our astonishment, quite a map-like appearance, with a far more accurate delineation of all the principal rivers of the plains—the road from Missouri to Santa Fé, and the different Mexican settlements, than is to be found in many of the engraved maps of those regions.

Tábba-quena's party consisted of about sixty persons, including several squaws and papooses, with a few Kiawa chiefs and warriors, who, although of a tribe so entirely distinct, are frequently found domiciled among the Comanches. As we were about to break up the camp they all started for Fort Gibson, for the purpose, as they informed us, of paying a visit to the 'Capitan Grande'—a Spanish phrase used by many prairie tribes, and applied, in their confused notions of rank and power, not only to the President of the United States himself, but to the seat of the federal government. These they are again apt to confound with Fort Gibson and the commanding officer of that station.

On the 18th of May, we set out from Chouteau's fort. From this forward our wagons were marched in two lines, and regularly 'formed' at every camp, so as to constitute a fortification and a *corral* for the stock.

On the following day we were again joined by old Tábba-quena, and another Comanche chief, with five or six warriors, and as many squaws, including Tab's wife and infant son. As we were jogging along in the afternoon, I held quite a long conversation in our semi-mute language with the squinting old chief. He gave me to understand, as well as he could, that his comrades had proceeded on their journey to see the Capitan Grande, but that he had concluded to return home for better horses. He boasted in no measured terms of his friendship for the Americans, and promised to exert his influence to prevent the turbulent and unruly spirits of his nation from molesting us. But he could not disguise his fears in regard to the Pawnees and Osages, who, he said, would be sure to run off with our stock while we were asleep at night. When I informed him that we kept a strict night-watch, he said, "*Está bueno*" (that's good), and allowed that our chances for safety were not so bad after all.

These friendly Indians encamped with us that night, and on the following morning the old chief informed us that some of his party had a few "mulas para *swap*" (mules to trade; for having learned the word *swap* of some American traders, he very ingeniously tacked it at the tail of his little stock of Spanish). A barter for five mules was immediately concluded upon, much to our advantage, as our teams were rather in a weak condition. Old Tab and his party then left us to join his band, which, he said, was located on the Faux Ouachittâ river, and we never saw aught of them more.

After leaving the Fort we generally kept on the ridge between the Canadian and the North Fork, crossing sometimes the tributary brooks of the one and sometimes those of the others. Having travelled in this manner for about eighty miles, we entered one of the most charming prairie vales that I have ever beheld, and which in the plenitude of our enthusiasm, we named 'Spring Valley,' on account of the numerous spring-fed rills and gurgling rivulets that greeted the sight in every direction; in whose limpid pools swarms of trout and perch were carelessly playing. It was somewhere along the border of this enchanting vale that a little picket fort was erected in 1822 by an unfortunate trader named Mc-Knight, who was afterwards betrayed and murdered by the faithless Comanches. The landscape is beautifully variegated with stripes and fringes of timber: while the little herds of buffalo that were scattered about in fantastic groups imparted a degree of life and picturesqueness to the scene, which it was truly delightful to contemplate.

It was three days previous that we had first met with these 'prairie cattle.' I have often heard backwoodsmen speak of the 'buck ague,' but commend me to the 'buffalo fever' of the Prairies for novelty and amusement. Very few of our party had ever seen a buffalo before in its wild state; therefore at the first sight of these noble animals the excitement surpassed anything I had ever witnessed before. Some of our dragoons, in their eagerness for sport, had managed to frighten away a small herd that were quietly feeding at some distance, before our 'still hunters,' who had crawled towards them, had been able to get within rifle-shot of them. No sooner were the movements of our mounted men perceived, than the whole extent of country, as far as the eye could reach, became perfectly animate with living objects, fleeing and scampering in every direction. From the surrounding valleys sprang up numerous herds of these animals which had hitherto been unobserved, many of which, in their indiscriminate flight, passed so near the wagons, that the drivers, carried away by the contagious excitement of the moment, would leave the teams and keep up a running fire after them. I had the good fortune to witness the exploits of one of our Northern greenhorns, who, mounted upon a sluggish mule, and without any kind of weapon, amused himself by chasing every buffalo that came scudding along, as if he expected to capture him by laying hold of his tail. Plying spur and whip, he would gallop after one division till he was left far behind: and then turn to another and another with the same earnestness of purpose, until they had all passed out of sight. He finally came back disheartened and sullen, with his head hanging down like one conscious of having done something supremely ridiculous; but still cursing his lazy mule, which, he said, might have caught the buffalo, if it had had a mind to.

On the night after the first buffalo scamper, we encamped upon a woodless ravine, and were obliged to resort to 'buffalo chips' (dry ordure) for fuel. It is amusing to witness the bustle which generally takes place in collecting this offal. In dry weather it is an excellent substitute for wood, than which it even makes a hotter fire; but when moistened by rain, the smouldering pile will smoke for hours before it condescends to burn, if it does at all. The buffalo meat which the hunter roasts or broils upon this fire, he accounts more savory than the steaks dressed by the most delicate cooks in civilized life.

16. A New Route Out

As it now appeared that we had been forced at least two points north of the course we had originally intended to steer, by the northern bearing of the Canadian, we made an effort to cross a ridge of timber to the south, which, after considerable labor, proved successful. Here we found a multitude of gravely, bright-flowing streams, with rich bottoms, lined all along with stately white oak, black-walnut, mulberry, and other similar growths, that yielded us excellent materials for wagon repairs, of which the route from Missouri, after passing Council Grove, is absolutely in want.

Although we found the buffalo extremely scarce westward of Spring Valley, yet there was no lack of game; for every nook and glade swarmed with deer and wild turkeys, partridges and grouse.

We now continued our line of march between the Canadian and the timbered ridge with very little difficulty. Having stopped to 'noon' in a bordering valley, we were quite surprised by the appearance of an Indian with no other protection than his squaw. From what we could gather by their signs, they had been the victims of a 'love scrape.' The fellow, whom I found to be a Kiawa, had, according to his own account, stolen the wife of another, and then fled to the thickets, where he purposed to lead a lonely life, in hopes of escaping the vengeance of his incensed predecessor. From this, it would appear that affairs of gallantry are not evils exclusively confined to civilization. Plausible, however, as the Indian's story seemed to be, we had strong suspicions that others of his band were not far off; and that he, with his 'better half,' had only been skulking about in hopes of exercising their "acquisitiveness' at our expense; when, on finding themselves discovered, they deemed it the best policy fearlessly to approach us. This singular visit afforded a specimen of that confidence with which civilization inspires even the most untutored savages. They remained with us, in the utmost nonchalance, till the following morning.

Shortly after the arrival of the visitors, we were terribly alarmed at a sudden prairie conflagration. The old grass of the valley in which we were encamped had not been burned off, and one of our cooks having unwittingly kindled a fire in the midst of it, it spread at once with wonderful rapidity, and a brisk wind springing up at the time, the flames were carried over the valley, in spite of every effort we could make to check them. Fortunately for us, the fire had broken out to the leeward of our wagons, and therefore occasioned us no damage; but the accident itself was a forcible illustration of the danger that might be incurred by pitching a camp in the midst of dry grass, and the advantages that might be taken by hostile savages in such a locality.

After the fire had raged with great violence for a few hours, a cloud suddenly obscured the horizon, which was almost immediately followed by a refreshing shower of rain: a phenomenon often witnessed upon the Prairies after an extensive conflagration; and affording a practical exemplification of Professor Espy's celebrated theory of artificial showers.

We now continued our journey without further trouble, except that of being still forced out of our proper latitude by the northern bearing of the Canadian. On the 30th of May, however, we succeeded in 'doubling' the spur of the Great North Bend. Upon ascending the dividing ridge again, which at this point was entirely destitute of timber, a 'prairie expanse' once more greeted our view. This and the following day, our route lay through a region that abounded in gypsum, from the finest quality down to ordinary plaster. On the night of the 31st we encamped on a tributary of the North Fork, which we called Gypsum creek, in consequence of its being surrounded with vast quantities of that substance.

Being compelled to keep a reckoning of our latitude, by which our travel was partly governed, and the sun being now too high at noon for the use of the artificial horizon, we had to be guided entirely by observations of the meridian altitude of the moon, planets, or fixed stars. At Gypsum creek our latitude was 36° 10′ —being the utmost northing we had made. As we were now about thirty miles north of the parallel of Santa Fé, we had to steer, henceforth, a few degrees south of west in order to bring up on our direct course.

Although we had encountered but very few buffalo since we left Spring Valley, they now began to make their appearance again, though not in very large droves; together with the deer and the fleet antelope, which latter struck me as being much more tame in this wild section of the Prairies than I had seen it elsewhere. The graceful and majestic mustang would also now and then sweep across the naked country, or come curvetting and capering in the vicinity of our little caravan, just as the humor prompted them. But what attracted our attention most were the little ⌊prairie⌋ dog settlements, or, as they are more technically called, 'dogtowns,' so often alluded to by prairie travellers. As we were passing through their 'streets,' multitudes of the diminutive inhabitants were to be seen among the numerous little hillocks which marked their dwellings, where they frisked about, or sat perched at their doors, yelping defiance, to our great amusement —heedless of the danger that often awaited them from the rifles of our party; for they had perhaps never seen such deadly weapons before.

On the 5th of June, we found ourselves once more travelling on a firm rolling prairie, about the region, as we supposed,* of the boundary between the United States and Mexico; when Lieut. Bowman, in pursuance of his instructions, began to talk seriously of returning. While the wagons were stopped at noon, a small party of us, including a few dragoons, advanced a few miles ahead to take a survey of the route. We had just ascended the highest point of a ridge to get a prospect of the country beyond, when we descried a herd of buffalo in motion and two or three horsemen in hot pursuit. "Mexican Ciboleros!" we all exclaimed at once; for we supposed we might now be within the range of the buffalo hunters of New Mexico. Clapping spurs to our horses, we set off towards them at full speed. As we might have expected, our precipitate approach frightened them away and we soon lost sight of them altogether. On reaching the spot where they had last been seen, we found a horse and two mules saddled, all tied to the

---

* From subsequent observations, this point appears to have been some miles west of the 100th degree of longitude.

carcass of a slain buffalo which was partly skinned. We made diligent search in some copses of small growth, and among the adjacent ravines, but could discover no further traces of the fugitives. The Indian rigging of the animals, however, satisfied us that they were not Mexicans.

We were just about giving up the pursuit, when a solitary Indian horseman was espied upon a ridge about a mile from us. My brother and myself set out towards him, but on seeing us approach, he began to manifest some fear, and therefore my brother advanced alone. As soon as he was near enough he cried out *"Amigo!"* to which the Indian replied *"Comantz!"* and giving himself a thump upon the breast he made a graceful circuit, and came up at full speed, presenting his hand in token of friendship. Nothing, however, could induce him to return to his animals with us, where the rest of our party had remained. He evidently feared treachery and foul play. Therefore we retraced our steps to the wagons, leaving the Indian's property just as we had found it, which, we subsequently discovered, was taken away after our departure.

In the afternoon of the same day, five more Indians (including a squaw), made their appearance, and having been induced by friendly tokens to approach us, they spent the night at our encampment. The next morning, we expressed a desire, by signs, to be conducted to the nearest point on our route where good pasturage and water might be found. A sprightly young chief, armed only with his bow and arrows, at once undertook the task, while his comrades still travelled along in our company. We had not progressed far before we found ourselves in the very midst of another large 'dog-town.' Our Comanche guide drew an arrow for the purpose of cutting short the career of a little citizen that sat yelping most doggedly in the mouth of his hole, forty or fifty paces distant. The animal was almost entirely concealed behind the hillock which encompassed the entrance of his apartment, so that the dart could not reach it in a direct line; but the Indian had resort to a manœuvre which caused the arrow to descend with a curve, and in an instant it quivered in the body of the poor little quadruped. The slayer only smiled at his feat, while we were perfectly astounded. There is nothing strange in the rifleman's being able to hit his mark with his fine-sighted barrel; but the accuracy with which these savages learn to shoot their feathered missiles, with such random aim, is almost incomprehensible. I had at the same time drawn one of Colt's repeating pistols, with a view of paying a similar compliment to another dog; when, finding that it excited the curiosity of the chief, I fired a few shots in quick succession, as an explanation of its virtues. He seemed to comprehend the secret instantly, and, drawing his bow once more, he discharged a number of arrows with the same rapidity, as a palpable intimation that he could shoot as fast with his instrument as we could with our patent fire-arms. This was not merely a vain show: there was more of reality than of romance in his demonstration.

Shortly after this we reached a fresh brook, a tributary of the North fork, which wound its silent course in the midst of a picturesque valley, surrounded by romantic hills and craggy knobs. Here we pitched our camp: when three of our visitors left us for the purpose of going to bring all the 'capitanes' of their tribe, who were said to be encamped at no great distance from us.

Our encampment, which we designated as 'Camp Comanche,' was only five or six miles from the North Fork, while, to the southward, the main Canadian was but a little more distant.

After waiting anxiously for the arrival of the Comanche chiefs, until our patience was well nigh exhausted, I ascended a high knoll just behind our camp, in company with the younger of the two chiefs who had remained with us, to see if anything could be discovered. By and by, the Comanche pointed anxiously towards the northwest, where he espied a party of his people, though at such a great distance, that it was some time before I could discern them. With what acuteness of vision are these savages endowed! Accustomed to the open plains, and like the eagle to look out for their prey at immense distances, their optical perception is scarcely excelled by that of the king of birds.

The party, having approached still nearer, assembled upon an eminence as if for the purpose of reconnoitering; but our chief upon the knoll hoisting his blanket, which seemed to say, 'come ahead,' they advanced slowly and deliberately—very unlike the customary mode of approach among all the prairie tribes.

The party consisted of about sixty warriors, at the head of whom rode an Indian of small stature and agreeable countenance, verging on the age of fifty. He wore the usual Comanche dress, but instead of moccasins, he had on a pair of long white cotton hose, while upon his bare head waved a tall red plume,—a mark of distinction which proclaimed him at once the *capitan mayor,* or principal chief. We addressed them in Spanish, inquiring if they had brought an interpreter, when a lank-jawed, grum-looking savage announced his readiness to officiate in that capacity. *"Sabes hablar en Español, amigo?"* (can you talk Spanish, friend?) I inquired. *"Si"* (yes), he gruffly replied. "Where are your people?" "Encamped just above on yonder creek." "How many of you are there?" "Oh, a great many—nearly all the Comanche nation; for we are *en junta* to go and fight the Pawnees." "Well, can you tell us how far it is to Santa Fé?"—But the surly savage cut short my inquiries by observing—*"Ahí platicarémos despues"* —"We will talk about that hereafter."

We then showed them a spot a few rods from us, where they might encamp so as not to intermix their animals with ours; after which all the *capitanes* were invited to our camp to hold a 'big talk.' In a very short time we had ten chiefs seated in a circle within our tent, when the pipe, the Indian token of peace, was produced: but, doubting perhaps the sincerity of our professions, they at first refused to smoke. The interpreter, however, remarked as an excuse for their conduct, that it was not their custom to smoke until they had received some presents: but a few Mexican *cigarritos* being produced, most of them took a whiff, as if under the impression that to smoke cigars was no pledge of friendship.

Lieut. Bowman now desired us to broach the subject of peace and amity betwixt the Comanches and our people, and to invite them to visit the 'Capitan Grande' at Washington, and enter into a perpetual treaty to that effect; but they would not then converse on the subject. In fact, the interpreter inquired, "Are we not at war?—how can we go to see the Capitan Grande?" We knew they held themselves at war with Mexico and Texas, and probably had mistaken us for Texans, which had no doubt caused the interpreter to speak so emphatically of their immense numbers. Upon this we explained to them that the United States was a distinct government and at peace with the Comanches. As an earnest of our friendly disposition, we then produced some scarlet cloth, with a small quantity of vermilion, tobacco, beads, etc., which

being distributed among them, they very soon settled down into
a state of placidness and contentment. Indeed, it will be found,
that, with wild Indians, presents are always the corner-stone of
friendship. "We are rejoiced," at last said the elder chief with a
ceremonious air, "our hearts are glad that you have arrived among
us: it makes our eyes laugh to see Americans walk in our land. We
will notify our old and young men—our boys and our maidens—
our women and children,—that they may come to trade with you.
We hope you will speak well of us to your people, that more of
them may hunt the way to our country, for we like to trade with
the white man." This was delivered in Comanche, but translated
into Spanish by the interpreter, who, although a full Indian, had
lived several years among the Mexicans and spoke that language
tolerably well. Our 'big talk' lasted several hours, after which the
Indians retired to sleep. The next morning, after renewing their
protestations of friendship, they took their departure, the principal chief saying, "Tell the Capitan Grande that when he pleases
to call us we are all ready to go to see him."

The project of bringing some of the chiefs of these wild prairie
tribes to Washington city, has been entertained, but never yet
carried into effect. The few who have penetrated as far as Fort
Gibson, or perhaps to a frontier village, have probably left with
more unfavorable impressions than they had before. Believing
the former to be our great Capital, and the most insignificant
among the latter, our largest cities, they have naturally come to
the conclusion that they surpass us in numbers and power, if not
in wealth and grandeur. I have no doubt that the chiefs of the
Comanches and other prairie tribes, if rightly managed, might be
induced to visit our veritable 'Capitan Grande,' and our large
cities, which would doubtless have a far better effect than all the
treaties of peace that could be concluded with them for an age to
come. They would then 'see with their own eyes and hear with
their own ears' the magnificence and power of the whites, which
would inspire them at once with respect and fear.

This was on the 7th of June. About noon, Lieut. Bowman and
his command finally took leave of us, and at the same time we
resumed our forward march. This separation was truly painful:
not so much on account of the loss we were about to experience, in
regard to the protection afforded us by the troops (which, to say

the truth, was more needed now than it had ever been before), as for the necessity of parting with a friend, who had endeared himself to us all by his affable deportment, his social manners and accommodating disposition.

There were perhaps a few timid hearts that longed to return with the dragoons, and ever and anon a wistful glance would be cast back at the receding figures in the distance. The idea of a handful of thirty-four men having to travel without guide or protection through a dreary wilderness, peopled by thousands of savages who were just as likely to be hostile as friendly, was certainly very little calculated to produce agreeable impressions. Much to the credit of our men, however, the escort was no sooner out of sight than the timorous regained confidence, and all seemed bound together by stronger ties than before. All we feared were ambuscades or surprise; to guard against which, it was only necessary to redouble our vigilance.

On the following day, while we were enjoying our noon's rest upon a ravine of the Canadian, several parties of Indians, amounting altogether to about three hundred souls, including women and children, made their appearance. They belonged to the same band of Comanches with whom we had had so agreeable an intercourse, and had brought several mules in the expectation of driving a trade with us. The squaws and papooses were so anxious to gratify their curiosity, and so very soon began to give such striking manifestations of their pilfering propensities, that, at the request of the chiefs, we carried some goods at a little distance, where a trade was opened in hopes of attracting their attention. One woman, I observed, still lingered among the wagons, who, from certain peculiarities of features, struck me very forcibly as not being an Indian. In accordance with this impression I addressed her in Spanish, and was soon confirmed in all my suspicions. She was from the neighborhood of Matamoros, and had been married to a Comanche since her captivity. She did not entertain the least desire of returning to her own people.

My attention was next attracted by a sprightly lad, ten or twelve years old, whose nationality could scarcely be detected under his Indian guise. But, though quite 'Indianized,' he was exceedingly polite. I inquired of him in Spanish, "Are you not a

Mexican?" "Yes, sir,—I once was." "What is your name?" "Bernardino Saenz, sir, at your service." "When and where were you taken?" "About four years ago, at the Hacienda de las Animas, near Parral." "Shan't we buy you and take you to your people?—we are going thither." At this he hesitated a little, and then answered in an affecting tone, *"No, señor; ya soy demasiado bruto para vivir entre los Cristianos"* (Oh, no, sir; I am now too much of a brute to live among Christians); adding that his owner was not there, and that he knew the Indian in whose charge he came would not sell him.

Out of half a dozen Mexican captives that happened to be with our new visitors, we only met with one who manifested the slightest inclination to abandon Indian life. This was a stupid boy about fifteen years of age, who had probably been roughly treated on account of his laziness. We very soon struck a bargain with his owner, paying about the price of a mule for the little outcast, whom I sent to his family as soon as we reached Chihuahua. Notwithstanding the inherent stupidity of my *protégé,* I found him abundantly grateful—much to his credit be it spoken—for the little service I had been able to render him.

We succeeded in purchasing several mules which cost us between ten and twenty dollars worth of goods apiece. In Comanche trade the main trouble consists in fixing the price of the first animal. This being settled by the chiefs, it often happens that mule after mule is led up and the price received without further cavil. Each owner usually wants a general assortment; therefore the price must consist of several items, as a blanket, a looking-glass, an awl, a flint, a little tobacco, vermilion, beads, etc.

The Santa Fé caravans have generally avoided every manner of trade with the wild Indians, for fear of being treacherously dealt with during the familiar intercourse which necessarily ensues. This I am convinced is an erroneous impression; for I have always found, that savages are much less hostile to those with whom they trade, than to any other people. They are emphatically fond of traffic, and, being anxious to encourage the whites to come among them, instead of committing depredations upon those with whom they trade, they are generally ready to defend them against every enemy.

17 . Santa Fé Again

The Comanches having all disappeared, we resumed our march, and soon emerged into an open plain or *mesa* which was one of the most monotonous I had ever seen, there being not a break, not a hill nor valley, nor even a shrub to obstruct the view. The only thing which served to turn us from a direct course pursued by the compass, was the innumerable ponds which bespeckled the plain, and which kept us at least well supplied with water. Many of these ponds seem to have grown out of 'buffalo wallows,'—a term used on the Prairies to designate a sink made by the buffalo's pawing the earth for the purpose of obtaining a smooth dusty surface to roll upon.

After three or four days of weary travel over this level plain, the picturesque valley of the Canadian burst once more upon our view, presenting one of the most magnificent sights I had ever beheld. Here rose a perpendicular cliff, in all the majesty and sublimity of its desolation;—there another sprang forward as in the very act of losing its balance and about to precipitate itself upon the vale below. A little further on a pillar with crevices and cornices so curiously formed as easily to be mistaken for the work of art; while a thousand other objects grotesquely and fantastically arranged, and all shaded in the sky-bound perspective by the blue ridge-like brow of the *mesa* far beyond the Canadian, constituted a kind of chaotic space where nature seemed to have indulged in her wildest caprices. Such was the confusion of ground-swells and eccentric cavities, that it was altogether impossible to determine whereabouts the channel of the Canadian wound its way among them.

It would seem that these mesas might once have extended up to the margin of the stream, leaving a *cañon* or chasm through which the river flowed, as is still the case in some other places. But the basis of the plain not having been sufficiently firm to resist the action of the waters, these have washed and cut the bordering *cejas* or brows into all the shapes they now present. The buffalo and other animals have no doubt assisted in these transmutations. Their deep-worn paths over the brows of the plains, form channels for the descending rains; which are soon washed into the size of ravines—and even considerable creeks. The beds of these continue to be worn down until veins of lasting water are opened, and constant-flowing streams thus established. Numerous were the embryo rivulets which might be observed forming in this way along the borders of those streams. The frequent isolated benches and mounds, whose tabular summits are on a level with the adjacent plains, and appear entirely of a similar formation, indicate that the intermediate earth has been washed away, or removed by some other process of nature—all seeming to give plausibility to our theory.

We had for some days, while travelling along the course of the Canadian, been in anxious expectation of reaching a point from whence there was a cart-road to Santa Fé, made by the Ciboleros; but being constantly baffled and disappointed in this hope, serious apprehensions began to be entertained by some of the party that we might after all be utterly lost. In this emergency, one of our Mexicans who pretended to be a great deal wiser than the rest, insisted that we were pursuing a wrong direction, and that every day's march only took us further from Santa Fé. There appeared to be so much plausibility in his assertion, as he professed a perfect knowledge of all the country around, that many of our men were almost ready to mutiny,—to take the command from the hands of my brother and myself and lead us southward in search of the Colorado, into the fearful *Llano Estacado*, where we would probably have perished. But our observations of the latitude, which we took very frequently, as well as the course we were pursuing, completely contradicted the Mexican wiseacre. A few days afterwards we were overtaken by a party of *Comancheros*, or Mexican Comanche traders, when we had the satisfaction of learning that we were in the right track.

These men had been trading with the band of Comanches we had lately met, and learning from them that we had passed on, they had hastened to overtake us, so as to obtain our protection against the savages, who, after selling their animals to the Mexicans, very frequently take forcible possession of them again, before the purchasers have been able to reach their homes. These parties of *Comancheros* are usually composed of the indigent and rude classes of the frontier villages, who collect together, several times a year, and launch upon the plains with a few trinkets and trumperies of all kinds, and perhaps a bag of bread and may-be another of *pinole*, which they barter away to the savages for horses and mules. The entire stock of an individual trader very seldom exceeds the value of twenty dollars, with which he is content to wander about for several months, and glad to return home with a mule or two, as the proceeds of his traffic.

These Mexican traders had much to tell us about the Comanches: saying, that they were four or five thousand in number, with perhaps a thousand warriors, and that the fiery young men had once determined to follow and attack us; but that the chiefs and sages had deterred them, by stating that our cannons could kill to the distance of many miles, and shoot through hills and rocks and destroy everything that happened to be within their range. The main object of our visitors, however, seemed to be to raise themselves into importance by exaggerating the perils we had escaped from. That they had considered themselves in great jeopardy, there could be no doubt whatever, for, in their anxiety to overtake us, they came very near killing their animals.

On the 20th of June we pitched our camp upon the north bank of the Canadian or Colorado, in latitude 35° 24′ according to a meridian altitude of Saturn. On the following day, I left the caravan, accompanied by three Comancheros, and proceeded at a more rapid pace towards Santa Fé. This was rather a hazardous journey, inasmuch as we were still within the range of the Pawnee and Comanche war-parties, and my companions were men in whom I could not repose the slightest confidence, except for pilotage; being fully convinced that in case of meeting with an enemy, they would either forsake or deliver me up, just as it might seem most conducive to their own interest and safety.

As we jogged merrily along, I often endeavored to while away the time by catechising my three companions in relation to the topography of the wild region we were traversing; but I soon found, that, like the Indians, these ignorant rancheros have no ideas of distances, except as compared with time or with some other distance. They will tell you that you may arrive at a given place by the time the sun reaches a certain point: otherwise, whether it be but half a mile or half a day's ride to the place inquired for, they are as apt to apply *está cerquita* (it is close by), or *está lejos* (it is far off), to the one as to the other, just as the impression happens to strike them, when compared with some other point more or less distant. This often proves a source of great annoyance to foreign travellers, as I had an opportunity of experiencing before my arrival. In giving directions, these people —in fact, the lower classes of Mexicans generally—are also in the habit of using very odd gesticulations, altogether peculiar to themselves. Instead of pointing with their hands and fingers, they generally employ the mouth, which is done by thrusting out the lips in the direction of the spot, or object, which the inquirer wishes to find out—accompanied by *aqui* or *allí está*. This habit of substituting labial gestures for the usual mode of indicating, has grown from the use of the *sarape*, which keeps their hands and arms perpetually confined.

From the place where we left the wagons, till we reached the *Angostura*, or narrows (a distance of 60 miles), we had followed a plain cart-road, which seemed everywhere passable for wagons. Here, however, we found the point of a table plain projecting abruptly against the river, so as to render it impossible for wagons to pass without great risk. The huge masses of solid rock, which occur in this place, and the rugged cliffs or brows of the table lands which rise above them, appear to have been mistaken by a detachment of the Texan Santa Fé expedition, for spurs of the Rocky Mountains; an error which was rational enough, as they not unfrequently tower to the height of two thousand feet above the valley, and are often as rocky and rough as the rudest heaps of trap-rock can make them. By ascending the main summit of these craggy promontories, however, the eastern ridge of the veritable Rocky Mountains may be seen, still very far off in the western horizon, with a wide-spread and apparently level table plain, intervening and extending in every direction, as far as the eye can reach; for even the deep-cut chasms of the intersecting rivers are rarely visible except one be upon their very brink.

Upon expressing my fears that our wagons would not be able to pass the *Angostura* in safety, my comrades informed me that there was an excellent route, of which no previous mention had been made, passing near the *Cerro de Tucumcari*, a round mound plainly visible to the southward. After several vain efforts to induce some of the party to carry a note back to my brother, and to pilot the caravan through the Tucumcari route, one of them, known as Tio Baca, finally proposed to undertake the errand for a bounty of ten dollars, besides high wages till they should reach the frontier. His conditions being accepted, he set out after breakfast, not, however, without previously recommending himself to the Virgin Guadalupe, and all the saints in the calendar, and desiring us to remember him in our prayers. Notwithstanding his fears, however, he arrived in perfect safety, and I had the satisfaction of learning afterward that my brother found the new route everything he could have desired.

I continued my journey westward with my two remaining companions; but, owing to their being provided with a relay of horses, they very soon left me to make the balance of the travel alone— though yet in a region haunted by hostile savages. On the following day, about the hour of twelve, as I was pursuing a horse-path along the course of the Rio Pecos, near the frontier settlements, I met with a shepherd of whom I anxiously inquired the distance to San Miguel. "O, it is just there," responded the man of sheep. "Don't you see that point of mesa yonder? It is just beyond that." This welcome information cheered me greatly; for, owing to the extraordinary transparency of the atmosphere, it appeared to me that the distance could not exceed two or three miles. *"Está cerquita,"* exclaimed the shepherd as I rode off; *"ahora está V. allá"*—"it is close by; you will soon be there."

I set off at as lively a pace as my jaded steed could carry me, confident of taking dinner in San Miguel. Every ridge I turned I thought must be the last, and thus I jogged on, hoping and anticipating my future comforts till the shades of evening began to appear; when I descended into the valley of the Pecos, which, although narrow, is exceedingly fertile and beautifully lined with verdant fields, among which stood a great variety of mud cabins. About eight o'clock, I called at one of these cottages and again inquired the distance to San Miguel; when a swarthy-looking ranchero once more saluted mine ears with *"Está cerquita; ahora está V. allá."* Although the distance was designated in precisely the same words used by the shepherd eight hours before, I had the consolation at least of believing that I was something nearer. After spurring on for a couple of miles over a rugged road, I at last reached the long-sought village.

The next day, I hired a Mexican to carry some flour back to meet the wagons; for our party was by this time running short of provisions. In fact, we should long before have been in danger of starvation, had it not been for our oxen; for we had not seen a buffalo since the day we first met with the Comanches. Some of our cattle being in good plight, and able, as we were, to spare a few from our teams, we made beef of them when urged by necessity: an extra advantage in ox-teams on these perilous expeditions.

On the 25th of June I arrived safely at Santa Fé,—but again rode back to meet the wagons, which did not reach the capital till the 4th of July. We did not encounter a very favorable reception from 'his majesty,' Gov. Armijo. He had just established his arbitrary impost of $500 per wagon, which bore rather heavily upon us; for we had an overstock of coarse articles which we had merely brought along for the purpose of increasing the strength of our company, by adding to the number of our wagons.

But these little troubles in a business way, were entirely drowned in the joyful sensations arising from our safe arrival, after so long and so perilous an expedition. Considering the character and our ignorance of the country over which we had travelled, we had been exceedingly successful. Instances are certainly rare of heavily-laden wagons' having been conducted, without a guide, through an unexplored desert; and yet we performed the trip without any important accident—without encountering any very difficult passes—without suffering for food or for water.

We had hoped that at least a few days of rest and quiet recreation might have been allowed us after our arrival; for relaxation was sorely needed at the end of so long a journey and its concomitant privations: but it was ordered otherwise. We had scarcely quartered ourselves within the town before a grand 'flare-up' took place between Gov. Armijo and the foreigners* in Santa Fé, which, for a little while, bid fair to result in open hostilities. It originated in the following circumstances.

In the winter of 1837–8, a worthy young American, named

---

* Among the New Mexicans, the terms *foreigner* and *American* are synonymous: indeed, the few citizens of other nations to be found there identify themselves with those of the United States. All foreigners are known there as *Americanos*; but south of Chihuahua they are indiscriminately called *Los Ingleses*, the English.

Daley, was murdered at the Gold Mines, by a couple of villains, solely for plunder. The assassins were arrested, when they confessed their guilt; but, in a short time, they were permitted to run at large again, in violation of every principle of justice or humanity. About this time they were once more apprehended, however, by the interposition of foreigners: and, at the solicitation of the friends of the deceased, a memorial from the Americans in Santa Fé was presented to Armijo, representing the injustice of permitting the murderers of their countrymen to go unpunished; and praying that the culprits might be dealt with according to law. But the governor affected to consider the affair as a conspiracy; and, collecting his ragamuffin militia, attempted to intimidate the petitioners. The foreigners were now constrained to look to their defence, as they saw that no justice was to be expected. Had Armijo persisted, serious consequences might have ensued; but seeing the 'conspirators' firm, he sent an apology, affecting to have misconstrued their motives, and promising that the laws should be duly executed upon the murderers.

Besides the incentives of justice and humanity, foreigners felt a deep interest in the execution of this promise. But a few years previous, another person had been assassinated and robbed at the same place; yet the authorities having taken no interest in the matter, the felons were never discovered: and now, should these assassins escape the merited forfeit of their atrocious crime, it was evident there would be no future security for our lives and property. But the governor's *due execution of the laws* consisted in retaining them a year or two in nominal imprisonment, when they were again set at liberty: yet by far the greater portion of this time they were merely the *criados sin sueldo* (servants without hire) of the governor, laboring for him as a remuneration for both the life and liberty which he granted them. Besides these, other foreigners have been murdered in New Mexico, and all with the same impunity.

18. Geography of the Prairies

While I have endeavored in the preceding pages to give the reader some general idea of life upon the Prairies, I feel that I have wholly failed thus far to convey any adequate notions of their natural history. I propose in the following pages to repair this deficiency as far as I am able, and to present a rapid sketch of the vastness of those mighty territories; of their physical geography; and of the life, as well vegetable as animal, which they sustain. It is to be regretted that this ample field for observation should have received so little of the consideration of scientific men; for there is scarcely a province in the whole wide range of Nature's unexplored domains, which is so worthy of study, and yet has been so little studied by the natural philosopher.

If we look at the Great Western Prairies, independently of the political powers to which portions of them respectively belong, we shall find them occupying the whole of that extensive territory lying between the spurs of the Rocky Mountains on the north, and the rivers of Texas on the south—a distance of some seven or eight hundred miles in one direction; and from the frontiers of Missouri and Arkansas on the east to the eastern branches of the southern Rocky Mountains on the west—about six hundred miles in the transverse direction: the whole comprising an area of about 400,000 square miles, some 30,000 of which are within the original limits of Texas, and 70,000 in those of New Mexico (if we extend them east to the United States boundary), leaving about 300,000 in the territory of the United States.

This vast territory is not interrupted by any important mountainous elevations, except along the borders of the great western sierras, and by some low, craggy ridges about the Arkansas frontier—skirts of the Ozark mountains. There is, it is true, high on the dividing ridge between Red River and the False Washita, a range of hills, the southwestern portion of which extends about to the 100th degree of longitude west from Greenwich; that is, to the United States boundary line.

With these exceptions, there are scarcely any elevations throughout these immense plains which should be dignified by the title of mountains. Those seen by the Texan Santa Fé Expedition about the sources of Red River, were without doubt the *cejas* or brows of the elevated table plains with which the Prairies abound, and which, when viewed from the plain below, often assume the appearance of formidable mountains; but once upon their summit, the spectator sees another vast plain before him.

These *table lands,* or *mesas,* as the Mexicans term them, of which there are many thousands of square miles lying between the frontier of the United States and the Rocky Mountains, are level plains, elevated a considerable distance above the surrounding country, and may be likened to the famous steppes of Asia. They are cut up with numerous streams, the largest of which are generally bordered for several miles back by hilly uplands, which are for the most part sandy, dry and barren.

The most notable of the great *plateaux* of the Prairies is that known to Mexicans as *El Llano Estacado,* which is bounded on the north by the Canadian river—extends east about to the United States boundary, including the heads of the False Washita and other branches of Red River—and spreads southward to the sources of Trinity, Brazos and Colorado rivers, and westward to Rio Pecos. It is quite an elevated and generally a level plain, without important hills or ridges, unless we distinguish as such the craggy breaks of the streams which border and pierce it. It embraces an area of about 30,000 square miles, most of which is without water during three-fourths of the year; while a large proportion of its few perennial streams are too brackish to drink of.

I have been assured by Mexican hunters and Indians, that, from Santa Fé southeastward, there is but one route upon which this plain can be safely traversed during the dry season; and even some of the watering-places on this are at intervals of fifty to eighty miles, and hard to find. Hence the Mexican traders and hunters, that they might not lose their way and perish from thirst, once staked out this route across the plain, it is said; whence it has received the name of *El Llano Estacado,* or the Staked Plain.

In some places the brows of these *mesas* approach the very borders of the streams. When this occurs on both sides, it leaves deep chasms or ravines between, called by the Mexicans *cañones,* and which abound in the vicinity of the mountains. The Canadian river flows through one of the most remarkable of these cañones for a distance of more than fifty miles—extending from the road of the Missouri caravans downward—throughout the whole extent of which the gorge is utterly impassable for wagons, and almost so for animals.

Nor are the flat prairies always free from this kind of annoyance to travellers. They are not unfrequently intersected by diminutive chasms or water-cuts, which, though sometimes hardly a rod in width, are often from fifty to a hundred feet deep. These little cañones are washed out by the rains, in their descent to the bordering streams, which is soon effected after an opening is once made through the surface; for though the clayey foundation is exceedingly firm and hard while dry, it seems the most soluble of earths, and melts almost as rapidly as snow under the action of water. The tenacious turf of the 'buffalo grass,' however, retains the marginal surface, so that the sides are usually perpendicular —indeed, often shelving inward at the base, and therefore utterly impassable. I have come unsuspectingly upon the verge of such a chasm; and though to a stranger, the appearance would indicate the very head of the ravine, I would sometimes be compelled to follow its meandering course for miles without being able to double its 'breaks.' These I have more especially observed high on the borders of the Canadian.

The geological constitution of the Prairies is exceedingly diversified. Along the eastern border, especially towards the north, there is an abundance of limestone, interspersed with sandstone, slate, and many extensive beds of bituminous coal. The coal is particularly abundant in some of the regions bordering the Neosho river; where there are also said to be a few singular bituminous or 'tar springs,' as they are sometimes called by the hunters. There are also many other mineral, and particularly sulphur springs, to be met with.

Further westward, the sandstone prevails; but some of the table plains are based upon strata of a sort of friable calcareous rock, which has been denominated 'rotten limestone: yet along the borders of the mountains the base of the plains seems generally to be of trap and greenstone. From the waters of Red River to the southwest corner of Missouri, throughout the range of the Ozark mountains, granite, limestone, flint and sandstone prevail. But much of the middle portion of the Prairies is without any apparent rocky foundation—we sometimes travel for days in succession without seeing even as much as a pebble.

On passing towards Santa Fé in 1839, and returning in 1840, I observed an immense range of plaster of Paris, both north and south of the Canadian river, and between thirty and fifty miles east of the United States western boundary. The whole country seemed based upon this fossil, and cliffs and huge masses of it were seen in every direction. It ranges from the coarsest compact sulphate of lime or ordinary plaster, to the most transparent gypsum or selenite, of which last there is a great abundance. By authentic accounts from other travellers, this range of gypsum extends, in a direction nearly north, almost to the Arkansas river.

Of metallic minerals, iron, lead, and perhaps copper, are found on the borders of the Prairies; and it is asserted that several specimens of silver ores have been met with on our frontier, as well as about the Witchita and the Rocky Mountains. Gold has also been found, no doubt, in different places; yet it is questionable whether it has anywhere been discovered in sufficient abundance to render it worth the seeking. Some trappers have reported an extensive gold region about the sources of the Platte river; yet, although recent search has been made, it has not been discovered.

The most valuable perhaps, and the most abundant mineral production of the Prairies is *Salt*. In the Choctaw country, on the waters of Red River, there are two salt-works in operation; and in the Cherokee nation salt springs are numerous, three or four of which are now worked on a small scale; yet a sufficient quantity of salt might easily be produced to supply even the adjoining States. The *Grand Saline*, about forty miles above Fort Gibson, near the Neosho river, was considered a curiosity of its kind, before its natural beauties were effaced by 'improvements.' In the border of a little valley, a number of small salt springs break out, around the orifice of each of which was formed, in the shape of a pot, a kind of calcareous saline concretion. None of the springs are very bold, but the water is strong, and sufficiently abundant for extensive works.

There have been several *Salines*, or mines (if we may so term them) of pure salt, discovered in different parts of the Prairies. The most northern I have heard of, is fifty or sixty miles west of the Missouri river, and thirty or forty south of the Platte, near a tributary called the Saline; where the Otoes and other Indians procure salt. It is described as resembling the *salinas* of New Mexico, and the quantity of salt as inexhaustible. South of the Arkansas river and a degree or two further westward, there are several of these salines, which are perhaps still more extensive.

Many of the low valleys of all the western streams (Red River

as well as Arkansas and its branches), are impregnated with sa-
linous qualities, and, during wet weather, ooze saltish exudations,
which effloresce in a thin scum. This is sometimes pure salt, but
more frequently compounded of different salts—not only of the
muriate, but of the sulphate of soda, and perhaps magnesia; often
strongly tinctured with nitre. Some of the waters of these sections
(particularly when stagnant) are so saturated with this compound
during dry weather, that they are insupportable even for brutes
—much to the consternation of a forlorn traveller. In these saline
flats nothing grows but hard wiry grass, which a famished beast
will scarcely eat.

It is from these exudations, as well as from the salines or salt
plains before mentioned, that our western waters, especially from
Arkansas to Red River, acquire their brackishness during the low
seasons; and not from the mountains, as some have presumed.
Such as issue from thence are there as pure, fresh and crystalline
as snow-fed rills and icy fountains can make them.

It will now readily be inferred that the Great Prairies from Red
River to the western sources of the Missouri, are, as has before
been intimated, chiefly uninhabitable—not so much for want of
wood (though the plains are altogether naked), as of soil and of
water; for though some of the plains appear of sufficiently fertile
soil, they are mostly of a sterile character, and all too dry to be
cultivated. These great steppes seem only fitted for the haunts of
the mustang, the buffalo, the antelope, and their migratory lord,
the prairie Indian. Unless with the progressive influence of time,
some favorable mutation should be wrought in nature's operations, to revive the plains and upland prairies, the occasional fertile valleys are too isolated and remote to become the abodes of
civilized man.

Like the table plains of Northern Mexico, these high prairies
could at present only be made available for grazing purposes,
and that in the vicinity of the water-courses. The grass with which
they are mostly clothed, is of a superior quality. The celebrated
'buffalo grass' is of two kinds, both of which are species of the
grama of New Mexico, and equally nutritious at all seasons. It
is the same, I believe, that is called 'mezquite grass' in Texas, from
the mezquite tree which grows there in the same dry regions with
it. Of this unequalled pasturage the great western prairies afford a

sufficiency to graze cattle for the supply of all the United States. It is particularly adapted to sheep-raising, as is shown by example of the same species in New Mexico.

But from the general sterility and unhabitableness of the Prairies is excepted, as will be understood, that portion, already alluded to, which borders our western frontier. The uplands from the Arkansas boundary to the Cross Timbers, are everywhere beautifully interspersed with isolated prairies and glades, many of which are fertile, though some are too flat, and consequently inclined to be marshy. The valleys of the streams are principally of a rich loam, rather subject to inundations, but mostly tillable. The timbered uplands are mostly of fair quality, except on the broken ridges and mountainous sections before referred to. Some of the uplands, however, known usually as 'post-oak flats,' like the marshy prairies, seem to be based upon quick-sand. The soil is of a dead unproductive character, and covered with small lumps or mounds of various sizes, and of irregular shapes.

The country lying west of Missouri, which includes the sources of the Neosho, the Verdigris, the Marais-des-Cygnes and other branches of the Osage, and the lower sections of the Kansas river, vies with any portion of the Far West in the amenity of its upland prairies—in the richness of its alluvial bottoms—in the beauty and freshness of its purling rills and rivulets—and in the salubrity of its atmosphere.

We have here then, along the whole border, a strip of country, averaging at least two hundred miles wide by five hundred long— and even more if we extend it up the Missouri river—affording territory for two States, respectable in size, and though more scant in timber, yet more fertile, in general, than the two conterminous States of Missouri and Arkansas. But most of this delightful region has been ceded to the different tribes of the Frontier Indians.

The chief natural disadvantage to which the Great Western Prairies are exposed, consists in the absence of navigable streams. Throughout the whole vast territory which I have been attempting to describe, there is not a single river, except the Missouri, which is navigable during the whole season. The remaining streams, in their course through the plains, are and must continue to be, for all purposes of commerce, comparatively useless.

The chief of these rivers are the Missouri, the Arkansas, and Red River, with their numerous tributaries. The principal western branches of the Missouri are the Yellow Stone, the Platte and the Kansas. Small 'flats' and 'buffalo boats' have passed down the two former for a considerable distance, during high water; but they are never navigable to any extent by steamboats.

The *Arkansas* river penetrates far into the Rocky Mountains, its ramifications, interlocking with some of the waters of the Missouri, Columbia, San Buenaventura, Colorado of the West, and Rio del Norte. The channel of this stream, in its course through the Prairies, is very wide and shallow, with banks in many places hardly five feet above low water. It will probably measure nearly 2000 miles in length, from its source to the frontier of Arkansas. It is called *Rio Napeste* by the Mexicans; but among the early French voyagers it acquired the name of *Arkansas,* or rather *Akansa,** from a tribe of the Dahcotah or Osage stock, who lived near its mouth. This river has numerous tributaries, some of which are of great length, yet there is not one that is at all navigable, except the Neosho from the north, which has been descended by small boats for at least a hundred miles.

Red River is much shorter and narrower from the frontier westward than the Arkansas, bearing but little over half the volume of water. Even in its serpentine course it can hardly exceed 1200 miles from the Arkansas boundary to its source. This river rises in the table plains of the Llano Estacado, and has not, as I have been assured by traders and hunters, any mountainous elevations about its source of any consequence; although we are continually hearing the inhabitants of its lower borders speak of the "*June freshets* produced by the melting of the snow in the mountains."

The upper portions of this river, and emphatically from the mouth of the False Washita (or Faux Ouachittâ) upward, present little or no facilities for navigation; being frequently spread out

---

* A stranger would be led to suppose we were without a system of orthography, from the fact of our so generally adopting the French spelling of Indian names, whereby all sight is soon lost of the original. The French first corrupt them, and we, by adapting our pronunciation to their orthography, at once transform them into new names. Thus 'polite usage' has converted into *Arkan'sas* the plural of the primitive *Arkansa* or *Arkonsah*; though an approximate, *Ar'kansaw*, is still the current 'vulgar' pronunciation. *Osage* and a great many others have suffered similar metamorphoses.

over sand-bars to the width of several hundred yards. A very credible Indian trader, who had been on Red River some two hundred miles above the False Washita, informed me, that, while in some places he found it not over fifty yards wide, in others it was at least five hundred. This and most other prairie streams have commonly very low banks with remarkably shallow channels, which, during droughts, sometimes go dry in their transit through the sandy plains.*

With regard to the productions of the soil of these regions, the reader will probably have formed, in the main, a tolerably correct idea already; nevertheless a few further specifications may not be altogether unacceptable.

The timber of that portion of the United States territory which is included between the Arkansas frontier and the Cross Timbers, throughout the highlands, is mostly oak of various kinds, of which black-jack and post-oak predominate, as these, and especially the former, seem only capable of withstanding the conflagrations to which they are exposed, and therefore abound along

---

* Of all the rivers of this character, the Cimarron, being on the route from Missouri to Santa Fé, has become the most famous. Its water disappears in the sand and reappears again, in so many places, that some travellers have contended that it 'ebbs and flows' periodically. This is doubtless owing to the fact, that the little current which may flow above the sand in the night, or in cloudy weather, is kept dried up, in an unshaded channel, during the hot sunny days. But in some places the sand is so porous that the water never flows above it, except during freshets.

I was once greatly surprised upon encountering one of these sandy sections of the river after a tremendous rain-storm. Our caravan was encamped at the 'Lower Cimarron Spring:' and, a little after night-fall, a dismal, murky cloud was seen gathering in the western horizon, which very soon came lowering upon us, driven by a hurricane, and bringing with it one of those tremendous bursts of thunder and lightning, and rain, which render the storms of the Prairies, like those of the tropics, so terrible. Hail-stones, as large as turkeys' eggs, and torrents of rain soon drenched the whole country; and so rapidly were the banks of the river overflowed, that the most active exertions were requisite to prevent the mules that were 'staked' in the valley from drowning. Next morning, after crossing the neck of a bend, we were, at the distance of about three miles, upon the river-bank again; when, to our astonishment, the wetted sand, and an occasional pool, fast being absorbed, were the only vestiges of the recent flood—no water was flowing there!

In these sandy stretches of the Cimarron, and other similar 'dry streams,' travellers procure water by excavating basins in the channel, a few feet deep, into which the water is filtrated from the saturated sand.

the prairie borders. The black-jack presents a blackened, scrubby appearance, with harsh rugged branches—partly on account of being so often scorched and crisped by the prairie fires. About the streams we find an intermixture of elm, hackberry, paccan (or pecan), ash, walnut, mulberry, cherry, persimmon, cottonwood, sycamore, birch, etc., with varieties of hickory, gum, dogwood, and the like. All of the foregoing, except paccan, gum and dogwood, are also found west of Missouri, where, although the uplands are almost wholly prairie, the richest growths predominate in the valleys.

In many of the rich bottoms from the Canadian to Red River, for a distance of one or two hundred miles west of the frontier, is found the celebrated *bois-d'arc* (literally, *bow-wood*), usually corrupted in pronunciation to *bowdark*. It was so named by the French on account of its peculiar fitness for *bows*. This tree is sometimes found with a trunk two or three feet in diameter, but, being much branched, it is rarely over forty or fifty feet high. The leaves are large, and it bears a fruit a little resembling the orange in general appearance, though rougher and larger, being four or five inches in diameter; but it is not used for food. The wood is of a beautiful light orange color, and, though coarse, is susceptible of polish. It is one of the hardest, firmest and most durable of timbers, and is much used by wagon-makers and millwrights, as well as by the wild Indians, who make bows of the younger growths.

On the Arkansas and especially its southern tributaries as far west as the Verdigris, and up those of Red River nearly to the False Washita, the bottoms are mostly covered with cane. And scattered over all the south to about the same distance westward, the sassafras abounds, which grows here in every kind of soil and locality.

The celebrated *Cross Timbers*, of which frequent mention has been made, extend from the Brazos, or perhaps from the Colorado of Texas, across the sources of Trinity, traversing Red River above the False Washita, and thence west of north, to the Red Fork of Arkansas, if not further. It is a rough hilly range of country, and, though not mountainous, may perhaps be considered a prolongation of that chain of low mountains which pass to the northward of Bexar and Austin city in Texas.

The Cross Timbers vary in width from five to thirty miles, and entirely cut off the communication betwixt the interior prairies and those of the great plains. They may be considered as the 'fringe' of the great prairies, being a continuous brushy strip, composed of various kinds of undergrowth; such as black-jacks, post-oaks, and in some places hickory, elm, etc., intermixed with a very diminutive dwarf oak, called by the hunters 'skin-oak.' Most of the timber appears to be kept small by the continual inroads of the 'burning prairies;' for, being killed almost annually, it is constantly replaced by scions of undergrowth; so that it becomes more and more dense every reproduction. In some places, however, the oaks are of considerable size, and able to withstand the conflagrations. The underwood is so matted in many places with grape-vines, green-briars, etc., as to form almost impenetrable 'roughs,' which serve as hiding-places for wild beasts, as well as wild Indians; and would, in savage warfare, prove almost as formidable as the hammocks of Florida.

South of the Canadian, a branch of these Cross Timbers projects off westward, and afterwards crosses the stream; and, having continued up for a hundred miles, it inclines northwest beyond the North Fork, and ultimately ceases, no doubt, in the great sandy plains in that direction.

The region of the Cross Timbers is generally well-watered; and is interspersed with romantic and fertile tracts. The bottoms of the tributaries of Red River, even for some distance west of the Cross Timbers (perhaps almost to the U. S. boundary), are mostly very fertile, and timbered with narrow stripes of elm, hackberry, walnut, hickory, mulberry, bur-oak and other rich growths.

But further north, and west of the Cross Timbers, even the streams are nearly naked. The Cimarron river for more than a hundred miles is absolutely without timber; and the Arkansas, for so large a stream, is remarkably scant. The southern border, being protected from the prairie fires by a chain of sand-hills, which extends for two hundred miles along it, is not so bare as the northern bank; though even here it is only skirted with occasional sparsely set groves of cottonwood in the nooks and bends. It is upon the abundance of islands which intersperse its channel, that the greatest quantity of timber (though purely cottonwood) is to be found; yet withal, there are stretches of miles without a tree in view. The banks of the Canadian are equally naked; and, having fewer islands, the river appears still more barren. In fact, there is scarce anything else but cottonwood, and that very sparsely scattered along the streams, throughout most of the far-western prairies.

It is unquestionably the prairie conflagrations that keep down the woody growth upon most of the western uplands. The occasional skirts and fringes which have escaped their rage, have been protected by the streams they border. Yet may not the time come when these vast plains will be covered with timber? It would seem that the prairie region, long after the discovery of America, extended to the very banks of the Mississippi. Father Marquette, in a voyage down this river, in 1673, after passing below the mouth of the Ohio, remarks:—"The banks of the river began to be covered with high trees, which hindered us from observing the country as we had done all along; but we judged from the bellowing of the oxen [buffalo] that the meadows are very near." —Indeed, there are parts of the southwest now thickly set with trees of good size, that, within the remembrance of the oldest inhabitants, were as naked as the prairie plains; and the appearance of the timber in many other sections indicates that it has grown up within less than a century. In fact, we are now witnessing the encroachment of the timber upon the prairies, wherever the devastating conflagrations have ceased their ravages.

The high plains seem too dry and lifeless to produce timber; yet might not the vicissitudes of nature operate a change likewise upon the seasons? Why may we not suppose that the genial influences of civilization—that extensive cultivation of the earth —might contribute to the multiplication of showers, as it certainly does of fountains? Or that the shady groves, as they advance upon the prairies, may have some effect upon the seasons? At least, many old settlers maintain that the droughts are becoming less oppressive in the West. The people of New Mexico also assure us that the rains have much increased of latter years, a phenomenon which the vulgar superstitiously attribute to the arrival of the Missouri traders. Then may we not hope that these sterile regions might yet be thus revived and fertilized, and their surface covered one day by flourishing settlements to the Rocky Mountains?

With regard to fruits, the Prairies are of course not very plenti-
fully supplied. West of the border, however, for nearly two
hundred miles, they are covered, in many places, with the wild
strawberry; and the groves lining the streams frequently abound
in grapes, plums, persimmons, mulberries, paccans, hackberries,
and other 'sylvan luxuries.' The high prairies beyond, however,
are very bare of fruits. The prickly pear may be found over most
of the dry plains; but this is neither very palatable nor wholesome, though often eaten by travellers for want of other fruits.
Upon the branches of the Canadian, North Fork, and Cimarron,
there are, in places, considerable quantities of excellent plums,
grapes, chokecherries, gooseberries, and currants—of the latter
there are three kinds, black, red, and white. About the ravines
and marshy grounds (particularly towards the east) there are
different kinds of small onions, with which the traveller may
season his fresh meats. On the plains, also, I have met with a
species resembling garlic in flavor.

But the flowers are among the most interesting products of the
frontier prairies. These gay meadows wear their most fanciful
piebald robes from the earliest spring till divested of them by the
hoary frosts of autumn. When again winter has fled, but before
the grassy green appears, or other vegetation has ventured to peep
above the earth, they are bespeckled in many places with a species
of *erythronium,* a pretty lilaceous little flower, which springs from
the ground already developed, between a pair of lanceolate leaves,
and is soon after in full bloom. But the floriferous region only
extends about two hundred miles beyond the border: the high
plains are nearly as destitute of flowers as they are of fruits.

The *climate* of most parts of the Prairies is no doubt healthy
in the extreme; for a purer atmosphere is hardly to be found. But
the cold rains of the 'wet season,' and the colder snows of winter,
with the annoying winds that prevail at nearly all times, often
render it very unpleasant. It can hardly be said, it is true, that the
Prairies have their regular 'dry and rainy seasons;' yet the sum-
mers are often so droughty, that, unless some change should be
effected in nature's functions, cultivators would generally find it
necessary, no doubt, to resort to irrigation. That portion, however,
which is conterminous with our western border, and to the distance of nearly two hundred miles westward, in every respect

resembles the adjacent States of Missouri and Arkansas in climate. The south is a little disposed to chills and fevers; but the northern portion is as healthy as the most salubrious uplands of Missouri.

19. Animals of the Prairies

The zoology of the prairies has probably attracted more attention than any other feature of their natural history. This has not arisen altogether from the peculiar interest the animals of the Prairies possess; but they constitute so considerable a portion of the society of the traveller who journeys among them, that they get to hold somewhat the same place in his estimation that his fellow-creatures would occupy if he were in civilization. Indeed, the animals are *par éminence* the communities of the Prairies.

By far the most noble of these, and therefore the best entitled to precedence in the brief notice I am able to present of the animals of those regions, is the *mustang** or wild horse of the Prairies. As he is descended from the stock introduced into America by the first Spanish colonists, he has no doubt a partial mixture of Arabian blood. Being of domestic origin, he is found of various colors, and sometimes of a beautiful piebald.

It is a singular fact in the economy of nature, that all *wild* animals of the same species should have one uniform color (with only occasional but uniform differences between males and females); while that of the *domestic* animals, whether quadruped or fowl, is more or less diversified.

The beauty of the mustang is proverbial. One in particular has been celebrated by hunters, of which marvellous stories are told. He has been represented as a medium-sized stallion of perfect symmetry, milk-white, save a pair of black ears—a natural 'pacer,' and so fleet, it has been said, as to leave far behind every horse that had been tried in pursuit of him, without breaking his 'pace.' But I infer that this story is somewhat mythical, from the difficulty which one finds in fixing the abiding place of its equine

---

* *Mustang* would most naturally seem a corruption of the Spanish adjective *mostrenco* (without owner), but the Mexicans call wild horses *mesteñas*, a synonym in one of its senses with *mostrenco*.

hero. He is familiarly known, by common report, all over the great Prairies. The trapper celebrates him in the vicinity of the northern Rocky Mountains; the hunter, on the Arkansas, or in the midst of the Plains; while others have him pacing at the rate of half a mile a minute on the borders of Texas. It is hardly a matter of surprise, then, that a creature of such an ubiquitary existence should never have been caught.

The wild horses are generally well formed, with trim and clean limbs; still their elegance has been much exaggerated by travellers, because they have seen them at large, abandoned to their wild and natural gaiety. Then, it is true, they appear superb indeed; but when caught and tamed, they generally dwindle down to ordinary ponies. Large droves are very frequently seen upon the Prairies, sometimes of hundreds together, gambolling and curvetting within a short distance of the caravans. It is sometimes difficult to keep them from dashing among the loose stock of the traveller, which would be exceedingly dangerous; for, once together, they are hard to separate again, particularly if the number of mustangs is much the greatest. It is a singular fact, that the gentlest wagon-horse (even though quite fagged with travel), once among a drove of mustangs, will often acquire in a few hours all the intractable wildness of his untamed companions.

The mustang is sometimes taken by the cruel expedient of 'creasing,' which consists in shooting him through the upper *crease* of the neck, above the cervical vertebræ; when, the ball cutting a principal nerve, he falls as suddenly as if shot in the brain, and remains senseless for a few minutes, during which he is secured with a rope. He soon recovers from the shock, however, and springs to his feet, but finds himself deprived of his liberty. He is easily tamed after this, and the wound heals without leaving any physical injury. But 'creasing' is so nice an operation that many are killed in the attempt. If the ball pass a little too low, it fractures a vertebra and kills the poor brute instantly.

But the most usual mode, among the Mexicans and Indians, of taking the *mesteña* (as the former call these animals), is with the lazo. They pursue them on fleet horses, and great numbers are thus noosed and tamed. The mustang has been taken in Texas in considerable numbers by preparing a strong pen at some passway or crossing of a river, into which they are frightened and caught.

The *buffalo*, though making no pretensions to the elegance and symmetry of the mustang, is by far the most important animal of the Prairies to the traveller. It is sufficiently well known that these animals bear but little resemblance to the buffalo of India; but that they are a species of bison, or *bos Americanus,* according to naturalists. They are called *Cíbolos* by the Mexicans; and it would certainly have prevented ambiguity, had they been distinguished by some other name than buffalo with us.

Their dusky black color becomes much paler during the season of long hair.* The phenomenon of a white buffalo has frequently been remarked upon the Prairies; but as the white skin is said to have been used in the mystic ceremonies of many of the northern tribes of Indians, this probably created such a demand for them, that they have become nearly extinct. Their unusual color has commonly been considered a *lusus naturæ,* yet it is probable that they stand in about the same relation to the black or brown buffalo that black sheep do to white ones. The horns of the buffalo are short and black, and almost concealed under the frightfully shaggy frontlets of long woolly hair that crown the foreheads of the bulls; which, with the goat-like beard, and ill-shapen hump, form the chief distinction between them and the domestic cattle: in fact, they are so nearly of the same species that they will breed together; though the offspring, like the mule, is said to be unfruitful. Between the males and females there is still a greater disproportion in size than among the domestic cattle. A buffalo cow is about as heavy as a common ox, while a large fat bull will weigh perhaps double as much.

These are very gregarious animals. At some seasons, however, the cows rather incline to keep to themselves; at other times they are mostly seen in the centre of the gang, while the bulls are scattered around, frequently to a considerable distance, evidently guarding the cows and calves. And on the outskirts of the buffalo range, we are apt to meet with small gangs of bulls alone, a day or two's travel distant, as though performing the office of piquet guards for the main herds.

The flesh of the buffalo is, I think, as fine as any meat I ever

---

* The bulls usually shed in the spring, from the shoulders back, but not in front, which imparts to them quite a lion-like appearance.

tasted: the old hunter will not admit that there is anything equal
to it. Much of its apparent savoriness, however, results perhaps
from our sharpened 'prairie appetites,' and our being usually upon
salt provisions awhile before obtaining it. The flesh is of a coarser
texture than beef, more juicy, and the fat and lean better distributed. This meat is also very easy of digestion,* possessing even
aperient qualities. The circumstance that bulls of all ages, if fat,
make good beef, is a further proof of the superiority of buffalo
meat. These are generally selected for consumption in the winter
and early spring, when the cows, unless barren, are apt to be
poor; but during most of the year, the latter are the fattest and
tenderest meat. Of these, the udder is held as hardly second to
the tongue in delicacy. But what the tail of the beaver is to the
trapper, the tongue of the buffalo is to the hunter. Next to this
are the 'marrow-bones,' the tender-loins, and the hump-ribs. Instead of a gristly substance, as sometimes stated, the hump is
produced by a convex tier of vertical ribs, which project from the
spine, forming a gradual curve over the shoulders: those of the
middle being sometimes nearly two feet in length. The 'veal' is
rarely good, being generally poor, owing to the scanty supply of
milk which their dams afford, and to their running so much from
hunters and wolves.

This animal furnishes almost the exclusive food of the prairie
Indians, as well as covering for their wigwams and most of their
clothing; also their bedding, ropes, bags for their meat, etc.,
sinews for bow-strings, for sewing moccasins, leggins, and the
like; besides sustenance for the numerous travellers and trappers
who range upon their grazing regions. Were they only killed for
food, however, their natural increase would perhaps replenish the
loss: yet the continual and wanton slaughter of them by travellers
and hunters, and the still greater havoc made among them by the
Indians, not only for meat, but often for the skins and tongues
alone (for which they find a ready market among their traders),
are fast reducing their numbers, and must ultimately effect their
total annihilation from the continent. It is believed that the annual

---

* It has often been remarked by travellers, that however much buffalo meat
one may eat, no inconvenience is ever suffered from it.

'export' of *buffalo rugs** from the Prairies and bordering 'buffalo range,' is about a hundred thousand: and the number killed wantonly, or exclusively for meat, is no doubt still greater, as the skins are fit to dress scarcely half the year. The vast extent of the prairies upon which they now pasture is no argument against the prospect of their total extinction, when we take into consideration the extent of country from which they have already disappeared; for it is well known, that, within the recollection of our oldest pioneers, they were nearly as abundant east of the Mississippi as they now are upon the western prairies; and from history we learn, that they once ranged to the Atlantic coast. Even within thirty years, they were abundant over much of the present States of Missouri and Arkansas; yet they are now rarely seen within two hundred miles of the frontier. Indeed, upon the high plains they have very sensibly decreased within the last ten years. Nevertheless, the number of buffalo upon the Prairies is still immense. But, as they incline to migrate *en masse* from place to place, it sometimes happens, that, for several days' travel to-gether, not a single one is to be met with; but, in other places, many thousands are often seen at one view.

The Indians, as well as Mexicans, hunt the buffalo mostly with the bow and arrows. For this purpose they train their fleetest horses to run close beside him; and, when near enough, with almost unerring aim, they pierce him with their arrows, usually behind the short ribs, ranging forward, which soon disables and brings him to the ground. When an arrow has been ill-directed, or does not enter deep enough, and even sometimes when it has penetrated a vital part, but is needed to use again, the hunter sometimes rides up and draws it out while the animal is yet running. An athletic Indian will not unfrequently discharge his darts with such force, that I have seen them (30 inches long) wholly buried in the body of a buffalo: and I have been assured by hunters that the arrows, missing the bones, have been known to pass entirely through the huge carcass and fall upon the ground.

The dexterity acquired by these wild hunters in shooting the buffalo, is very surprising. On one occasion, upon the prairies, a

---

* Often, but it would seem improperly, called 'buffalo *robes.*'

party of Witchita Indians were encamped near us; and a drove of buffalo passing in the vicinity, I requested a chief to take my horse and kill one 'upon the shares.' He delighted in the sport: so, gathering his arrows, he mounted the pony, which was slow, and withal very lean, and giving chase, in a few minutes he had two buffaloes lying upon the plain, and two others went off so badly wounded, that, with a little exertion, they might have been secured.

In all these modes of hunting, the buffalo is sometimes dangerous; for, becoming enraged from his wounds, he will often make desperate lunges at his pursuer; and, if the horse be not well trained, he may be himself disembowelled, leaving his rider at the mercy of the buffalo, as has happened on some occasions. But if the steed understand his business, he will dodge the animal with the expertness of a fencer.

Buffalo calves (but not full-grown buffalo) are often taken with a lazo by Mexicans and Indians; yet, being separated from their dams and the droves during chases, these simple little creatures not unfrequently take up with the riding animals of the hunters, and follow them to the camp as tamely as though they were their dams. If provided with domestic cows, they may be raised without much difficulty.

Some of the northern Indians, particularly the Assinaboins, are said to practice still a distinct mode of taking the buffalo. A staunch pound is erected at some convenient point, and, after a course of mystic rites by their medicine-men, they start upon the enterprise. A gang of buffalo is frightened towards the pen, while an Indian, covered with one of their woolly skins, runs at a distance ahead. Being seen by the animals, they mistake him for one of their kind, and follow him into the pen. Once secured in the enclosure, they leisurely dispatch them with their arrows, as they are said to believe it would offend the Great Spirit and render future hunts unpropitious to use fire arms in killing their imprisoned game.

However, of all other modes, our backwoodsmen prefer 'still-hunting'—that is, stealing upon their game afoot with the rifle. Buffalo are much more easily approached than deer. When the hunter perceives a herd at rest, or quietly feeding, he crawls upon them behind a bank, a shrub, or a tuft of grass, with the greatest facility, provided he 'has the wind of them,' as hunters say—that is, if the wind blows from the buffalo; but if the reverse, he will find it impossible to approach them, however securely he may have concealed himself from their sight. In fact, their scent being acute, they seem to depend more upon it than their sight; for if a gang of buffalo be frightened, from any quarter whatever, they are apt to shape their course against the wind, that they may scent an enemy in their way.

The tenacity of these animals for life is often very extraordinary. When one receives even a mortal shot, he frequently appears not hurt—he seems to disdain to flinch—but will curl his tail and step about as though he neither felt nor feared anything! If left undisturbed, however, he begins to stagger, and in a few moments expires: but if provoked, he might run for miles before he would fall. I have seen a party of hunters around a wounded and enraged bull, fire, at a few paces distance, a dozen or two shots, aimed at his very heart, without their seeming to have any effect till his anger cooled, when in an instant he would lie lifeless upon the ground. In such cases, the inexperienced hunter often aims to shoot them in the brain, but without success. Owing not only to the thickness of the skull, but to the matted wool upon it, I have never witnessed an instance of a rifle-ball's penetrating to the brain of a buffalo bull.

The buffalo never attacks, however, except when wounded. Even the largest droves (the opinion of some travellers to the contrary notwithstanding), though in the wildest career, are easily turned from their course by a single man who may intercept their way. I have crouched in the tall grass in the direct route of a frighted gang, when, firing at them on their near approach, they would spread in consternation to either side. Still their advance is somewhat frightful—their thundering rumble over the dry plain —their lion-like fronts and dangling beards— their open mouths and hanging tongues—as they come on, puffing like a locomotive engine at every bound, does at first make the blood settle a little heavy about the heart.

The gait of these animals is a clumsy gallop, and any common pony can overtake them in the chase; though, as the hunter would express it, they 'lumber' over the ground rather deceivingly. The cows are usually much faster than the bulls. It has been the remark of travellers that the buffalo jumps up from the ground differently from any other animal. The horse rises upon his fore feet first, and the cow upon her hind feet, but the buffalo seems to spring up on them all at once.

American hunters, as well as Indians, to butcher the buffalo, generally turn it upon the belly, and commence on the back. The hump-ribs, tender-loins, and a few other choice bits being appropriated, the remainder is commonly left for the wolves. The skin is chiefly used for buffalo rugs, but for which it is only preserved by the Indians during fall and winter (and then rarely but from the cows and bullocks), when the hair is long and woolly. I have never seen the buffalo hide tanned, but it seems too porous and spongy to make substantial leather. Were it valuable, thousands of hides might be saved that are annually left to the wolves upon the Prairies.

Although the buffalo is the largest, he has by no means the control among the prairie animals: the sceptre of authority has been lodged with the large *gray wolf*. Though but little larger than the wolf of the United States, he is much more ferocious. The same species abound throughout the north of Mexico, where they often kill horses, mules and cattle of all sizes; and on the Prairies they make considerable havoc among the buffalo.

Many curious tales are told of the wiles and expedients practised by these animals to secure their prey. Some assert that they collect in companies, and chase a buffalo by turns, till he is fatigued, when they join and soon dispatch him: others, that, as the buffalo runs with the tongue hanging out, they snap at it in the chase till it is torn off, which preventing him from eating, he is reduced by starvation, and soon overpowered: others, that, while running, they gnaw and lacerate the legs and ham-strings till they disable him, and then he is killed by the gang. Be this as it may, certain it is that they overcome many of the largest buffaloes, employing perhaps different means of subduing them, and among these is doubtless the last mentioned, for I have myself seen them with the muscles of the thighs cruelly mangled —a consequence no doubt of some of these attacks. Calves are constantly falling victims to the rapacity of these wolves; yet, when herds of buffalo are together, they defend their offspring with great bravery.

Though the color of this wolf is generally a dirty gray, they are sometimes met with nearly white. I am of opinion, however, that the diversity of color originates chiefly from the different ages of the hair, and partially from the age of the animal itself. The few white wolves I have seen, have been lean, long-haired, and apparently very old. There are immense numbers of them upon the Prairies. Droves are frequently to be seen following in the wake of caravans, hunting companies, and itinerant Indian bands, for weeks together—not, like the jackal, so much to disinter the dead (though this they sometimes do), as to feast upon the abandoned carcasses of the buffalo which are so often wantonly killed and wasted. Unless in these cases, they are rarely seen, except in the neighborhood of buffalo; therefore, when the hungry traveller meets with wolves, he feels some assurance that supplies of his favorite game are at hand.

I have never known these animals, rapacious as they are, extend their attacks to man, though they probably would, if very hungry and a favorable opportunity presented itself. I shall not soon forget an adventure with one of them, many years ago, on the frontier of Missouri. Riding near the prairie border, I perceived one of the largest and fiercest of the gray species, which had just descended from the west, and seemed famished to desperation. I at once prepared for a chase; and, being without arms, I caught up a cudgel, when I betook me valiantly to the charge, much stronger, as I soon discovered, in my cause than in my equipment. The wolf was in no humor to flee, however, but boldly met me full half-way. I was soon disarmed, for my club broke upon the animal's head. He then 'laid to' my horse's legs, which, not relishing the conflict, gave a plunge and sent me whirling over his head, and made his escape, leaving me and the wolf at close quarters. I was no sooner upon my feet than my antagonist renewed the charge; but, being without weapon, or any means of awakening an emotion of terror, save through his imagination, I took off my large black hat, and using it for a shield, began to thrust it towards his gaping jaws. My *ruse* had the desired effect; for, after springing at me a few times, he wheeled about and trotted off several paces, and stopped to gaze at me. Being apprehensive that he might change his mind and return to the attack, and conscious that, under the compromise, I had the best of the bargain, I very resolutely——took to my heels, glad of the opportunity of making a drawn game, though I had myself given the challenge.

There is a small species called the *prairie wolf* on the frontier, and *coyote* by the Mexicans, which is also found in immense numbers on the Plains. It is rather smaller than an ordinary dog, nearly the color of the common gray wolf, and though as rapacious as the larger kind, it seems too cowardly to attack stout game. It therefore lives upon the remains of buffalo killed by hunters and by the large wolves, added to such small game as hares, prairie dogs, etc., and even reptiles and insects. It will lie for hours beside a 'dog-hole,' watching for the appearance of the little animal, which no sooner peeps out than the enemy pounces upon it.

The coyote has been denominated the 'jackal of the Prairies;' indeed, some have reckoned it really a species of that animal, yet it would seem improperly, as this creature partakes much less of the nature of the jackal than of the common wolf. Still, however noisy the former may be, he cannot exceed the prairie wolf. Like ventriloquists, a pair of these will represent a dozen distinct voices in such quick succession—will bark, chatter, yelp, whine, and howl in such variety of note, that one would fancy a score of them at hand. This, added to the long and doleful bugle-note of the large wolf, which often accompanies it, sometimes makes a night upon the Prairies perfectly hideous. Some hunters assert that the coyote and the dog will breed together. Be this as it may, certain it is that the Indian dogs have a wonderfully wolfish appearance.

The *elk* as well as the *deer* is found somewhat abundant upon the Arkansas river, as high as the Santa Fé road, but from thence westward they are both very scarce; for these animals do not resort to the high prairie plains. Further south, however, in the prairies bordering the brushy tributaries of the Canadian and Red River, deer are exceedingly plenty—herds of hundreds are sometimes seen together; but in these southern regions there are but few elks.

About the thickety streams above-mentioned, as well as among the Cross Timbers, the *black bear* is common, living chiefly upon acorns and other fruits. The grape vines and the branches of the scrubby oaks, and plum-bushes, are in some places so torn and broken by the bear in pursuit of fruits, that a stranger would conclude a violent hurricane had passed among them.

That species of gazelle known as the *antelope* is very numerous upon the high plains. This beautiful animal, though reckoned a link between the deer and goat, is certainly much nearest the latter. It is about the size and somewhat of the figure of a large goat. Its horns also resemble those of the latter, being likewise persistent; but they are more erect, and have a short prong projecting in front. The ground of this animal's color a little resembles that of the common deer, but it is variegated with a whitish section or two on each side.

The antelope is most remarkable for its fleetness: not bounding like the deer, but skimming over the ground as though upon skates. The fastest horse will rarely overtake them. I once witnessed an effort to catch one that had a hind-leg broken, but it far out-stripped our fleetest 'buffalo-horse.' It is, therefore, too swift to be hunted in the chase. I have seen dogs run after this animal, but they would soon stop and turn about, apparently much ashamed of being left so far behind.

The flesh of the antelope is, like that of the goat, rather coarse, and but little esteemed: consequently, no great efforts are made to take them. Being as wild as fleet, the hunting of them is very difficult, except they be entrapped by their curiosity. Meeting a stranger, they seem loth to leave him until they have fully found him out. They will often take a circuit around the object of their curiosity, usually approaching nearer and nearer, until within rifle-shot—frequently stopping to graze. Also, they are often decoyed with a scarlet coat, or a red handkerchief attached to the tip of a ramrod, which will sometimes allure them within reach of the hunter's aim. But this interesting animal, like the buffalo, is now very rarely seen within less than 200 miles of the frontier: though early voyagers tell us that it once frequented regions east of the Mississippi.

The *bighorn* (*carnero cimarron*, as called by Mexicans, and sometimes known to trappers as the mountain sheep), so abundant in most of the Rocky Mountain chain, is found in the spurs and table-plain cliffs about the sources of the Cimarron river (whence this stream acquired its name), as well as in the highland gorges, and other parts of those mountain borders. Its flesh is said to be excellent, and is preferred by many hunters to venison. It is larger than a common sheep, and covered with brownish hair instead of wool—darker than the deer, but whitish on the belly. It is most remarkable for its huge spiral horns, resembling in shape and curvature those of the sheep, but sometimes over three feet long, and four to six inches in diameter at the base.

The bighorn is quite celebrated for its agility, and its habit of secluding itself among the most inaccessible mountain crags. It seems to delight in perching and capering upon the very verge of the most frightful precipices and overhanging cliffs, and in skipping from rock to rock, regardless of the yawning chasms, hundreds of feet in depth, which intervene. In fact, when pursued, it does not hesitate, as I have been assured, to leap from a cliff into a valley a hundred or more feet below, where, lighting upon its huge horns, it springs to its feet uninjured; for the neck is so thick and strong as to support the greatest shock the animal's weight can bring upon it. Being exceedingly timorous, it rarely descends to the valleys, but feeds and sleeps about such craggy fastnesses as are inaccessible to the wolves and other animals of prey. The animal seems greatly to resemble the *moufflon* of Buffon, in color, figure and horns, but the *chamois* in habits.

But of all the prairie animals, by far the most curious, and by no means the least celebrated, is the little *prairie dog*. This singular quadruped is but little larger than a common squirrel, its body being nearly a foot long, with a tail of three or four inches. The color ranges from brown to a dirty yellow. The flesh, though often eaten by travellers, is not esteemed savory. It was denominated the 'barking squirrel,' the 'prairie ground-squirrel,' etc., by early explorers, with much more apparent propriety than the present established name. Its yelp, which resembles that of the little toy-dog, seems its only canine attribute. It rather appears to occupy a middle ground betwixt the rabbit and squirrel—like the former in feeding and burrowing—like the latter in frisking, flirting, sitting erect, and somewhat so in its barking.

The prairie dog has been reckoned by some naturalists a species of the marmot (*arctomys hudoviciana*); yet it seems to possess scarce any other quality in common with this animal except that of burrowing. Some have supposed, it is true, that like the marmot, they lie torpid during the cold season; and it is observed in 'Long's Expedition,' that, "as they pass the winter in a lethargic state, they lay up no provisions," etc.: but this is no doubt errone- ous; for I have the concurrent testimony of several persons, who have been upon the Prairies in winter, that, like rabbits and squirrels, they issue from their holes every soft day; and therefore lay up no doubt a hoard of 'hay' (as there is rarely anything else to be found in the vicinity of their towns), for winter's use.

A collection of their burrows has been termed by travellers a 'dog town,' which comprises from a dozen or so, to some thou- sands in the same vicinity; often covering an area of several square miles. They generally locate upon firm dry plains, coated with fine short grass, upon which they feed; for they are no doubt exclusively herbivorous. But even when tall coarse grass sur- rounds, they seem commonly to destroy this within their 'streets,' which are nearly always found 'paved' with a fine species suited to their palates. They must need but little water, if any at all, as their 'towns' are often, indeed generally, found in the midst of the most arid plains—unless we suppose they dig down to sub- terranean fountains. At least they evidently burrow remarkably deep. Attempts either to dig or drown them out of their holes have generally proved unsuccessful.

Approaching a "village,' the little dogs may be observed frisk- ing about the "streets'—passing from dwelling to dwelling ap- parently on visits—sometimes a few clustered together as though in council—here feeding upon the tender herbage—there cleans- ing their 'houses,' or brushing the little hillock about the door— yet all quiet. Upon seeing a stranger, however, each streaks to its home, but is apt to stop at the entrance, and spread the general alarm by a succession of shrill yelps, usually sitting erect. Yet at the report of a gun or the too near approach of the visitor, they dart down and are seen no more till the cause of alarm seems to have disappeared.

Two other animals are said to live in communion with the prairie dogs—the *rattlesnake* and a small *owl*,* but both are no doubt intruders, resorting to these burrows for shelter, and to feed, it is presumed, upon the 'pups' of the inmates.

---

* This has been called the *Coquimbo owl*. Its note, whether natural or imita- tive, much resembles that of the prairie dog.

Rattlesnakes are exceedingly abundant upon these plains: scores of them are sometimes killed in the course of a day's travel; yet they seem remarkably harmless, for I have never witnessed an instance of a man's being bitten, though they have been known to crawl even into the beds of travellers.* Mules are sometimes bitten by them, yet very rarely, though they must daily walk over considerable numbers.

The *horned frog,* as modern travellers have christened it, or horned lizard, as those of earlier times more rationally called it, is the most famed and curious reptile of the plains. Like the prairie dog, it is only found in the dry regions, often many miles from water. It no doubt lives nearly, if not wholly, without drink. Its food probably consists chiefly of ants and other insects; though many Mexicans will have it, that the *camaleon* (as they call it) *vive del aire*—lives upon the air. It has been kept several months without partaking of a particle of aliment. I once took a pair of them upon the far-western plains, which I shut up in a box and carried to one of the eastern cities, where they were kept for several months before they died,—without having taken food or water, though repeatedly offered them.

The whole length of the horned frog is from two to five inches —body flattened horizontally, oval-shaped, and between one and two inches wide in the middle. The back is beautifully variegated, with white and brown, and sometimes a yellowish purple. The belly is whitish and covered with brown specks. It acquired its name from a pair of short horns projecting from the top of the head—with other smaller horny protuberances upon the head and body. It has a short tail, which gives it a lizard-like appearance. It is a very inoffensive creature, and may be handled with perfect impunity, notwithstanding its uncouth appearance, and sometimes vicious demonstrations.

As birds mostly incline to the timbered regions, there is but a scant variety to be met with upon the plains. About the Cross Timbers and indeed on all the brushy creeks, especially to the southward, are quantities of wild *turkeys,* which are frequently seen ranging in large flocks in the bordering prairies. That species

---

* Though I never saw it tried, it has been said that snakes will not crawl over a hair-rope stretched upon the ground, and that consequently these form good barriers to keep these reptiles out of a bed.

of American grouse, known west as the *prairie-hen,* is very abundant on the frontier, and is quite destructive, in autumn, to the prairie corn-fields. This fowl is rarely seen over two hundred miles beyond the border. Of *partridges,* the same is true; but their number is quite limited anywhere beyond the precincts of the settlements. About the streams there are different species of geese and ducks, as well as both sand-hill and white cranes: also flocks of a species of plover and curlew. Add to these numbers of hawks and ravens, and we have most of the fowls of the Prairies. Flocks of the latter follow in the wake of caravans with even greater constancy than wolves.

The *bee,* among Western pioneers, is the proverbial precursor of the Anglo-American population: in fact, the aborigines of the frontier have generally corroborated the notion; for they used to say, they knew the whites were not far behind, when bees appeared among them. This partial coincidence, I suppose, is the result of their emigration westward being at nearly an even pace with that of the settlers. As yet no honey-bees seem to have been discovered as far westward as any part of the Rocky Mountains. They are scattered, however, to the distance of two or three hundred miles west of the Missouri and Arkansas frontier, where there is timber affording them suitable habitations. On the Santa Fé route but few have been found beyond the Council Grove.

20. Indians of the Prairies

Those savage hordes which may be considered as the Prairie Indians proper, have made little or no perceptible progress in civilization. They mostly live by plunder and the chase: a few eke out a subsistence by agriculture. They consist of various distinct tribes, but among whom there is a greater diversity of language than of habitudes. I would not have it understood, however, that all the customs of every band are entirely similar: it is this assumption, together with the practice of setting down as standing customs what they have observed on some particular occasions, that has frequently created such a discrepancy between the accounts of transient travellers.

The tribes inhabiting near the borders of the frontier Indians differ from those that range the far-western prairies in several traits of general character. The former have their fixed villages, and, for the most part, combine the pursuits of agriculture and the chase. They form, indeed, a sort of intermediate class between the frontier and the wild tribes, resembling the one or the other in all important particulars. I will merely notice in this place a few of the characteristics by which the more conspicuous of these tribes are distinguished.

Their village wigwams differ from the lodges of the wilder tribes, in their being much more substantial, and usually covered with grass and earth instead of skins. The Indians commonly remain in their villages during the inclement portion of the winter; yet most of them spend the early spring upon the Prairies in buffalo-hunting; as well as such portions of the summer and autumn as are not occupied in the cultivation and gathering of their crops, which they secure in *caches* till their return.

In dress they differ but little from the wilder tribes, except that, having more communication with the whites, they make greater use of our fabrics—blankets, coarse cloths, calicoes and the like. Their most striking peculiarity consists in the cut of their hair. Most of them, instead, like the Indians of the Plains, of wearing the hair long, trim and arrange it in the most fantastic style. In the care bestowed upon this part of their toilet, they cannot be excelled by the most *soigneux* of civilized dandies. They shave a large portion of the head, but leave a fanciful lock upon the crown as a scalp-crest (an indispensable trophy for the enemy), which is in general gorgeously bedecked with painted feathers and gewgaws.

The *Pawnees*, who now have their principal village on the Loup Fork of the Platte river, are perhaps the most famous of these tribes. Small bands of their war-parties roam on foot through every portion of the Prairies, often to the Mexican frontier, though they generally contrive to return well mounted. When upon these expeditions, they may properly enough be considered the Ishmaelites of the Prairies—their hands are against every man, and every man's hand is against them. They will skulk about in the vicinity of a prize of mules or horses for several days unsuspected, till a favorable opportunity offers to pounce upon them.

The *Osages* are at present the most important western branch of the Dahcotah stock, after the Sioux. There are two bands of them, the Big and Little Osages. Though the Pawnees stand most prominent as prairie marauders, these are unsurpassed in simple rogueries. Expertness at stealing appears indeed to constitute a part of their faith, and an all-important branch of education, in which degrees are conferred in true 'academic order;' for I have been assured, that, in their councils, the claims of the candidates to the honors of rogueship are duly considered, and to the most proficient is awarded an honorary badge—the right to wear a fancy feather stuck athwart his scalp-crest.

The habitudes of the Osages do not appear to have undergone any material change, notwithstanding the exertions of the government and the missionaries to civilize and to christianize them. Some of their matrimonial customs are very curious and rather peculiar. The eldest daughter seems not only 'heiress apparent,' but, when married, becomes absolute owner of the entire property and household of her parents—family and all. While single, however, she has no authority, but is herself held as a piece of merchantable property, estimated somewhat as in civilized life, in proportion to her 'charms,' and to the value of her 'hereditaments.' She is therefore kept under the strictest watch by her parents, that she may not diminish her worth by any improper conduct.

When some warrior 'beau' has taken a fancy to the heiress and wishes to possess her and her estate of sisters, dogs, rugs and household, he takes his finest horses, (and if she be a 'belle' he need not attempt it unless he have some of the noblest), and tying them at her lodge door departs without saying a word; leaving them, like a slow-match, silently to effect his purpose. After the 'pretender' has disappeared, the matron of the premises and her lord inspect the valuables, the 'demure damsel' barely venturing a sly peep through some crevice of the wigwam. If the offer be found unworthy, the horses are sent back to the owner as silently as they came, or maybe with some apology, provided he be a warrior whom they are afraid of offending. But if accepted, the father takes instead some of his own horses and ties them at the door of the proposer, as a token of admission. If the parties be without horses some other valuables are employed in lieu. After this the marriage is solemnized with a joyous fête and their primitive ceremonies.

But now the son-in-law is fully indemnified for his heavy 'disbursement' in the *purchase* of his bride; for he at once becomes possessor of the entire wealth of his father-in-law—master of the family-lodge and all the household: if there be a dozen younger daughters, they are all his *de droit*—his wives or slaves as we may choose to consider them: in fact, the 'heiress' herself seems in the same predicament, and the wife among them all who may have the tact to gain the husband's affections, generally becomes mistress of the 'harem.' From the refuse of this estate of 'fair ones' the indigent warriors and inferior Indians who are not able to purchase an 'heiress' are apt to supply themselves with wives upon a cheaper scale.

The Osages bury their dead according to the usual Indian mode; and, though it seems always to have been the custom among most savage nations, to keep up a chorus of hideous cries and yells for a long while after the death of a relative, yet the Osages are by far the most accomplished mourners of them all. Being once encamped near a party of them, I was wakened at the dawn of day by the most doleful, piteous, heart-rending howls and lamentations. The apparently distressed mourner would cry with a protracted expiration till completely out of breath. For some instants he seemed to be in the very last agonies: then he would recover breath with a smothered, gurgling inspiration: and thus he continued for several minutes, giving vent to every variety of hideous and terrific sounds. Looking around, I perceived the weeper standing with his face towards the faint gleam which flitted from the still obscured sun. This was perhaps his idol; else he was standing thus because his deceased relation lay in that direction. A full 'choir' of these mourners (which is always joined by the howls and yelps of their myriad of dogs), imparts the most frightful horror to a wilderness camp.

It is considered among these as well as other 'crying' tribes, quite a merit to be a graceful weeper: it becomes even a profitable vocation to those whose eyes and lungs are most capacious of such things. If you tell an Osage that you have lost a kinsman or friend for whom you wish him to mourn, he will undertake the service for a trifling reward—and acquit himself with more 'credit'—

more to the spirit than the best tragic actor. He will mimic every exterior indication of grief and the most heart-felt wailing, till the tears trickle in torrents down his cheeks.

The Osages seem generally to worship a good and evil spirit, and to believe in the most usual Indian paradise. No people can have more implicit faith in witchcraft and all kinds of sorcery and superstitions—such as holding converse with deceased friends or relations—appointing a time to die, etc.: and instances are related of their fancying themselves thus called to the world of spirits, which would so powerfully affect the imagination as to cause them to pine away, and sometimes die even to the appointed day.

Owing partially, no doubt, to the burdensome life they lead, the squaws of all the tribes are, for the most part, much more inclined to corpulency than the men. They are generally chubby and ill-favored, while the males are usually tall, erect, well-turned and active. For their proverbial straightness, however, the Osages are perhaps more famous than any of the other prairie Indians.

The *Wacoes, Witchitas* and their kindred tribes on Red River, are, for the most part, a very indigent race. They are chiefly remarkable for their profuse tattooing, whereby they have some-times acquired the title of 'Pawnee Picts:' the females particularly make a perfect calico of the whole under-jaw, breast and arms, and the mammæ are fancifully ornamented with rings and rays. The tattoo, in fact, seems to constitute the chief female ornament of these tribes; for their only gown consists of about a yard and a half of strouding, or else a small dressed skin, suspended from the waist, and constituting a sort of primitive petticoat. The upper portion of the body remains uncovered, except by a blanket or small skin, thrown loosely over the shoulders. The men are often without any other vesture than the flap, and sometimes a buffalo rug or blanket.

As the remaining tribes of this intermediate class present few or no distinctive characteristics, we will pass at once to the consideration of the *wild tribes* proper of the Great Western Prairies. These neither cultivate the soil nor live in fixed villages, but lead a roving life in pursuit of plunder and game, and without ever submitting themselves to that repose—to those fixed habits, which must always precede any progress in civilization. But as the

Comanches are the only tribe of these 'wandering Arabs' of the Plains which present any distinguishing features of interest—any prominent points of national character—the remarks that follow will be devoted almost exclusively to them.

The relationship of the Comanches to the Snakes or Shoshonies, shows them to have descended from the north: in fact, it is but half a century since their range was from the Arkansas river northward; but at present this stream is their *ultima Thule*. Yet they even now acknowledge no boundaries, but call themselves the lords of the entire Prairies—all other are but 'tenants at will.' They lead a wandering sort of life, betaking themselves whithersoever the seasons or the habits of the buffalo, their chief object of pursuit, may lead them. Although during summer they are not unfrequently found as far north as the Arkansas river, their winters they usually pass about the head branches of the Brazos and Colorado rivers of Texas.

In their domestic habits, these Indians, for the most part, resemble the other wild tribes; yet in some respects they differ materially. One of the most interesting traits of difference is to be found in their distaste for ardent spirits: but few of them can be induced to taste a drop of intoxicating liquors; thus forming an exception, I believe, to the entire race of the 'red man,' who appears to have a constitutional appetite for strong drinks. The frontier as well as the prairie tribes—the Mexican as well as the Mountain Indians—all are equally slaves to their use.

The Comanches are divided into numerous petty bands, each under the control of its own particular chief. When a chief becomes old and care-worn, he exercises but the 'civil authority' of his clan; while his son, if deemed worthy, otherwise some distinguished brave, assumes, by 'common consent,' the functions of war-chief. As is the case with all barbarous tribes, their chiefs assume every judicial and executive authority. Complaints are made to them and sentence summarily pronounced, and often as summarily executed. For most offences, the chief, if he considers his authority sufficiently well established, freely uses the rod upon his subjects. He rarely attempts this, however, upon noted warriors or 'braves,' whose influence and resentment he may have reason to fear. The punishment of murder among these, as among most of the savage nations, devolves upon the bereaved relatives, who are free to pursue and punish the perpetrators according to their own liking, which is seldom short of death. But the offended party, if disposed to compromise, has also the privilege of accepting a commutation and releasing the murderer.

The husband seems to have complete power over the destinies of his wife and children. For adultery, his punishment is most usually to cut off the nose or ears, or both; and he may even take the life of his unfaithful wife with impunity. The squaw who has been mutilated for such a cause, is *ipso facto* divorced, and, it is said, for ever precluded from marrying again. The consequence is, that she becomes a confirmed harlot in the tribe. Owing in part, no doubt, to such severity in their customs, the Comanche squaws have ever been noted for their chastity. This may result also, in some degree, from the circumstance, that the Comanche husbands, fathers and brothers, seldom or never subject their wives, daughters and sisters, to that debasing traffic practised among so many of the northern nations.

Like the other wild tribes, the Comanches tolerate polygamy, the chiefs and braves sometimes taking as many as eight or ten wives at a time. Three is considered the usual number, however, for 'subjects' or common warriors, and nine for the chiefs. Their marriage ceremonies vary in different bands; but the following has been represented as the most usual. Unlike most other tribes, the consent of the maiden has to be obtained. This done, the lover, from apparent delicacy, goes not to the father of his intended, but, in accordance with a custom which prevails among some other tribes, communicates his desire to an uncle or other aged relative, who enters into the marriage contract. The parties, however, are not yet fully betrothed; but, as a test of the submission of the bride to the service of her proposed lord, the latter ties his riding-horse at her lodge door. If she turn him loose, she has resolved finally to reject him; but if she lead him to the *caballada*, it is an unequivocal agreement to take the charge of his horses and other property; and the marriage is soon concluded. The 'uncle' now communicates the engagement to the chief, who causes the 'bans' to be published, that no other wooer may interfere. As the horse is with them the type of every important interest, the bridegroom next proceeds to kill the least valuable one that he is possessed of; and, taking out the heart, hangs it at the door of his betrothed, who takes and roasts it, and then dividing it into two parts, each eats a half, which perfects the bond of wedlock. The heart of the buffalo or other animal may perhaps be substituted, if the bridegroom has not a superabundance of horses. Should the circumstances of the parties admit of it, the marriage is usually celebrated with feasting and dances; though, in general, the Comanches are less fond of dancing than most other Indians.

The Comanche dress consists of the usual leggins, moccasins, flap and blanket or robe. Many wear in addition a kind of leathern jerkin, or tight jacket closed before. Their moccasins differ from those of other tribes, by having a lengthy tassel of leathern fringes attached to the heels, which trail the ground as they walk. Instead of this fringe, the tassel sometimes consists of the tail of a polecat or some other animal. When he can procure it, the young warrior is wont to wear a mantle and leggins of strouding. Both of these articles, according to the 'latest fashions,' should be one-half red, the other blue. The bi-colored mantle, as well as the blanket or buffalo rug, is carelessly thrown over the shoulders, and must be long enough to drag the ground; for they seem to have an instinct for the 'regal grandeur of a sweeping gown.'

Though all the far-western Indians wear their hair long, the Comanche seems to take most pride in the voluminousness of his 'tresses,' and the length of his *queue*, which is sometimes eked out with buffalo or other hair, till its tip reaches the ground, and is bedaubed with gum, grease and paint, and decorated with beads and other gewgaws. We are not to think that foppery and coxcombry are generated exclusively in civilized life. I am sure I never saw a vainer creature than a Comanche brave in full costume, of dress, trinkets and paint. He steps as if he disdained the very ground upon which he walks.

The dress of the Comanche squaw is usually a kind of loose gown or tunic of leather, or cotton if it can be procured, which hangs from the shoulders and is bound around the waist with a girdle; thus presenting a resemblance in its appearance to our ordinary female costume. They wear moccasins, to which short leggins are attached, and which constitute a sort of leathern hose. They are not permitted to wear long hair: that 'manly' prerogative would be degraded by such an association. It is therefore kept docked so as scarcely to reach the shoulders.

A style of dress similar to that of the Comanche females, is worn by those of most of the erratic tribes. The squaws of the north usually embroider their leathern frocks in a fanciful manner with colored porcupine quills and beads, and bedeck the borders with rattling shells, tags, hawk-bells, and the like. Such as have the fortune to marry Canadian or American trappers, are those who usually dress most gaily.

The prairie Indians generally are an equestrian race; yet in horsemanship the Comanches stand decidedly pre-eminent; and can only be equalled by the Northern Mexicans, and perhaps the Arabs. Like the latter, they dote upon their steeds: one had as well undertake to purchase a Comanche's child as his favorite riding-horse. They have a peculiar mark for their animals: every one which has pertained to them may always be recognized by a slit in the tip of each ear; a practice apparently universal among all their tribe.

In their warlike expeditions they avail themselves of their equestrian skill with wonderful success. As they always fight on horseback, they depend chiefly upon the charge, at which they use their arrows and javelins* with wonderful efficacy. On such occasions a Comanche will often throw himself upon the opposite side of his charger, so as to be protected from the darts of the enemy; and, while clinging there, he will discharge his arrows with extraordinary dexterity from underneath his horse's neck. Different from the 'prowling' tribes, they seldom attack at night, or in timbered or rough regions; for they would then be unable to manœuvre their coursers to advantage.

Although not meriting the title of brave Indians, they are held by the Mexicans as the most valiant of their border: but when they come in contact with Americans or any of our frontier tribes, they generally appear timid and cowardly. Their predatory forays are therefore directed mostly westward. They make continual inroads upon the whole eastern frontier of Mexico, from Chihuahua to the coast; driving off immense numbers of horses and mules, and killing the citizens they may encounter, or making them prisoners —particularly the females and boys. Of the latter they make

---

* The Comanches employ usually short-handled javelins or lances, declaring, like the Spartan mother, that cowards only need long weapons.

slaves, to perform such menial service as usually pertains to the squaws, particularly the herding of the stock. It is perhaps this alleviation of their labor by slaves, that has contributed to elevate the Comanche women above those of many of the northern tribes. Of their female captives they often make wives; a fate which has befallen some of those taken from Texas.

Strange as it may appear, their captives frequently become attached to their masters and to the savage life, and with difficulty are induced to leave them after a few years' captivity. In fact, these prisoners, it is said, in time often turn out to be the most formidable savages. Combining the subtlety of the Mexican with the barbarity of the Indian, they sometimes pilot into their native frontier and instigate horrid outrages. The department of Chihuahua has been the greatest sufferer from their inroads.

But, though at continual war with the south of the republic, for many years the Comanches have cultivated peace with the New Mexicans—not only because the poverty of the country offers fewer inducements for their inroads, but because it is desirable, as with the interior Mexican tribes, to retain some friendly point with which to keep an amicable intercourse and traffic. Parties of them have therefore sometimes entered the settlements of New Mexico for trading purposes; while every season numerous bands of New Mexicans, known as *Comancheros*, supplied with arms, ammunitions, trinkets, provisions and other necessities, launch upon the Prairies to barter for mules, and the different fruits of their ravages upon the South.

As these Indians always go to war on horseback, several days are often spent previous to a campaign in equestrian exercises and ceremonies, which seem partly to supply the place of the war-dance of other tribes; though they sometimes join in preparatory dances also. It is not an unusual custom, when a campaign is in agitation, for a band of about twenty Comanche maidens to chant, for three nights in succession, the victories of their ancestors, the valor of their brothers and contemporaries, and the individual prowess of all such young warriors as they consider should engage in the contemplated enterprise: and all those designated by the serenading band are held as drafted for the campaign. Fired by the encomiums and excitations of the 'fair *cantatrices*,' they fly at once to the standard of their favorite chief: and the ceremony is concluded by a war-dance.

Upon their return from a successful expedition, the 'war-worn corps' halts on some elevation at a distance from the village, and a herald is sent forward to announce their arrival. Thereupon, one of their most respectable and aged matrons issues forth to receive them, carrying with her a very long-handled lance kept for the purpose. On the top of this the victorious Indians fasten all the scalps they may have taken, so arranged that each shall be conspicuous. The matron squaw then approaches the wigwams, holding her scalp-garnished lance high in the air, and chanting some favorite war-legend. She is soon joined by other squaws and Indian lasses, who dance around as the procession moves through the entire circuit of the village. If the victory has been brilliant, the dancing and feasting are apt to be kept up for several days, all parties joining in the general jubilee.

If the conquerors bring any prisoners with them, these have to encounter the scourging and insults of the squaws and children. Each seems entitled to a blow, a kick, a pinch, a bite, or whatever simple punishment they may choose to inflict upon the unfortunate captives. This done, they are delivered over to the captors as slaves, and put to the service and drudgery of the camp.

After their first entrance it seems rare for them to treat their captives with much cruelty: though an instance was related to me by some Mexican prisoners, of a very barbarous massacre which they witnessed during their captivity. Two white men, supposed to be Texans, were tied to a stake, and a number of their marksmen, retiring to a distance and using the naked bodies of their victims as target, began wantonly to fire at them, and continued their horrid sport, until some fatal balls put an end to their sufferings! The capture of these had probably been attended with some aggravating circumstances, which induced the savages to resort to this cruel method of satiating their revenge.

If a campaign has been unsuccessful, the warriors separate upon their return, and drop into the village one by one. Nothing is now heard for several days, but the wailings and howlings of the bereft relatives and friends. They will also scarify their arms and legs, and subject themselves to other carnal mortifications of the most powerful character. On these occasions their previous captives, and particularly such as may belong to the nation of their victorious enemy, are sure to be roughly treated, and sometimes massacred by the enraged relatives of the slain.

When a Comanche dies, a similar course of mourning is prac-tised; and he is usually wrapped in his best blankets or robes, and interred with most of his 'jewelry' and other articles of esteem; accompanying which, it is said, an awl and some moccasin leather is generally added, as a provision, it would appear, for his use during his long journey to the 'happy hunting ground' beyond the grave. They also kill the favorite horses of the deceased, which are often buried by his side, doubtless with the same object.

The religious notions of the Comanches resemble, in most particulars, those of the other prairie tribes; yet they appear to have an occasional peculiarity. Some say the dry buffalo head or cranium is their idol. True it is that they show it great reverence, and use it in many of their mystic ceremonies. The Pawnees also hold these buffalo heads, with which the plains are strewed, in great reverence; and usually for many leagues around, these skulls are set up facing towards their villages, in the belief that the herds of buffalo will thus be conducted by them into their neighbor-hood. Of the Comanches the sun is no doubt the principal deity. When preparing for a campaign, it is said they do not fail to place their arms betimes every morning on the east side of their lodges, that they may receive the blessing of the fountain of light at his first appearance. This indeed seems the usual time for offering their devotions to the sun, of many tribes of the American aborigines.

21. Chihuahua

After passing the custom-house ordeal, and exchanging some of our merchandise for 'Eagle Dollars'—an operation which occu-pied us several weeks, I prepared to set out for the Chihuahua market, whither a portion of stock had been designed. Upon this expedition I was obliged to depart without my brother, who was laboring under the 'home fever,' and anxious to return to his family. "He that hath wife and children," says Lord Bacon, "hath given hostages to fortune; for they are impediments to great enterprises, either of virtue or mischief." Men under such bonds are peculiarly unfitted for the chequered life of a Santa Fé trader. The domestic hearth, with all its sacred and most endearing recollections, is sure to haunt them in the hour of trial, and almost every step of their journey is apt to be attended by melancholy reflections of home and domestic dependencies.

Before starting on this new journey I deem it proper to make a few observations relative to the general character of the *Chihuahua Trade*. I have already remarked, that much surprise has frequently been expressed by those who are unacquainted with all the bearings of the case, that the Missouri traders should take the circuitous route to Santa Fé, instead of steering direct for Chihuahua, inasmuch as the greatest portion of their goods is destined for the latter city. But as Chihuahua never had any port of entry for foreign goods till the last six or eight years, the market of that department had to be supplied in a great measure from Santa Fé. By opening the ports of El Paso and Presidio del Norte, the commercial interest was so little affected, that when Santa Anna's decree for closing them again was issued, the loss was scarcely felt at all.

The mode of transmitting merchandise from the ports to the interior, is very different from what it is in the United States. It is not enough to have to pass the tedious ordeal of custom-houses on the frontier;—we have not only to submit to a supervision and repayment of duty on arriving at our point of destination, but our cargo is subject to scrutiny at every town we have to pass through on our journey. Nor would it be advisable to forsake the main route in order to avoid this tyrannical system of taxation; because, according to the laws of the country, every *cargamento* which is found out of the regular track (except in cases of unavoidable necessity), is subject to confiscation, although accompanied by the necessary custom-house documents.

There are also other risks and contingencies very little dreamed of in the philosophy of the inexperienced trader. Before setting out, the entire bill of merchandise has to be translated into Spanish; when, duplicates of the translation being presented to the custom-house, one is retained, while the other, accompanied by the *guia* (a sort of clearance or mercantile passport), is carried along with the cargo by the conductor. The trader can have three points of destination named in his *guia,* to either of which he may direct his course, but to no others: while in the drawing up of the *factura,* or invoice, the greatest care is requisite, as the slightest mistake, even an accidental slip of the pen, might, according to the terms of the law, subject the goods to confiscation.

The *guia* is not only required on leaving the ports for the interior, but is indispensable to the safe conveyance of goods from one department of the republic to another: nay, the simple transfer of property from town to town, and from village to village, in the same department, is attended by precisely the same proportion of risk, and requires the same punctilious accuracy in the accompanying documents. Even the produce and manufactures of the country are equally subject to these embarrassing regulations. New Mexico has no internal custom-houses, and is therefore exempt from this rigorous provision; but from Chihuahua south every village has its revenue officers; so that the same stock of merchandise sometimes pays the internal duty at least half-a-dozen times before the sale is completed.

Now, to procure this same *guia*, which is the cause of so much difficulty and anxiety in the end, is no small affair. Before the authorities condescend to draw a single line on paper, the merchant must produce an endorser for the *tornaguía*, which is a certificate from the custom-house to which the cargo goes directed, showing that the goods have been legally entered there. A failure in the return of this document within a prescribed limit of time, subjects the endorser to a forfeiture equal to the amount of the impost. Much inconvenience and not a little risk are also occasioned on this score by the irregularity—I may say, insecurity of the mails.

Speaking of mails, I beg leave to observe, that there are no conveniences of this kind in New Mexico, except on the route from Santa Fé to Chihuahua, and these are very irregular and uncertain. Before the Indians had obtained such complete possession of the highways through the wilderness, the mails between these two cities were carried semi-monthly; but now they are much less frequent, being mere expresses, in fact, dispatched only when an occasion offers. There are other causes, however, besides the dread of marauding savages, which render the the transportation of the mails in New Mexico very insecure: I mean the dishonesty of those employed in superintending them. Persons known to be inimical to the post-master, or to the 'powers that be,' and wishing to forward any communication to the South, most generally either wait for a private conveyance, or send their letters to a post-office (the only one besides that of Santa Fé in all New Mexico) some eighty miles on the way; thus avoiding an overhauling at the capital. Moreover, as the post-rider often carries the key of the mail-bag (for want of a supply at the different offices), he not unfrequently permits whomsoever will pay him a trifling *douceur*, to examine the correspondence. I was once witness to a case of this kind in the Jornada del Muerto, where the entire mail was tumbled out upon the grass, that an individual might search for letters, for which luxury he was charged by the accommodating carrier the moderate price of one dollar.

Having at last gone through with all the vexatious preparations necessary for our journey, on the 22d of August we started for Chihuahua. I fitted out myself but six wagons for this market, yet joining in company with several other traders, our little caravan again amounted to fourteen wagons, with about forty men. Though our route lay through the interior of Northern Mexico, yet, on account of the hostile savages which infest most of the country through which we had to pass, it was necessary to unite in caravans of respectable strength, and to spare few of those precautions for safety which are required on the Prairies.

The road we travelled passes down through the settlements of New Mexico for the first hundred and thirty miles, on the east side of the Rio del Norte. Nevertheless, as there was not an inn of any kind to be found upon the whole route, we were constrained to put up with very primitive accommodations. Being furnished from the outset, therefore, with blankets and buffalo rugs for bedding, we were prepared to bivouac, even in the suburbs of the villages, in the open air; for in this dry and salubrious atmosphere it is seldom that travellers go to the trouble of pitching tents.* When travelling alone, however, or with but a comrade or two, I have always experienced a great deal of hospitality from the rancheros and villageois of the country. Whatever sins these

---

* How scant soever our outfit of 'camp comforts' might appear, our Mexican muleteers were much more sparely supplied. The exposure endured by this hardy race is really surprising. Even in the coldest winter weather, they rarely carry more than one blanket apiece—the *sarape*, which serves as a cloak during the day, and at night is their only 'bed and bedding.'

ignorant people may have to answer for, we must accord to them at least two glowing virtues—gratitude and hospitality. I have suffered like others, however, from one very disagreeable custom which prevails among them. Instead of fixing a price for the services they bestow upon travellers, they are apt to answer, "*Lo que guste,*" or "*Lo que le dé la gana*" (whatever you please, or have a mind to give), expecting, of course, that the liberal foreigner will give more than their consciences would permit them to exact.

In about ten days' drive we passed the southernmost settlements of New Mexico, and twenty or thirty miles further down the river we came to the ruins of Valverde. This village was founded about twenty years ago, in one of the most fertile valleys of the Rio del Norte. It increased rapidly in population, until it was invaded by the Navajoes, when the inhabitants were obliged to abandon the place after considerable loss, and it has never since been repeopled. The bottoms of the valley, many of which are of rich alluvial loam, have lain fallow ever since, and will perhaps continue to be neglected until the genius of civilization shall have spread its beneficent influences over the land. This soil is the more valuable for cultivation on account of the facilities for irrigation which the river affords; as it too frequently happens that the best lands of the settlements remain unfruitful for want of water.

Our next camping place deserving of mention was *Fray Cristóbal,* which, like many others on the route, is neither town nor village, but a simple isolated point on the river-bank—a mere *parage,* or camping-ground.

We arrived at Fray Cristóbal in the evening, but this being the threshold of the famous *Jornada del Muerto,* we deemed it prudent to let our animals rest here until the following afternoon. The road over which we had hitherto been travelling, though it sometimes traverses upland ridges and undulating sections, runs generally near the border of the river, and for the most part in its immediate valley: but here it leaves the river and passes for nearly eighty miles over a table-plain to the eastward of a small ledge of mountains, whose western base is hugged by the circuitous channel of the Rio del Norte. The craggy cliffs which project from these mountains render the eastern bank of the river altogether impassable. As the direct route over the plain is entirely destitute of water, we took the precaution to fill all our kegs at Fray Cristóbal, and late in the afternoon we finally set out. We generally find a great advantage in travelling through these arid tracts of land in the freshness of the evening, as the mules suffer less from thirst, and move on in better spirits—particularly in the season of warm weather.

Early the next morning we found ourselves at the *Laguna del Muerto*, or 'Dead Man's Lake,' where there was not even a vestige of water. This *lake* is but a sink in the plain of a few rods in diameter, and only filled with water during the rainy season. The *marshes*, which are said by some historians to be in this vicinity, are nowhere to be found: nothing but the firmest and driest table land is to be seen in every direction. To procure water for our thirsty animals, it is often necessary to make a halt here, and drive them to the *Ojo del Muerto* (Dead Man's Spring), five or six miles to the westward, in the very heart of the mountain ridge that lay between us and the river. This region is one of the favorite resorts of the Apaches, where many a poor arriero has met with an untimely end. The route which leads to the spring winds for two or three miles down a narrow cañon or gorge, overhung on either side by abrupt precipices, while the various clefts and crags, which project their gloomy brows over the abyss below, seem to invite the murderous savage to deeds of horror and blood.

There is a tradition among the arrieros from which it would appear that the only road known in ancient time about the region of the *Jornada*, wound its circuitous course on the western side of the river. To save distance, an intrepid traveller undertook to traverse this desolate tract of land in one day, but having perished in the attempt, it has ever after borne the name of *La Jornada del Muerto*, 'the Dead Man's Journey,' or, more strictly, 'the Day's Journey of the Dead Man.' One thing appears very certain, that this dangerous pass has cost the life of many travellers in days of yore; and when we at last reached Robledo, a camping-site upon the river, where we found abundance of wood and water, we felt truly grateful that the arid *Jornada* had not been productive of more serious consequences to our party. We now found ourselves within the department of Chihuahua, as the boundary betwixt it and New Mexico passes not far from Robledo.

We were still some sixty miles above Paso del Norte, but the balance of the road now led down the river valley or over the low bordering hills. During our journey between this and El Paso we passed the ruins of several settlements, which had formerly been the seat of opulence and prosperity, but which have since been abandoned in consequence of the marauding incursions of the Apaches.

On the 12th of September we reached the usual ford of the Rio del Norte, six miles above El Paso; but the river being somewhat flushed we found it impossible to cross over with our wagons. The reader will no doubt be surprised to learn that there is not a single ferry on this 'Great River of the North' till we approach the mouth. But how do people cross it? Why, during three-fourths of the year it is everywhere fordable, and when the freshet season comes on, each has to remain on his own side or swim, for canoes even are very rare. But as we could neither swim our wagons and merchandise, nor very comfortably wait for the falling of the waters, our only alternative was to unload the vehicles, and ferry the goods over in a little 'dug-out' about thirty feet long and two feet wide, of which we were fortunate enough to obtain possession.

We succeeded in finding a place shallow enough to haul our empty wagons across: but for this good fortune we should have been under the necessity of taking them to pieces (as I had before done), and of ferrying them on the 'small craft' before mentioned. Half of a wagon may thus be crossed at a time, by carefully balancing it upon the canoe, yet there is of course no little danger of capsizing during the passage.

On the 14th we made our entrance into the town of *El Paso del Norte*, which is the northernmost settlement in the department of Chihuahua. Here our cargo had to be examined by a stern, surly officer, who, it was feared, would lay an embargo on our goods upon the slightest appearance of irregularity in our papers; but notwithstanding our gloomy forebodings, we passed the ordeal without any difficulty.

After leaving El Paso, our road branched off at an angle of

about two points to the westward of the river, the city of Chihuahua being situated nearly a hundred miles to the west of it. At the distance of about thirty miles we reached *Los Médanos*, a stupendous ledge of sand-hills, across which the road passes for about six miles. As teams are never able to haul the loaded wagons over this region of loose sand, we engaged an *atajo* of mules at El Paso, upon which to convey our goods across. These Médanos consist of huge hillocks and ridges of pure sand, in many places without a vestige of vegetation. Through the lowest gaps between the hills, the road winds its way.

What renders this portion of the route still more unpleasant and fatiguing, is the great scarcity of water. All that is to be found on the road for the distance of more than sixty miles after leaving El Paso, consists in two fetid springs or pools, whose water is only rendered tolerable by necessity. A little further on, however, we very unexpectedly encountered, this time, quite a superabundance of this necessary element. Just as we passed Lake Patos, we were struck with astonishment at finding the road ahead of us literally overflowed by an immense body of water, with a brisk current, as if some great river had suddenly been conjured into existence by the aid of supernatural arts. A considerable time elapsed before we could unravel the mystery. At last we discovered that a freshet had lately occurred in the streams that fed Lake Patos, and caused it to overflow its banks, which accounted for this unwelcome visitation. We had to flounder through the mud and water for several hours, before we succeeded in getting across.

The following day we reached the *acequia* below Carrizal, a small village with only three or four hundred inhabitants, but somewhat remarkable as being the site of a *presidio* (fort), at which is stationed a company of troops to protect the country against the ravages of the Apaches, who, notwithstanding, continue to lay waste the ranchos in the vicinity, and to depredate at will within the very sight of the fort.

About twelve miles south of Carrizal there is one of the most charming warm springs called Ojo Caliente, where we arrived the next day. It forms a basin some thirty feet long by about half that width, and just deep and warm enough for a most delightful bath at all seasons of the year. Were this spring (whose outlet forms a bold rivulet) anywhere within the United States, it would doubtless soon be converted into a place of fashionable resort. There appears to be a somewhat curious phenomenon connected with this spring. It proceeds, no doubt, from the little river of Cármen which passes within half a mile, and finally discharges itself into the small lake of Patos before mentioned. All the water of this stream disappears in the sand several miles above the spring; and what medium it traverses in its subterranean passage to impart to it so high a temperature, before breaking out in this fountain, would afford to the geologist an interesting subject of inquiry.

After fording the Rio Cármen, which, though usually without a drop of water in its channel, we now found a very turbulent stream, we did not meet with any object particularly worthy of remark, until we reached the *Laguna de Encinillas*. This lake is ten or twelve miles long by two or three in width, and seems to have no outlet even during the greatest freshets, though fed by several small constant-flowing streams from the surrounding mountains. The water of this lake during the dry season is so strongly impregnated with nauseous and bitter salts, as to render it wholly unpalatable to man and beast. The most predominant of these noxious substances is a species of alkali, known there by the title of *tequesquite*. It is often seen oozing out from the surface of marshy grounds, about the table plains of all Northern Mexico, forming a grayish crust, and is extensively used in the manufacture of soap, and sometimes by the bakers even for raising bread. Here we had another evidence of the alarming effects of the recent flood, the road for several miles along the margin of the lake being completely inundated. It was, however, in the city of Chihuahua itself that the disastrous consequences of the freshet were most severely felt. Some inferior houses of *adobe* were so much soaked by the rains, that they tumbled to the ground, occasioning the loss of several lives.

The valley of Encinillas is very extensive and fertile, and is the locale of one of those princely estates which are so abundant further south, and known by the name of *Haciendas*. It abounds in excellent pasturage, and in cattle of all descriptions. In former times, before the Apaches had so completely devastated the country, the herds which grazed in this beautiful valley presented much the appearance of the buffalo of the plains, being almost as wild and generally of dark color. Many of the proprietors of these princely haciendas pride themselves in maintaining a uniformity in the color of their cattle: thus some are found stocked with black, others red, others white—or whatsoever shade the owner may have taken a fancy to.

As we drew near to Chihuahua, our party had more the appearance of a funeral procession than of a band of adventurers about to enter into the full fruition of 'dancing hopes,' and the realization of 'golden dreams.' Every one was uneasy as to what might be the treatment of the revenue officers. For my own part, I had not quite forgotten sundry annoyances and trials of temper I had been made to experience in the season of 1837, on a similar occasion. Much to our surprise, however, as well as delight, we were handled with a degree of leniency by the custom-house deities, on our arrival, that was almost incomprehensible. But the charm which operated in our favor, when understood, was very simple. A caravan had left Chihuahua direct for the United States the spring previous, and was daily expected back. The officers of the custom-house were already compromised by certain cogent arguments to receive the proprietors of this caravan with striking marks of favor, and the *Señor Administrador de Rentas*, Zuloaga himself, was expecting an *ancheta* of goods. Therefore, had they treated us with their wonted severity, the contrast would have been altogether too glaring.

We arrived at Chihuahua on the first of October, after a trip of forty days, with wagons much more heavily laden than when we started from the United States.

It is usual for each trader, upon his arrival in that city, to engage a store-room, and to open and exhibit his goods, as well for the purpose of disposing of them at wholesale as retail. His most profitable custom is that of the petty country merchants from the surrounding villages. Some traders, it is true, continue in the retail business for a season or more, yet the greater portion are transient dealers, selling off at wholesale as soon as a fair bargain is offered.

The usual mode of selling by the lot in Chihuahua is somewhat singular. All such cottons as calicoes and other prints, bleached, brown and blue domestics both plain and twilled, stripes, checks, etc., are rated at two or three *reales* per *vara*, without the least reference to quality or cost, and the 'general assortment' at 60 to 100 per cent upon the bills of cost, according to the demand. The *varage* is usually estimated by adding eight per cent to the yardage, but the *vara* being thirty-three inches (nearly), the actual difference is more than nine. In these sales, cloths—indeed all measurable goods, except ribands and the like, sometimes enter at the *varage* rate. I have heard of some still more curious contracts in these measurement sales, particularly in Santa Fé, during the early periods of the American trade. Everything was sometimes rated by the vara—not only all textures, but even hats, cutlery, trinkets, and so on! In such cases, very singular disputes would frequently arise as to the mode of measuring some particular articles: for instance, whether pieces of riband should be measured in bulk, or unrolled, and yard by yard; looking glasses, cross or lengthwise; pocketknives, shut or open; writing-paper, in the ream, in the quire, or by the single sheet; and then, whether the longer or shorter way of the paper; and many others.

Before the end of October, 1839, I had an opportunity of selling out my stock of goods to a couple of English merchants, which relieved me from the delays, to say nothing of the inconveniences attending a retail trade: such, for instance, as the accumulation of copper coin, which forms almost the exclusive currency in petty dealings. Some thousands of dollars' worth are frequently accumulated upon the hands of the merchant in this way, and as the copper of one department is worthless in another, except for its intrinsic value, which is seldom more than ten per cent of the nominal value, the holders are subjected to a great deal of trouble and annoyance.

With regard to the city, there is but little to be said that is either very new or unusually interesting. When compared with Santa Fé and all the towns of the North, Chihuahua might indeed be pronounced a magnificent place; but, compared with the nobler cities of *tierra afuera*, it sinks into insignificance. According to Capt. Pike, the city of Chihuahua was founded in 1691. The ground-plan is much more regular than that of Santa Fé, while a much greater degree of elegance and classic taste has been exhibited in the style of the architecture of many buildings; for though the bodies be of *adobe*, all the best houses are cornered with hewn stone, and the doors and windows are framed in the same. The streets, however, remain nearly in the same state as Nature formed them, with the exception of a few roughly-paved side-walks. Although situated about a hundred miles east of the main chain of the Mexican Cordilleras, Chihuahua is surrounded on every side by detached ridges of mountains, but none of them of any great magnitude. The elevation of the city above the ocean is between four and five thousand feet; its latitude is 28° 36'; and its entire population numbers about ten thousand souls.

The most splendid edifice in Chihuahua is the principal church, which is said to equal in architectural grandeur anything of the sort in the republic. The steeples, of which there is one at each front corner, rise over a hundred feet above the azotea. They are composed of very fancifully-carved columns; and in appropriate niches of the frontispiece, which is also an elaborate piece of sculpture, are to be seen a number of statues, as large as life, the whole forming a complete representation of Christ and the twelve Apostles. This church was built about a century ago, by contributions levied upon the mines (particularly those of Santa Eulalia, fifteen or twenty miles from the city), which paid over a per centage on all the metal extracted therefrom; a *medio*, I believe, being levied upon each *marco* of eight ounces. In this way, about a million of dollars was raised and expended in some thirty years, the time employed in the construction of the building.

No better evidence can be found of the extensive operations which have been carried on in this the greatest mining district of Northern Mexico, than in the little mountains of *scoria* which are found in the suburbs of the city. A great number of poor laborers make a regular business of hammering to pieces these metallic excrescences, from which they collect silver enough to buy their daily bread. An opinion has often been expressed by persons well acquainted with the subject, that a fair business might be done by working this same scoria over again. There are still in operation several furnaces in the city, where silver ores extracted from the mines of the surrounding mountains are smelted. There is also a rough mint in Chihuahua (as there is indeed in all the mining departments), yet most of its silver and all of its gold have been coined in the cities further south.

When I arrived at Chihuahua, in 1839, a great fête had just come off for the double purpose of celebrating the anniversary of the Emperor Iturbide's birth day (Sept. 27, 1783), and that of his triumphal entrance into the city of Mexico in 1821. It will be remembered, that, after Mexico had been struggling for independence several years, General Iturbide, who had remained a faithful officer of the crown, and an active agent in persecuting the champions of Mexican liberty, finding himself, about the close of 1820, at the head of a large division of the royal army sent against the patriot Guerrero, suddenly turned over his whole force to the support of the republican cause, and finally succeeded in destroying the last vestige of Spanish authority in Mexico. How he was afterwards crowned emperor, and subsequently dethroned, outlawed by a public decree and eventually executed, is all matter of history. But it is not generally known, I believe, that this unfortunate soldier has since received the honors of the Father of the Republic, a dignity to which he was probably as much entitled as any one else—absurd though the adoption of such a hero as the 'champion of liberty,' may appear to 'republicans of the Jefferson school.' A *grande fête d'hilarité* takes place annually, in honor of his political canonization, which 'comes off' at the date already mentioned. To this great ball, however, no Americans were invited, with the exception of a Mexicanized denizen or two, whose invitation tickets informed the *honored party* that the price of admission to this famous feast,—a ball given by the governor and other magnates of the land, in honor of the hero of independence, —was twenty-five dollars.

Balls or reunions of this kind, however, seem not as frequent in Chihuahua as in New Mexico: and to those we hear of, claiming the title of 'fashionable,' Americans are very rarely invited. There is, in fact, but little social intercourse between foreigners and the natives, except in a business way, or with a certain class of the former, at the gambling-table. This want of hospitable feelings is one of the worst traits in the character of the Chihuahueños, and when placed in contrast with the kind and courteous treatment those who visit the United States invariably experience from the lawgivers of fashion among us, their illiberality will appear a hundred fold more ungracious. These exclusive laws are the more severely felt in Chihuahua, because in that city there are no *cafés*, nor reading rooms, nor in short any favorite public resorts, except of a gambling character, at which gentlemen can meet to lounge or amuse themselves.

Besides the cock-pit, the gaming-table, and the *Alameda*, which is the popular promenade for the wealthy and the indolent, one of the most favorite pastimes of the females generally is shopping; and the most fashionable time for this is by candle-light, after they have partaken of their chocolate and their *cigarritos*. The streets and shops are literally filled from dusk till nine or ten o'clock; and many a time have I seen the counter of a store actually lined till a later hour, with the fairest and most fashionable señoritas of the city. On such occasions it is not a little painful as well as troublesome to be compelled to keep a strict eye to the rights of property, not that the dealers are all dishonest, but because there never fail to be some present who are painfully afflicted with the self-appropriating mania, even among the fairest-looking señoritas. This, with other purposes no less culpable, has no doubt tended to establish the custom of night-shopping.

Having closed all my affairs in Chihuahua and completed my preparations for departing, I took my leave of that city for the North, on the 31st of October, 1839, and on the 6th of December we reached Santa Fé, in fine health and spirits.

22. The Return Home

About the beginning of February, 1840, and just as I was making preparations to return to the United States, the small-pox broke out among my men in a manner, which at first occasioned at least as much astonishment as alarm. One of them, who had travelled in a neighboring district, where there were some cases of small-pox, complained of a little fever, which was followed by slight eruptions, but so unlike true variolous pustules, that I treated the matter very lightly; not even suspecting a varioloid. These slight symptoms having passed off, nothing more was thought of it until eight or ten days after, when every unvaccinated member of our company was attacked by that fell disease, which soon began to manifest very malignant features. There were no fatal cases, however; yet much apprehension was felt, lest the disease should break out again on the route; but, to our great joy, we escaped the second scourge.

On the 25th of February we set out from Santa Fé; but owing to some delays, we did not leave San Miguel till the 1st of March. As the pasturage was yet insufficient for our animals, we here provided ourselves with over six hundred bushels of corn, to feed them on the way. This time our caravan consisted of twenty-eight wagons, two small cannons, and forty-seven men, including sixteen Mexicans and a Comanche Indian who acted in the capacity of guide.*

Instead of following the trail of the year before, I determined to seek a nearer and better route down the south side of the Canadian river, under the guidance of the Comanche; by which movement, we had again to travel a distance of four hundred miles over an entirely new country. We had just passed the Laguna Colorada, where, the following year, a division of Texan volunteers, under General McLeod, surrendered to Col. Archuleta, when our fire was carelessly permitted to communicate with the prairie grass. As there was a head-wind blowing at the time, we very soon got out of reach of the conflagration: but the next day, the wind having changed, the fire was again perceived in our rear approaching us at a very brisk pace. The terror which these prairie conflagrations are calculated to inspire, when the grass is tall and dry, as was the case in the present instance, has often been described, and though the perils of these disasters are not unfrequently exaggerated, they are sometimes sufficient to daunt the stoutest heart. Mr. Kendall relates a frightful incident of this kind which occurred to the Texan Santa Fé Expedition; and all those who have crossed the Prairies have had more or less experience as to the danger which occasionally threatens the caravans from these sweeping visitations. The worst evil to be apprehended with those bound for Santa Fé is from the explosion of gun-powder, as a keg or two of twenty-five pounds each, is usually to be found in

---

* Manuel *el Comanche* was a full Indian, born and bred upon the great prairies. Long after having arrived at the state of manhood, he accompanied some Mexican *Comancheros* to the frontier village of San Miguel, where he fell in love with a Mexican girl—married her—and has lived in that place, a sober, 'civilized' citizen for the last ten or twelve years—endowed with much more goodness of heart and integrity of purpose than a majority of his Mexican neighbors. He had learned to speak Spanish quite intelligibly, and was therefore an excellent Comanche interpreter: and being familiar with every part of the prairies, he was very serviceable as a guide.

every wagon. When we saw the fire gaining so rapidly upon us, we had to use the whip very unsparingly; and it was only when the lurid flames were actually rolling upon the heels of our teams, that we succeeded in reaching a spot of short-grass prairies, where there was no further danger to be apprehended.

The headway of the conflagration was soon after checked by a small stream which traversed our route; and we had only emerged fairly from its smoke, on the following day (the 9th), when our Comanche guide returned hastily from his accustomed post in advance, and informed us that he had espied three buffaloes, not far off. They were the first we had met with, and, being heartily anxious for a change from the dried beef with which we were provided, I directed the Comanche, who was by far our surest hunter, to prepare at once for the *chasse*. He said he preferred to hunt on horseback and with his bow and arrow; and believing my riding-horse the fleetest in company (which, by the by, was but a common pony, and thin in flesh withal), I dismounted and gave him the bridle, with many charges to treat him kindly, as we still had a long journey before us. "Don't attempt to kill but one—that will serve us for the present!" I exclaimed, as he galloped off. The Comanche was among the largest of his tribe—bony and muscular —weighing about two hundred pounds: but once at his favorite sport, he very quickly forgot my injunction, as well as the weakness of my little pony. He soon brought down two of his game— and shyly remarked to those who followed in his wake, that, had he not feared a scolding from me, he would not have permitted the third to escape.

On the evening of the 10th our camp was pitched in the neighborhood of a ravine in the prairie, and as the night was dark and dreary, the watch tried to comfort themselves by building a rousing fire, around which they presently drew, and commenced 'spinning long yarns' about Mexican fandangoes, and black-eyed damsels. All of a sudden the stillness of the night was interrupted by a loud report of fire-arms, and a shower of bullets came whizzing by the ears of the heedless sentinels. Fortunately, however, no one was injured; which must be looked upon as a very extraordinary circumstance, when we consider what a fair mark our men, thus huddled round a blazing fire, presented to the rifles of the Indians. The savage yells, which resounded from every part of the ravine, bore very satisfactory testimony that this was no false alarm; and the 'Pawnee whistle' which was heard in every quarter, at once impressed us with the idea of its being a band of that famous prairie banditti.

Every man sprang from his pallet with rifle in hand; for, upon the Prairies, we always sleep with our arms by our sides or under our heads. Our Comanche seemed at first very much at a loss what to do. At last, thinking it might possibly be a band of his own nation, he began a most boisterous harangue in his vernacular tongue, which he continued for several minutes; when finding that the enemy took no notice of him, and having become convinced also, from an occasional Pawnee word which he was able to make out, that he had been wasting breath with the mortal foes of his race, he suddenly ceased all expostulations, and blazed away with his rifle, with a degree of earnestness which was truly edifying, as if convinced that that was the best he could do for us.

It was now evident that the Indians had taken possession of the entire ravine, the nearest points of which were not fifty yards from our wagons: a warning to prairie travellers to encamp at a greater distance from whatsoever might afford shelter for an enemy. The banks of the gully were low, but still they formed a very good breastwork, behind which the enemy lay ensconced, discharging volleys of balls upon our wagons, among which we were scattered. At one time we thought of making an attempt to rout them from their fortified position; but being ignorant of their number, and unable to distinguish any object through the dismal darkness which hung all around, we had to remain content with firing at random from behind our wagons, aiming at the flash of their guns, or in the direction whence any noise appeared to emanate. Indeed their yelling was almost continuous, breaking out every now and then in the most hideous screams and vociferous chattering, which were calculated to appal such timorous persons as we may have had in our caravan. All their screeching and whooping, however, had no effect—they could not make our animals break from the enclosure of the wagons, in which they were fortunately shut up; which was no doubt their principal object for attacking us.

Although sundry scores of shots had been fired at our people, we had only two men wounded. One, a Mexican, was but slightly injured in the hand, but the wound of the other, who was an Italian, bore a more serious aspect, and deserves especial mention. He was a short, corpulent fellow, and had been nicknamed 'Dutch'—a loquacious, chicken-hearted *fainéant*, and withal in the daily habit of gorging himself to such an enormous extent, that every alternate night he was on the sick list. On this memorable occasion, Dutch had 'foundered' again, and the usual prescription of a double dose of Epsom salts had been his supper potion. The skirmish had continued for about an hour, and although a frightful groaning had been heard in Dutch's wagon for some time, no one paid any attention to it, as it was generally supposed to be from the effects of his dose. At length, however, some one cried out, "Dutch is wounded!" I immediately went to see him, and found him writhing and twisting himself as if in great pain, crying all the time that he was shot. "Shot!—where?" I inquired. "Ah! in the head, sir?" "Pshaw! Dutch, none of that; you've only bumped your head in trying to hide yourself." Upon lighting a match, however, I found that a ball had passed through the middle of his hat, and that, to my consternation, the top of his head was bathed in blood. It turned out, upon subsequent examination, that the ball had glanced upon the skull, inflicting a serious-looking wound, and so deep that an inch of sound skin separated the holes at which the bullet had entered and passed out. Notwithstanding I at first apprehended a fracture of the skull, it very soon healed, and Dutch was 'up and about' again in the course of a week.

Although teachers not unfrequently have cause to deplore the thickness of their pupils' skulls, Dutch had every reason to congratulate himself upon possessing such a treasure, as it had evidently preserved him from a more serious catastrophe. It appeared he had taken shelter in his wagon at the commencement of the attack, without reflecting that the boards and sheets were not ball-proof: and as Indians, especially in the night, are apt to shoot too high, he was in a much more dangerous situation than if upon the ground.

The enemy continued the attack for nearly three hours, when they finally retired, so as to make good their retreat before daylight. As it rained and snowed from that time till nine in the morning, their 'sign' was almost entirely obliterated, and we were unable to discover whether they had received any injury or not. It was evidently a foot party, which we looked upon as another proof of their being Pawnees; for these famous marauders are well known to go forth on their expeditions of plunder without horses, although they seldom fail to return well mounted.

Their shot had riddled our wagons considerably: in one we counted no less than eight bullet-holes. We had the gratification to believe, however, that they did not get a single one of our animals: the horse which broke away at the first onset, doubtless made his escape; and a mule which was too badly wounded to travel, was dispatched by the muleteers, lest it should fall into the hands of the savages, or into the mouths of the wolves; and they deemed it more humane to leave it to be eaten dead than alive. We also experienced considerable damage in our stock of sheep, a number of them having been devoured by wolves. They had been scattered at the beginning of the attack; and, in their anxiety to fly from the scene of action, had jumped, as it were, into the very jaws of their ravenous enemies.

On the 12th of March, we ascended upon the celebrated *Llano Estacado,* and continued along its borders for a few days. The second night upon this dreary plain, we experienced one of the strongest and bleakest 'northwesters' that ever swept across those prairies; during which, our flock of sheep and goats, being left unattended, fled over the plain, in search of some shelter, it was supposed, from the furious element. Their disappearance was not observed for some time, and the night being too dark to discern anything, we were obliged to defer going in pursuit of them till the following morning. After a fruitless and laborious search, during which the effects of the mirage proved a constant source of annoyance and disappointment, we were finally obliged to relinquish the pursuit, and return to the caravan without finding one of them.

These severe winds are very prevalent upon the great western prairies, though they are seldom quite so inclement. At some seasons, they are about as regular and unceasing as the 'trade winds' of the ocean. It will often blow a gale for days, and even weeks together, without slacking for a moment, except occasionally at night. It is for this reason, as well as on account of the rains, that percussion guns are preferable upon the Prairies, particularly for those who understand their use. The winds are frequently so severe as to sweep away both sparks and priming from a flint lock, and thus render it wholly ineffective.

The following day we continued our march down the border of the Llano Estacado. Knowing that our Comanche guide was about as familiar with all those great plains as a landlord with his premises, I began to question him, as we travelled along, concerning the different streams which pierced them to the southward. Pointing in that direction, he said there passed a water-course, at the distance of a hard day's ride, which he designated as a *cañada* or valley, in which there was always water to be found at occasional places, but that none flowed in its channel except during the rainy season. This cañada he described as having its origin in the Llano Estacado some fifty or sixty miles east of Rio Pecos, and about the same distance south of the route we came, and that its direction was a little south of east, passing to the southward of the northern portion of the Witchita mountains, known to Mexican Ciboleros and Comancheros as *Sierra Jumanes*. It was, therefore, evident that this was the principal northern branch of Red River. The False Washita, or *Rio Negro*, as the Mexicans call it, has its rise, as he assured me, between the Canadian and this cañada, at no great distance to the southeastward of where we were then travelling.

On the 15th, our Comanche guide, being fearful lest we should find no water upon the plain, advised us to pursue a more northwardly course, so that, after a hard day's ride, we again descended the *ceja* or brow of the Llano Estacado, into the undulating lands which border the Canadian; and, on the following day, we found ourselves upon the southern bank of that stream.

Although, but a few days' travel above where we now were, the Canadian runs pent up in a narrow channel, scarcely four rods across, we here found it spread out to the width of from three to six hundred yards, and so full of sand-bars (only interspersed with narrow rills) as to present the appearance of a mere sandy valley instead of the bed of a river. In fact, during the driest seasons, the water wholly disappears in many places. Notwithstanding it presents the face of one of the greatest rivers of the west during freshets, yet even then it would not be navigable on account of its rapidity and shallowness. It would appear almost incredible to those unacquainted with the prairie streams, that a river of about 1500 miles in length, and whose head wears a cap of perennial snow (having its source in the Rocky Mountains), should scarcely be navigable, for even the smallest craft, over fifty miles above its mouth.

We pursued our course down the same side of the river for several days, during which time we crossed a multitude of little streams which flowed into the Canadian from the adjoining plains, while others presented nothing but dry beds of sand. One of these was so remarkable, on account of its peculiarity and size, that we named it 'Dry River.' The bed was at least 200 yards wide, yet without a vestige of water; notwithstanding, our guide assured us that it was a brisk-flowing stream some leagues above: and from the drift-wood along its borders, it was evident that, even here, it must be a considerable river during freshets.

While travelling down the course of the Canadian, we sometimes found the buffalo very abundant. On one occasion, two or three hunters, who were a little in advance of the caravan, perceiving a herd quietly grazing in an open glade, they 'crawled upon' them after the manner of the 'still hunters.' Their first shot having brought down a fine fat cow, they slipped up behind her, and, resting their guns over her body, shot two or three others, without occasioning any serious disturbance or surprise to their companions; for, extraordinary as it may appear, if the buffalo neither see nor smell the hunter, they will pay but little attention to the crack of guns, or to the mortality which is being dealt among them.

The slaughter of these animals is frequently carried to an excess, which shows the depravity of the human heart in very bold relief. Such is the excitement that generally prevails at the sight of these fat denizens of the prairies, that very few hunters appear able to refrain from shooting as long as the game remains within reach of their rifles; nor can they ever permit a fair shot to escape them. Whether the mere pleasure of taking life is the incentive of these brutal excesses, I will not pretend to decide; but one thing is very certain, that the buffalo killed yearly on these prairies far exceeds the wants of the traveller, or what might be looked upon as the exigencies of rational sport.*

Not long after crossing Dry River, we ascended the high grounds, and soon found ourselves upon the high ridge which divides the waters of the Canadian and False Washita, whose 'breaks' could be traced descending from the Llano Estacado far to the southwest.

By an observation of an eclipse of one of Jupiter's satellites, on the night of the 25th of March, in latitude 35° 51′ 30″, I found that we were very near the 100th degree of longitude west from Greenwich. On the following day, therefore, we celebrated our entrance into the United States territory. Those who have never been beyond the purlieus of the land of their nativity, can form but a poor conception of the joy which the wanderer in distant climes experiences on treading once more upon his own native soil! Although we were yet far from the abodes of civilization, and further still from home, nevertheless the heart within us thrilled with exhilarating sensations; for we were again in our own territory, breathed our own free atmosphere, and were fairly out of reach of the arbitrary power which we had left behind us.

As we continued our route upon this narrow dividing ridge, we could not help remarking how nearly these streams approach each other: in one place they seemed scarcely five miles apart. On this account our Comanche guide, as well as several Mexicans of our party, who had some acquaintance with these prairies, gave it as their opinion that the Washita or *Rio Negro* was in fact a branch of the Canadian; for its confluence with Red River was beyond the bounds of their peregrinations.

As the forest of Cross Timbers was now beginning to be seen in the distance, and fearing we might be troubled to find a pass-way through this brushy region, south of the Canadian, we forded this river on the 29th, without the slightest trouble, and very soon entered our former trail, a little west of Spring Valley. This gave a

* The same barbarous propensity is observable in regard to wild horses. Most persons appear unable to restrain this wanton inclination to take life, when a mustang approaches within rifle-shot. Many a stately steed thus falls a victim to the cruelty of man.

new and joyful impulse to our spirits; for we had been travelling over twenty days without even a trail, and through a region of which we knew absolutely nothing, except from what we could gather from our Comanche pilot. This trail, which our wagons had made the previous summer, was still visible, and henceforth there was an end to all misgivings.

If we take a retrospective view of the country over which we travelled, we shall find but little that can ever present attractions to the agriculturist. Most of the low valleys of the Canadian, for a distance of five hundred miles, are either too sandy or too marshy for cultivation; and the upland prairies are, in many places, but little else than sand-hills. In some parts, it is true, they are firm and fertile, but wholly destitute of timber, with the exception of a diminutive branch of the Cross Timbers, which occupies a portion of the ridge betwixt the Canadian and the North Fork. The Canadian river itself is still more bare of timber than the upper Arkansas. In its whole course through the plains, there is but little except cottonwood, and that very scantily scattered along its banks—in some places, for leagues together, not a stick is to be seen. Except it be near the Mountains, where the valleys are more fertile, it is only the little narrow valleys which skirt many of its tributary rivulets that indicate any amenity. Some of these are rich and beautiful in the extreme, timbered with walnut, mulberry, oak, elm, hackberry, and occasionally cedar about the bluffs.

We now continued our journey without encountering any further casualty, except in crossing the Arkansas river, where we lost several mules by drowning; and on the 22d of April we made our entrance into Van Buren. This trip was much more tedious and protracted than I had contemplated—owing, in the first part of the journey, to the inclemency of the season, and a want of pasturage for our animals; and, towards the conclusion, to the frequent rains, which kept the route in a miserable condition.

Concerning this expedition, I have only one or two more remarks to offer. As regards the two different routes to Santa Fé, although Missouri, for various reasons which it is needless to explain here, can doubtless retain the monopoly of the Santa Fé trade, the route from Arkansas possesses many advantages. Besides its being some days' travel shorter,* it is less intersected with large streams; there are fewer sandy stretches, and a greater variety of wood-skirted brooks, affording throughout the journey very agreeable camping-places. Also, as the grass springs up nearly a month earlier than in Upper Missouri, caravans could start much sooner, and the proprietors would have double the time to conduct their mercantile transactions. Moreover, the return companies would find better pasturage on their way back, and reach their homes before the season of frost had far advanced. Again, such as should desire to engage in the 'stock trade' would at once bring their mules and horses into a more congenial climate— one more in accordance with that of their nativity; for the rigorous winters of Missouri often prove fatal to the unacclimated Mexican animals.

This was my last trip across the Plains, though I made an excursion, during the following summer, among the Comanche Indians, and other wild tribes, living in the heart of the Prairies, but returned without crossing to Mexico.

Since that time I have striven in vain to reconcile myself to the even tenor of civilized life in the United States; and have sought in its amusements and its society a substitute for those high excitements which have attached me so strongly to Prairie life. Yet I am almost ashamed to confess that scarcely a day passes without my experiencing a pang of regret that I am not now roving at large upon those western plains. Nor do I find my taste peculiar; for I have hardly known a man, who has ever become familiar with the kind of life which I have led for so many years, that has not relinquished it with regret.

There is more than one way of explaining this apparent incongruity. In the first place—the wild, unsettled and independent life of the Prairie trader, makes perfect freedom from nearly every kind of social dependence an absolute necessity of his being. He is in daily, nay, hourly exposure of his life and property, and in the habit of relying upon his own arm and his own gun both for protection and support. Is he wronged? No court or jury is

---

* The latitude of Independence, Mo., is 39° 8', while that of Van Buren is 35° 26',—within a few miles of the parallel of Santa Fé: and being on about the same meridian as Independence, the distance, of course, is considerably shorter.

called to adjudicate upon his disputes or his abuses, save his own conscience; and no powers are invoked to redress them, save those with which the God of Nature has endowed him. He knows no government—no laws, save those of his own creation and adoption. He lives in no society which he must look up to or propitiate. The exchange of this untrammelled condition—this sovereign independence, for a life in civilization, where both his physical and moral freedom are invaded at every turn, by the complicated machinery of social institutions, is certainly likely to commend itself to but few,—not even to all those who have been educated to find their enjoyments in the arts and elegancies peculiar to civilized society;—as is evinced by the frequent instances of men of letters, of refinement and of wealth, voluntarily abandoning society for a life upon the Prairies, or in the still more savage mountain wilds.

A 'tour on the Prairies' is certainly a *dangerous* experiment for him who would live a quiet contented life at home among his friends and relatives: not so dangerous to life or health, as prejudicial to his domestic habits. Those who have lived pent up in our large cities, know but little of the broad, unembarrassed freedom of the Great Western Prairies. Viewing them from a snug fireside, they seem crowded with dangers, with labors and with sufferings; but once upon them, and these appear to vanish—they are soon forgotten.

There is another consideration, which, with most men of the Prairies, operates seriously against their reconciliation to the habits of civilized life. Though they be endowed naturally with the organs of taste and refinement, and though once familiar with the ways and practices of civilized communities, yet a long absence from such society generally obliterates from their minds most of those common laws of social intercourse, which are so necessary to the man of the world. The awkwardness and the *gaucheries* which ignorance of their details so often involves, are very trying to all men of sensitive temperaments. Consequently, multitudes rush back to the Prairies, merely to escape those criticisms and that ridicule, which they know not how to disarm.

It will hardly be a matter of surprise then, when I add, that this passion for Prairie life, how paradoxical soever it may seem, will be very apt to lead me upon the Plains again, to spread my bed

with the mustang and the buffalo, under the broad canopy of
heaven,—there to seek to maintain undisturbed my confidence in
men, by fraternizing with the little prairie dogs and wild colts,
and the still wilder Indians—the *unconquered Sabœans* of the
Great American Deserts.